The Arabs
and the English

The Arabs
and the English

Sari J Nasir

Longman

LONGMAN GROUP LTD

London

Associated companies, branches and representatives throughout the world

© Longman Group Ltd 1976

First published 1976

ISBN 0 582 78046 2

Printed in Great Britain by William Clowes & Sons, Limited
London, Beccles and Colchester

To my father and mother in Arab Jerusalem
and to all Palestinian fathers and mothers
wherever they may be

"What cannot totally be known, ought not to be totally neglected; for the knowledge of a part is better than the ignorance of the whole."

Abulfida Ismail
14th Century Arab Cosmographer

"Men are short of vision, and they see but that for which they look. Some look for evil and they find evil; some look for good and it is good that they find . . ."

Conversation between an
Arab guide and Gertrude Bell
as reported in her book
The Desert and the Sown

Acknowledgements

My first thanks and gratitude go to my brother, Dr Jamal Nasir. Without his assistance, help and encouragement I could not have finished writing this book.

Next, I should like to thank the Ford Foundation for its research award in 1972 and 1973, which enabled me to complete the bulk of the research. The British Council also helped me for two months in the summer of 1975.

I am most grateful to Vivien Hamer for her patience in reading the manuscripts and in providing helpful comments. To my friend Professor Albert Butros I owe much. Besides his never-failing encouragement, he was always ready to read and discuss this work. I am most grateful for his advice and help.

I want, also, to thank the following: Professor A. A. Duri, Dr Amin Mahmoud, Dr Mohammad Shaheen, Dr Suhail Khoury, Dr Afif Kafena, Mr James Auty, Mr Roger Hardy, and my son Jamil Nasir. A special word of appreciation goes to Sir Anthony Nutting and Mr Michael Adams for the time they gave to conversations about the general topic of the image of Arabs in Britain.

Finally, the section of the book which deals with films is based on a chapter in my unpublished Ph.D. thesis entitled "The Image of the Arabs in American Popular Culture", which I completed at the University of Illinois in 1962.

The publishers are grateful to the following for permission to reproduce copyright material:

Executors of the Charles Montagu Doughty Estate for extracts from *Travels in Arabia Deserta* by Charles Montagu Doughty; extracts from William Zinsser's article 'In Search of Lawrence of Arabia' reprinted by permission of *Esquire Magazine* © 1961 by Esquire Inc: John Murray (Publishers) Limited and Doreen Ingrams for extracts from *Palestine Papers 1917–1922*.

We regret we have been unable to trace copyright holder for extracts taken from *A Paladin of Arabia* by N. N. E. Bray.

The publishers are grateful to the following for permission to reproduce the photographs: Radio Hulton Picture Library; the Mansell Collection; Cinegate Ltd.; Columbia-Warners; Cinema International Corporation; London Films; MGM for the still from *Ben Hur*; Paramount for the stills from *Beau Geste* and *Beau Sabreur*; the still from *Charlie Chan in Egypt* by courtesy of Twentieth Century-Fox Film Company Limited; Pan Books for the illustrations from *The Parlour Song Book* by Michael R. Turner. The illustrations at the beginnings and the ends of chapters are taken from Lane's translation of *The Arabian Nights*, 1882.

Preface

"The Aarab, in their suffering manner of life (their cup of life is drawn very low and easily stirred at the dregs), which eagers the blood and weakens the heart . . ." Thus wrote Charles M. Doughty, the Victorian traveller who journeyed among the Arabs in the second half of the nineteenth century.

Doughty was one of a long list of British voyagers who had journeyed to the Middle East from the time of the Crusades and even earlier. The motives which sent these people to the Arabs varied: religious zeal, trade, scholarly interest, love of adventure, and, later, political and military missions. Many such travellers into the Arab World reported their experiences in the accounts of their travels, thus adding to the growing amount of information about the Arab people.

At present, the average British individual is bombarded with news and views about the Arabs. Therefore it becomes important to raise these questions: what ideas, impressions, and notions do the British have of the Arabs? How and from where did these ideas reach them?

This book is concerned with the study of the origins and development in Britain of the image of Arabs. More particularly, it is concerned with the cultural portrayal of Arabs, with emphasis on the ideas, impressions, and notions provided by English writers who came in contact with the Arabs, primarily in the Levant and the Arabian Peninsula. Furthermore, there will be an examination of the manner in which Arabs have been portrayed in films, which, though for the most part made in America, have been popular enough in Britain to make a profound impression on thoughts and attitudes.

The aim of this work is twofold: first, to contribute to the general quest of understanding the fundamental British attitudes towards the Arabs; and secondly it is hoped that this study will be the basis for further enquiries into the image of Arabs.

The word "English" in the title of this book is used because all natives of the British Isles are generally referred to by the Arabs as *Engleeze*. But the word must be taken to imply not only the British as a whole but also those many English-speaking peoples, in America and elsewhere, whose general picture of the Arabs has been constructed largely from those influences examined in this book.

Sari J. Nasir
University of Jordan
Amman, Jordan, 1976

Contents

Contents

Chapter One

A Bird's-eye View

Early Sources

A search for the origins of the contemporary British image of the Arabs leads one inevitably to two very early sources: first, the works of the ancient classical authors, such as Herodotus, Strabo and Pliny; and secondly the Bible.

In the sixth century BC, Herodotus, the Greek historian, referred to Arabia as a land of spices, these commodities, such as frankincense, myrrh, cassia, cinnamon and ledanum (gum), being of great value in his homeland. Herodotus' Arabia, however, was a strange land; a riot of fantasies and peril, where winged creatures stood guarding various spices. For example, colourful snakes with wings were said to shield the frankincense trees. These strange serpents had to be driven off by the fumes of "styrax". The cassia, which grew in shallow lakes, could be obtained, we are told, only by having the seeker cover his body with hides of oxen to protect himself against animals with wings. But the procurement of cinnamon needed originality and ingenuity. According to Herodotus, this valuable commodity was stuck in the muddy nests of huge birds on high inaccessible cliffs. The way to obtain it was first to slaughter an ox, then to scatter its meat below the heights, upon which birds would swoop down and carry the heavy pieces of flesh back to their nests. The additional weight caused the collapse of the nests and the cinnamon fell with it.

The gum was easily obtained; it had to be collected from the beards of he-goats, since it adhered there from the bushes amongst which they browsed.

Herodotus claimed that the rich perfumes and spices filled the whole air of Arabia with a sweet odour. He was one of the early writers to describe the Phoenix, the mythical bird of ancient Egypt. The legend describes the bird first as consuming itself by fire of its own will, then arising from the ashes for resurrection. Furthermore, the bird was said to have inhabited Arabia and to have lived more than five hundred years. The "Phoenix of Arabia" became widely used in literature to symbolise immortality.[1]

The ancient Greeks had also heard about the Arabs and Arabia at the time of Alexander the Great, who, according to legend, "intended . . . even to make it (Arabia) his royal abode. . . ."[2] Alexander had despatched his Admiral Nearchus to explore a sea route to the Euphrates. Nearchus reported seeing during the course of his journey shoals, reefs, frankincense-trees, "sea hedgehogs" and pearls.

The Romans, who penetrated into the area generally known now as the Middle East, also reported that Arabian goods included spices, ivory, perfumes, gums and precious stones. Arabia was known to the Romans as the "happy" country.[3] The notions and impressions the Romans entertained about the inhabitants of the Arabian Peninsula, whom they called the Sabaeans, were that they formed a race of prosperous and powerful merchants. The source of their wealth was thus said to be derived from the export of such commodities as aromatics, gold, pearls and precious stones.

In his work *Geography*, written shortly before the birth of Christianity, Strabo, a Greek historian, referred to Arabia as "Arabia the blest". Strabo saw the Arabs as people who "till the land either little or none, but they keep herds of all kinds, particularly of camels."[4] He described the natives of Gerrha (a coastal town on the Gulf), as people who inhabit a district where "the soil contains salt and the people live in houses made of salt; and since flakes of salt continually scale off, owing to the scorching heat of the rays of the sun, and fall away, the people frequently sprinkle the houses with water and thus keep the walls firm."[5]

Strabo's accounts further portrayed Arabia and its peoples (the Sabaean country) as a fertile land, rich with spices and strange creatures and inhabited by an indolent people, especially the impoverished classes.

"On the coast is found balsam and also another kind of herb of very fragrant smell," but which he found soon dispersed. "There are also sweet-smelling palms and reeds," he continued. "There are serpents a span in length, which are dark-red in colour, can leap even as far as a hare, and inflict an incurable bite." He believed that "on account of fruits the people are lazy and easy going in their modes of life. Most of the populace sleep on the roots of trees," he remarked.[6]

Strabo spoke of Arab traders who handled "loads of aromatics" and who, according to him, became "drowsy by the sweet odours, they overcame drowsiness by inhaling the incense of asphaltus and goats' beard." The "Sabaeans", were also portrayed as a sensual people who "pass their lives in effeminate luxury." Nevertheless, they were also portrayed as prosperous traders who lived lavishly. As seen by Strabo, "from their trafficking both the Sabaeans and the Gerrhaeans have become richest of all; and they have a vast equipment of both gold and silver articles, such as couches and tripods and bowls, together with drinking-vessels and very costly houses, for doors and walls and ceilings are variegated with ivory and gold and silver set with precious stones."[7]

As a contrast to the coastal town of Gerrha Strabo described the desert of Arabia as a "sandy waste, with only few palms and pits of water". The Bedouin, living in tents, were said to exist as robbers and camel drivers subsisting primarily on animal milk and flesh.

Pliny, the Roman author of the first century AD, was one of the first to speak of the nomads and desert dwellers, in contrast to the city Arabs described at length by Strabo. In his accounts, Pliny noted that trade was the prime concern of the city dwellers, who trafficked their merchandise across the desert routes. The caravans carried goods such as ivory, ostrich feathers, gold, pearls, silver, spices and precious stones.

Taken as a whole, the ancient Greek and Roman writers pictured Arabia as a mysterious and strange land, containing various riches and valuable products. The Arab inhabitants were depicted partly as nomads who lived in deserts, their main vocation being plunder; partly as city dwellers, described as prosperous and sensual merchants.

Another and exceedingly important early source portraying Arabs was of course the Bible. This book is indeed crucial, especially since it was and became increasingly established as the cornerstone for the Christian faith. Christians generally accept the information given in the Bible as the ultimate truth (although less now in modern times). The Bible makes allusions to Arabs, depicting them in general as tent dwellers with evil characteristics.

According to James A. Montgomery in his book, *Arabia and the Bible*, the first reference to the Arab appeared in the Old Testament in Isaiah 13:20, depicting him as a nomadic Bedou; "The Arab shall not tent there." The second appearance is more menacing: in an address to Judah: "thou hast sat (lurking) for them like an Arab in the wilderness" (Jeremiah 3:2).

The Arab is generally referred to in the Bible as a wily politician whose main intention is to control the trade routes and the consequent wealth. He is also seen as a mercenary: the enemies of Judas could "hire Arabs" against him (Maccabees 5:59).

Most biblical references, according to Montgomery, portray Arabs as nomads and "lurking" mercenaries. They are spoken of as people in conflict over the trade routes of Palestine, which were the main concern of the trading classes for wealth and livelihood.[8]

For some centuries after the Roman historians, we have no written records of contact between the people of Western Europe and the Arabs. It appears that the inhabitants of the West had little occasion to make contact with the Arabs, who were generally envisaged as living in a mysterious land and occasionally doing a little trade with Egypt and Syria. Fisher, in his book *A History of Europe*, described Arabia according to European impressions in AD 500 as being "remote and inhospitable as the frozen North. Nothing is likely to be reported from this scorching wilderness. . . . Arabian society was still in the tribal stage, and the hawk-eyed Bedouin tribes might be confidently expected to rob and massacre each other till the crack of doom." Of the Arabs, Fisher wrote, "The Arabs were poets, dreamers, fighters, traders; they were not politicians."[9]

At the beginning of the seventh century AD an event took place in Arabia which was to bring the Arabs into the mainstream of world history and into the full focus of European view.

The birth of Muhammad in Arabia in the year 571 was destined to transform Arabian society and influence the life and thought of Europe.

Muhammad, an Arab, brought into being the concept of Islam

as a new religion. Although Islam emanated from the main springs of both Judaism and Christianity, it became a major cause of concern to the latter. In the first place, it was considered by Christians as a rival to the power and influence of their own religion. Secondly, the subsequent Arab conquests were seen as a positive menace to the security of European lands.

Initial reactions against Muhammad and Islam came from a number of Christians who were living in Muslim lands. These criticisms were later passed on to Europe and ultimately absorbed, adapted and adopted by the Latinate Christian West.

It is believed that St John of Damascus, who was Muhammad's contemporary, was the first to spread the unfavourable portrayal of Muhammad and Islam. Claims were made to discredit the new religion and its founder on the grounds that Muhammad, acting on the advice of an Arian Monk called Bahira, manufactured the Qur'an, primarily from the Old and New Testament, to satisfy his own personal interests.

Norman Daniel, in his book *Islam and the West*, notes that in attacking Muhammad St John introduced such elements as power, infidelity and sexual indulgence into the image of Islam. Of this aspect he writes: "St John also introduced other elements that would long survive: he descended to ridicule, for example, of what he mistakenly took to be Quranic belief, the *Camel of God*, in a petty way; and he began the long tradition of attacking Muhammad for bringing in God-simulating revelation in order to justify his own sexual indulgence."[10]

According to Daniel, Muhammad was viewed in European mediaeval accounts as the "Prince of the Arabs". The Arabs themselves were considered as "pagans" and ignorant in accepting the "cunning pseudo-prophet". They were generally seen as soldiers, farmers and idolators; furthermore, they were depicted as "rough" men wandering in the desert. In addition, the mediaeval accounts pictured Muhammad as advocating what he believed would best please the Arabs, "especially lust". Mecca, the Holy City of Islam, was described as a "prostitute". Islam was perceived as being forced on people by the sword, this explaining the reason for its spread and its success.

By the end of the year 732 the Arabs had erupted from the desert and had swiftly galloped their horses to carve an Empire and build a civilisation. Hitti describes this tremendous conquest thus: "One hundred years after the death of Muhammad his followers were the masters of an empire greater than that of Rome at its

5

zenith, an empire extending from the Bay of Biscay to the Indies and the confines of China and from the Aral Sea to the upper cataracts of the Nile. The name of the prophet-son of Arabia, joined with the name of Almighty Allah, was being called five times a day from thousands of minarets scattered over South Western Europe, Northern Africa and Western and Central Asia."[11]

Although Arab conquests in Europe were halted in 732 by Charles Martel in the battle of Tours, there had been time enough to develop a flourishing civilisation far superior to anything found as yet in Europe. As Hitti noted, "Arab scholars were studying Aristotle when Charlemagne and his lords were learning to write their names."[12] Despite Europe's awareness of the superior civilisation of the Arabs, the Europeans still naturally held them as the conquering race and as suspect and dangerous. In the ninth century AD Charlemagne and Harun El Rashid, the Abassid Caliph, entered into a friendly relationship. Gifts were exchanged between the two men and ultimately a mutual pact was concluded. Harun El Rashid wanted the Franks to help him against the Omayyads of Spain, while Charlemagne looked to Harun as a possible ally against his Byzantine foes.

In 778 Charlemagne despatched troops to fight the Omayyad Moors in Spain, but was beaten back. On their retreat the Frankish army was attacked by the Basques and suffered heavy losses in both men and armoury. One of the Frankish leaders who fought heroically was Roland, later immortalised in the *Chanson de Roland*. Although the actual adversaries of Roland were Christian Basque brigands from Northern Spain and Southern France, the chivalric poem portrayed the Arabs, "the wild golden-armoured Saracens", as the enemy. For centuries, Western school children have read the *Chanson de Roland*, whose theme was the Christian battle against the "Mahometan" Arabs.

The religion of the Arabs never appealed to European sensibilities. It was to them completely alien to Christian precepts. Hostility to Islam was not forgotten. Christian writers vehemently attacked the "infidels", accusing them of usurping lands that had once been Christian and of profaning and polluting Christian churches.

It was partly against the background of this hostile climate of opinion in the Latin West that the concept of the Crusading Movement began to develop. The aim was to fight the infidel and free Jerusalem for Christianity and the "right and only" God.

Pope Urban, in a speech well-known in history (1095), appealed to all Christians to "enter upon the road to the Holy Sepulchre, wrest it from the wicked race and subject it to Christendom." "God wills it," echoed through the continent of Europe.

The Christians who rallied to fight the "infidels" were not all motivated by religion. "The romantic, the restless and the adventurous, in addition to the devout, found a new rallying point and many criminals sought penance thereby."[13]

Crusades and After

The Crusades mark the beginning of a period of direct contact between Arabs and Europeans. The Franks, who as Crusaders came to save the Holy Land, considered themselves far superior to the Arabs, whom they regarded as idolaters, worshipping Muhammad as a God. To the Arab Moslem the Crusaders left the impression of, as one Arab historian said, "Animals possessing the virtues of courage and fighting, but nothing else."

While the Crusaders were engaged in long and tedious battles in Palestine, stories about the Arabs' barbaric attitudes towards Christians and Christianity circulated in Europe: the Golden Cross being thrown down from the Dome of the Rock; the Crucifix dragged through the streets at the tail of an ass; holy pictures put to insult; Christian children captured and forced to spit upon the Crucifix; the massacre of defenceless Christians, and many other stories.

"To kill the Muslim Arab was to slay for God's love," became the slogan in Europe. Daniel refers to several "serious writers" who advocated complete annihilation of all the "infidels".

Nonetheless, the fighting Crusaders eventually began to discern superior qualities in the Arabs. They learned that their enemy possessed "chivalry", a quality which they admired and adopted. One of the most celebrated Arab personalities to acquire a favourable reputation in Europe was Salah-el-Din (Saladin). He was the Muslim Sultan who led a successful campaign against the Crusaders led by Richard the Lionheart. Saladin's popularity in Europe was the result of his honourable dealings with the Franks. He was witnessed as showing mercy towards his enemy. Europeans saw in Saladin a humanity which they did not expect the infidel to possess or to understand. A new awareness began to develop about the Arabs in Europe: Arabs, after all, were not as bad as the Crusaders had been led to believe. They were recognised as human beings, who were capable not only of living up to universal values but also of showing superior qualities unknown to Western man.

In Europe Saladin became the central character in many fictional stories and a hero of purely romantic adventures. One story even saw him travelling incognito in Europe, convinced of the validity of Christianity. Daniel describes the true Saladin of history: "It would probably be true to say that his legend was known over a wider area for a longer period of time than that of any political figure of the Mediaeval West, and almost as favourably. The famous Europeans, Frederick II and Louis IX, for example, had all in some ways a more provincial reputation than Saladin."[14]

The Crusades established communication between Christian Europe and the Muslim Arab world. Both peoples were drawn together for the first time on a day-to-day basis. Christian soldiers, considering their vows fulfilled, returned to their countries with new experiences and ideas regarding the Arabs and their religion. Many others settled in the Holy Land and intermarried. Hitti describes the Franks who settled in the Holy Land as discarding their European dress "in favour of the more comfortable and more suitable native clothing. They acquired new tastes in food, especially those varieties involving the generous use of sugar and spices. They preferred oriental houses, with their spacious open courts and running water."[15] It is assumed that the Crusaders must have heard stories of the *Arabian Nights* and carried them back to Europe. Boccaccio is said to have incorporated some of these tales in the *Decameron*. Chaucer's *Squire's Tale* is considered to have been influenced by the *Nights*.

With the eventual failure of the Crusades and the recapture of the Holy Land by the Arabs, European Christian theologians began to search for an explanation for this great setback. One justification for the failure of the Franks in their religious wars cited as a prophecy in the Book of Genesis: "He shall be a wild man. His hand will be against all men, and all men's hands against him: and he shall pitch his tents against all his brethren." Another explanation for the defeat of the Crusades was said to be the sins of the Christians, indeed a blow to a proud religious race.

The Crusades were one of the first important cultural contacts between Europe and the Arabs. This inevitably led to a change in the prevailing European attitudes towards the Arabs and Islam. Many of the earlier polemics were reinforced. For example, Islam became more feared and suspect. However, at the same time, more favourable elements, such as chivalry and nobility of spirit, found their way to the conglomeration of concepts concerning Arabs in Europe.

The Crusaders were not the only Christians who were conveying ideas and impressions about Arabs in Europe during this period. There were also other European travellers, such as adventurers, pilgrims and traders.

The accounts of the voyages of the Venetian Marco Polo were published at the end of the thirteenth century. The fantasy of Marco Polo's stories about the East became widely read and caught the imagination of the European. Marco Polo related many peculiar anecdotes, such as the "Old Man of the Mountain" who was a "Saracen" prince named "Alo-eddin" whose "religion was that of Mahomet". This character, we are told, lived in a "beautiful valley enclosed betwen two lofty mountains", which he had turned into a garden. This garden had palaces, elegant pavilions and "every fragrant shrub that could be procured", also "streams of wine, milk, honey, and some pure water . . ." Beautiful women were seen loitering around, singing and dancing. The old man, according to Marco Polo, wanted his people to believe that he was a prophet and the garden was the paradise of "Mahomet".

However, the old man prohibited anyone from entering his "paradise" except those whom "he should choose to favour".

Furthermore, the old man recruited youths "between twelve to twenty years" and trained them as "assassins". The method which he used to inure his "assassins" was to remove the youths from "paradise" after putting them to sleep by means of opium. Once they were out of the garden the old man would order them to go and kill anyone he wished, promising them that they would return to paradise dead or alive. "We have the assurances of our prophet that he who defends his lord shall inherit paradise, and if you show yourselves devoted to the obedience of my orders, that happy lot awaits you." This was the manner in which the "assassins" gladly obeyed and did what the old man desired.[16]

Marco Polo, in his adventures, spoke of many fantastic feats and strange creatures and spirits. He portrayed the East as a dangerous and perilous land, apparently, it must be suspected, to enhance his own reputation as a fearless adventurer and intrepid explorer.

Other Christian voyagers, especially the Venetian and Genoese, long famous as travelling merchants, also journeyed into Arab lands and left accounts of their travels, in which the Arabs were described. One such narrative, according to the English Hakluyt's *Navigations*, one of the most famous accounts, concerned a Venetian merchant, Caesar Frederick, who travelled in the area in 1563.

In his account, Frederick mentioned the hardships of trading in the Levant and his various encounters with Arabs. Writing of a trade route used by early merchants, Frederick described the various perils to be met:

"From Bir where the marchants imbarke themselves to Feluchis over against Babylon, if the river have good store of water, they shall make their voyage in fifteene or eighteene dayes downe the river, and if the water be lowe, and it hath not rained, then it is much trouble, and it will be forty or fifty dayes journey downe, because that when the barks strike on the stones that be in the river, then they must unlade them, which is great trouble, and then lade them againe when they have mended them: therefore it is not necessary, neither doe the marchants go with one boat alone, but with two or three, that if one boat split and be lost with striking on the sholdes, they may have another ready to take in their goods, untill such time as they have mended the broken boat, and if they draw the broken boat on land to mend her, it is hard to defend her in the night from the great multitude of Arabians that will come downe there to robbe you: and in the rivers every night when you make fast your boat to the banckeside, you must keepe good watch against the Arabians which are theeves in number like to ants, yet when they come to robbe, they will not kill, but steale and run away. Harquebuzes are very good weapons against them, for that they stand greatly in feare of the shot. And as you passe the river Euphrates from Bir to Feluchia, there are certain places which you must passe by, where you pay custome certaine medines upon a bale, which custome is belonging to the sonne of Aborise king of the Arabians and of the desert, who hath certaine cities and villages on the river Euphrates."[17]

Among the Renaissance adventurers who journeyed to Arab lands was the Italian Ludovico Di Varthema, in 1503. It is believed that Varthema was the first Christian European to enter Arabia and report on the Holy Cities of Islam. It is said that he enrolled in the Mameluke's army after apparent conversion to Islam, and adopted the name of Yunas. Thus he became the first in a long list of Westerners to travel to Arab lands in disguise, this being considered essential for their own safety. Varthema is said to have joined the *Haj* caravan and to have made the holy trip to Mecca and Medina as a Muslim pilgrim. He thus became the first Westerner to enter the tomb area in the Holy City of Mecca.

Varthema's adventures were printed in Rome in 1510. The first English translation appeared in 1576–77 (in Richard Eden's

History of Travayle), and Samuel Purchas's *Purchas His Pilgrims* and the Hakluyt Society published extracts from his work. Varthema's accounts included a description of the Bedouin, whom he saw as essentially nomadic tribes and characterised as horsemen and plunderers.

He portrays them thus: "Sometimes he runs a whole day and a night with his said mares without stopping, and when they have arrived at the end of their journey they give them camels milk to drink because it is very refreshing. Truly it appears to me that they do not run, but fly like falcons; for I have been with them, and you must know that they ride for the most part without saddles, and in their shirts, except some of the principal men. Their arms consist of a lance of Indian cane ten or twelve cubits in length, and when they go on any expedition they keep as close together as starlings. The said Arabians are very small men, and are of a dark tawny colour, and they have a feminine voice, and long, stiff, and black hair. And truly these Arabs are in such vast numbers that they cannot be counted, and they are constantly fighting amongst themselves. They inhabit the mountain, and come down when the caravan passes through to go to Mecca, in order to lie in wait at the passes for the purpose of robbing the said caravan. They carry their wives, children, and all their furniture, and also their houses, upon camels, which houses are like the tents of soldiers and are of black wool and of a sad appearance."[18]

Varthema also denied the belief current in Europe that the prophet's tomb was suspended in mid-air.

Varthema's journey into Arabia was followed by those of other travellers, as we shall see in later chapters.

Arabia not only attracted the attention of individual adventurers, it also aroused the curiosity of a number of European governments. About the middle of the eighteenth century, Frederick V of Denmark showed interest in an idea for an expedition into Arabia with both Biblical and geographical aims in view.

The Danish expedition left in January, 1761. It consisted of six men, a doctor-botanist, a surgeon-zoologist, a philologist-orientalist, an artist, a surveyor and a Swedish ex-cavalryman as an attendant. The surveyor, by name one Carsten Niebuhr, of peasant stock, had spent eighteen months prior to the voyage studying mathematics and Arabic.

The expedition resulted in the death of all but one man: Niebuhr survived to tell Europe of their adventures and experiences with the Arabs.

Niebuhr's book *Travels through Arabia* was first published in German in 1772. The English translation appeared in 1792.

The book is divided into two parts. The first narrates the journeys made in the Yemen, and the second depicts the character of the Arab, his manners and customs.

Niebuhr tells us that he travelled on a donkey, disguised as a poor man, to avoid Arab thieves: "A turban, a great coat wanting the sleeves, a shirt, linen drawers and a pair of slippers were all the dress I wore," he wrote. "It being the fashion of the country to wear arms in travelling, I had a sabre and two pistols hung by my girdle. A piece of an old carpet was my saddle, and served me likewise for a seat at table and various other purposes. To cover me at night, I had the linen cloak which the Arabs wrap about their shoulders, to shelter me from the sun and rain. A bucket of water, an article of indispensable necessity to a traveller in these arid regions, hung by my saddle. I had for some time endeavoured to suit myself to the Arabian manner of living, and now could spare many conveniences to which I had been accustomed in Europe, and could content myself with bad bread, the only article to be obtained in most of the inns."[19]

Niebuhr reported that he and the members of the expedition discovered in the Yemen coffee plantations whose trees "were all in flower . . . and exhaled an exquisitely agreeable perfume." He described how the coffee trees were planted upon terraces "in the form of an amphitheatre".

Niebuhr preferred the lively Arabs, who took delight in their poetry and songs, to the "ignorant, grave and silent" Turks. He also distinguished between the city Arabs and the Bedouin. Of the former, he wrote, "The Arabs settled in cities, and especially those in the sea-port towns, have lost somewhat of their distinctive national manners by their intercourse with strangers." Niebuhr praised the Bedouin, "the genuine Arabs", for their love of freedom and their "natural hospitality". He noted, however, that "They are said to be addicted to robbery," adding "and the accusation is not entirely unfounded". Nevertheless, he does not wholly support this ill repute and points out that the same accusation "may be laid equally to the charge of all nations that lead an erratic life."

Niebuhr depicts the Bedouin as practising true democracy: "The schiechs ride continually about on their horses or dromedaries inspecting the conduct of their subjects. . . . Little or no revenue is paid to the great schiech, and the other schiechs are rather like equals than subjects. If dissatisfied with his government they depose him, or go away with their cattle and join another tribe."

In addition Niebuhr criticises some prevalent European attitudes which tend to degrade the Arabs, stating: "The Europeans who live among Mohammedans would be more beloved and respected if they did not vilify themselves in the eyes of orientals by amusements which they might surely spare."

Niebuhr held Arab manners and general way of life in high regard, stressing, "If any people in the world afford in their history an instance of high antiquity, and of great simplicity of manners, the Arabs surely do . . . Coming among them one can hardly help fancying oneself suddenly carried backward to the age which succeeded immediately after the Flood. We are here tempted to imagine ourselves among the old patriarchs, with whose adventures we have been so much amused in our infant day. The language which has been spoken for time immemorial, and which so nearly resembles that which we have been accustomed to regard as that of the most distant antiquity, completes the illusion which the analogy of manners began."

Niebuhr's portrayal of the Arabs, and especially of the Bedouin, reflected a highly favourable image, due to the simplicity and unpretentiousness he observed in them.

Nonetheless, the development in eighteenth century Europe which most significantly influenced the image of Arabs in the West was the publication in 1704 of Antoine Galland's translation of the *One Thousand and One Nights*, more commonly known as the *Arabian Nights*. The book is a collection of tales believed to be of Indian or Persian origin. It rapidly attained universal popularity and among those who translated it into English were E. W. Lane in 1840 and in 1855 Sir Richard Burton. *The Nights*, in the complete edition, contains over two hundred tales, all woven into one main story, which is essentially as follows. Shahriar, the King, finding his wife unfaithful, kills her, and afterwards each successive bride on the morning following the marriage meets the same fate. This distressing situation causes Sheherezade, the Vizier's daughter, to offer herself "to be a ransom for the daughters of the Mohammadans on the cause of their deliverance." She "beguiles the waking hour" of the King by beginning a story which she interrupts at a point of suspense, whereupon her life is spared that she may continue the tale. She repeats the device, linking tale to tale, or involving one in another, until at the end of the one thousand and first night she asks that her life be spared. Her request is granted and the King also makes Sheherezade his Queen.

The *Nights* apparently provided the West with an escape from the undesirable realities of their own culture and society. It introduced to them a new world in which men and women interacted freely with no inhibitions, guilt, shame or strict moral values; a world of genies, fairies and miracles. Westerners seemed to have a need to escape, a need to reside in such an exotic world, so different from their own. Young and old were fascinated to such an extent that the book of tales was printed in more languages than any other book with the exception of the Bible. The stories of the *Nights* have provided rich material for the entertainment industry in the West until this day, and will doubtless continue to do so.

It is generally believed in the West that the *Arabian Nights* contains a true account of the life of the Arab people. They are "consulted by scholars for their pictures of the customs and manners of the Orient". The tales are described by *The World Book Encyclopedia*: "The stories of the Arabian Nights are of many countries and times, but whatever their age or source all have been so transformed that they are Moslem to the core, thoroughly Arabian in temper and spirit."[20] The *Nights* have had a lasting influence on the sensibilities of great and unknown Western writers alike. Travellers to the Arab world went with great expectations to the exotic lands of the *Nights*; many were disappointed. Many tourists, for example, were deflated upon discovering that the realities of the Arab world were far removed from the exotic world of the *Arabian Nights*. The "wretchedness" and "squalor" of the city Arab was reported in many letters sent back to the West both by famous and by little-known writers. In 1874 the French writer Flaubert, in a letter to his mother from Cairo, wrote "Yesterday, for example, we were at a cafe which is one of the best in Cairo, and where there were, at the same time as ourselves, inside, a donkey shitting and a gentleman was pissing in a corner. No-one finds that odd; no-one says anything."[21]

The Eighteenth Century

Up until the end of the eighteenth century Arabs were not viewed as an entity by the West; they were lumped together with the rest of the peoples of the Ottoman Empire. Nevertheless, very soon after, Arabs became a focal point of Western attention. This was for several reasons: changing conditions in Europe, especially the French Revolution, romantic sentiments in literature now more accessible to the public, and the beginning of modern imperialism.[22]

The Arabs, as a distinct group, became the subject of deliberate thought by serious writers, especially by the French and shortly before the Napoleonic military campaign in Egypt. The dreaded Turk was abhorred in Europe. The powerful Ottoman Empire was resented; intellectuals, thinkers, military men were searching for new approaches to weaken and destroy the "Empire of the Crescent". The French philosopher and traveller, Volney, advocated the destruction of the Ottoman Empire, and believed that Arabs might revolt and reconstruct a new state. The "Arab Nation" began to be discussed in important French circles. The Arab, the "Noble Savage", the "freedom loving" Bedouin was expected to rise and fight the Turks from within the Empire.[23]

Another French traveller, C. E. Savary, classified Arabs in Egypt into three categories.

First come the urban Arabs, who, according to Savary, are corrupt and brigands. Second are the Arabs of the desert, a semi-nomadic breed, whose Sheiks are men of benevolence; "under this paternal Government man enjoys all his freedom and is attached to his prince only by ties of respect and gratitude." These were the Arabs who should fight the Turks, because in case of failure they may return to their deserts: "If these leaders were to unite their forces, if they would form a League against the Turks, they would chase them out of Egypt without difficulty and make themselves sovereigns." According to Savary this category of Arabs represented "the best people upon earth. They do not know the vices of the policed nations."

The third category of Arabs are the Bedouin, who also love freedom and independence and are hospitable but on the other hand are marauders and robbers of caravans.[24]

C. S. Sonnini agreed that Bedouin are virtuous, extend extensive hospitality and have "simple manners" and "generous habits", but he thought that they should be encouraged to settle on their lands and continue to perform their function as suppliers of camels and sheep.[25]

According to Norman Daniel, Volney was the ablest analyst of the Arabs, because of the important fact that he was fully cognisant of the enmity between Arabs and Turks. Volney stated that "on their side, the Arabs regard the Turks as usurpers and traitors and only seek opportunities to hunt them." Although he admired the Bedouin simplicity and hospitality, he claimed that the Arabs' industry was limited to the making of tents, mats and butter, and their literature consisted of stories like the *Thousand and One Nights*. Volney described Bedouin society: "Good faith reigns there, a disinterestedness, a generosity which would do honour to the most civilised of men." Volney believed nevertheless that the Bedouin exercised a spirit of rapine which they used only against their enemies.[26]

Praise for the Bedouin Arabs in Europe reached a high peak at the end of the eighteenth century. It is interesting to note that, since the earliest contacts with Arabs, Westerners assumed a degree of identification with them, either by adopting Arab dress and habits, as did many of the Crusaders when they discarded their European garments in favour of Arab dress, or by disguising themselves and assuming Arab identity, as in the case of Varthema of Rome who in 1503 visited Egypt, and later Burckhardt and Burton, who will be discussed at a later stage. This theme became familiar in Europe, especially among travellers to the Arab lands. Perhaps the Western mentality assumed that Arabs were too "simple" and naive to detect their clever disguises, and thus the Westerner enjoyed a small sense of superiority over them. In the undertones of politics, the Bedouin aspect of robbery was conveniently ignored.

This proved to be an important development in the attitude of Westerners towards Arabs in imperial relations. The French and later the British entertained notions of Arab naivety and simplicity. Both governments used this formula in a variety of ways in their subsequent dealings with Arab leaders. Westerners identifying themselves with the interests of Arabs increased in numbers, believing they were exploiting the simplicity of the Arab by so doing.

In the latter part of the eighteenth century the Ottoman Empire had gradually become weaker, to the point that the West began to refer to it as the "Sick Man of Europe". Napoleon conquered Egypt in 1798. He arrived well aware of the ideas and notions circulating concerning the Arab and was not alone in his conviction that Arabs were true to the portrayal of them in Europe. In one of Napoleon's early dispatches he writes, "the Arabs of the desert . . . have not ceased harassing us for two days, but yesterday I managed to conclude a treaty with them, not only of friendship but of alliance. . . . I seated myself among them and we had a very long conversation. . . . This nation is no less than the travellers and writers of accounts have painted it: it is calm, proud and brave." Napoleon later admitted that his Army reacted unfavourably to

Egypt, "The whole Army was in a revolt at the sight of such a country, where there was neither bread nor wine . . . none of our customs were known there," but he proceeded to analyse the country and its people in terms of the notions put forward by European travellers and writers. He perceived the Arabs as constituting the bulk of the nation led by "grand Scheiks", who were "leaders of the nobility and the doctors of the law". At once Napoleon seized upon the Arab *ulamma*, religious men of wisdom, and gave them all the preponderance. He believed that the *ulamma* are even respected by the "wild Arabs of the desert" whether "bandits" or "noble savages". From then on Napoleon spoke to the people through these men: "sherifs, ulemas, orators of mosques, make the people know well that those who, from frivolity of heart, declare themselves my enemies will have no refuge in this world or the next. Is there a man so blind as not to see that destiny itself directs my operations? Could there be anyone so incredulous as to call in doubt that this vast universe is subject to the empire of destiny?"[27]

Napoleon came to the Arabs for the purpose of conquest and thus disguised his intentions, proclaiming his identification with them. "People of Egypt, you will be told that I come to destroy your religion; do not believe it. Answer that I come to restore your rights, punish the usurpers, and that more than the Mameloucks do, I respect God, his prophet and the Koran." Napoleon went as far as "playing at being a Muslim". On occasions he dressed like an Arab and, as Scott pointed out, he used "the inflated language of the East . . . and he himself pertained in some sort to their religion being an envoy of the Deity"; he regarded himself as a man of destiny, which "fitted the romantic picture of Islam".

Napoleon had a special respect for the Arabs: he condemned the Turks as mercenaries and the Mamelukes as his enemies. Throughout his stay in Egypt Napoleon was acting, like the true Machiavellian he was, a role of a Westerner who had come to the Arabs to help them because he regarded himself as one of them. This is what T. E. Lawrence later tried to do, although initial motives and characteristics were very different. Daniel commented on the similarity of the missions of the two men: "The difference was in the actors, not in the play."[28]

Chapter Two

The Beginnings

Direct Contact

The first significant British contacts with Arabs, both culturally and politically, came at a time when the Arab World was subject to the Ottoman Empire.

Until then, as we have seen, ideas about Arabs and Arab lands had reached England from various sources. First there was the Bible, which gave focus to the Middle East as being the scene of Christ's life. Many countries in the area became familiar to Christians; Egypt, the country where Moses lived and from which he led the Hebrews; Palestine, where Christ was born, raised and crucified; Syria, the land in which Saint Paul and Saint Peter travelled. Many other biblical places and names also became current usage: places such as Jerusalem, Bethlehem and Nazareth; names such as the Queen of Sheba, Ruth and Salome. The Holy Land held the attention of people and evoked an interest both religious and mystical.

A second source was the tales and fables circulating about the "inscrutable Orient"; the dreadful "hiddeous Egiptian beast" and the enigmatic "Phoenix of Arabia", derived from the works of early Greek and Roman writers. There were also the stories of the assassins and frightful "evil spirits of the desert", as told by Marco Polo.

Then there were the European polemics about Islam and Moslems, the "religion of the sword" and the dark "infidels" who threatened Christianity and Christians. The legends of the Crusades provided another source of information for Christian bias. According to these fables, King Richard accomplished "such mighty deeds that the Saracens stood in great fear of him", as reported in Jonville's *Chronicles* in the thirteenth century. When the Saracen children cried, their mothers called out, "Wisht! here is King Richard," in order to keep them quiet, and when the horses of the Saracens and the Bedouin started at a tree or bush, their masters said to the horses, "Do you think that is King Richard of England?"[1]

In general these legends and fables painted the Middle East as a land inhabited by demons and saints; a world full of wonders and of the supernatural.

In contrast to these ideas very few Englishmen were aware of Arab contributions to human knowledge.

In subsequent centuries new concepts in the portrayal of Arabs began to appear in the accounts of English merchants, travellers, scholars and adventurers; these first travellers were later followed by diplomats and soldiers.

The making of the modern image of the Arabs in England began in the twelfth century. Two men, a scholar and a traveller, added two basic and opposing themes to the image.

The first came from Adelard of Bath "the pioneer of Arab learning in the West", who travelled extensively in Spain and Syria in the first quarter of the twelfth century. His aim was to study Arabic and Arab science, "being of good wit and being desirous to increase and enrich the same with the best things." Adelard translated many Arabic books into Latin and served as tutor to King Henry II. In his book *The Natural Questions*, Adelard wrote "I shall plead the cause of the Arabs, not my own." He then proceeded to show the superiority of the Arab method of learning and was instrumental in spreading it in the West. Adelard addressing his nephew on the method he learnt from the Arabs in Spain:

"I, with reason for my guide, have learned one thing from my Arab teachers, you, something different; dazzled by the outward show of authority you wear a head-stall. For what else should we call authority but a head-stall? Just as brute animals are led by the head-stall where one pleases, without seeing why or where they are being led, and only follow the halter by which they are held, so many of you, bound and fettered as you are by a low credulity, are led into danger by the authority of writers. . . . Reason has been given to individuals that, with it as chief judge, distinction may be drawn between the true and false. . . . We must first search after reason, and when it has been found, and not until then, authority, if added to it, may be received. Authority by itself can inspire no confidence in the philosopher, nor ought it to be used for such a purpose."[2] This same theme of the "superiority" of Arab learning was reinforced in the twelfth century within the same era by Robert of Chester and Daniel of Morley. The latter, dissatisfied with the Frankish Universities, went to the Arabs to "seek the wider philosophers of the Universe."

However, in the same century a diametrically opposed theme appeared in the accounts of the English traveller Mandeville. In his *Travels*,[3] Mandeville, while on a journey to the Holy Land in the latter part of the twelfth century, speaks of the "Arabians" and "Bedouins" who inhabit the "deserts" between Jerusalem and Syria, and describes them as "evil", wicked and "of malice": "In those deserts dwell mickle people that men call Arabians, Bedouins and Ascopards. They are folk of full evil conditions, and full of all manner of wickedness and malice," he wrote. "They are right foul folk and cruel and of evil kind." The Arabs are perceived by Mandeville as an "evil kind", thus setting them aside from his own "kind", regarding them as an "outgroup", a theme which has survived to this day. Mandeville proceeds to describe the Arabs as roaming nomads who live in tents. "Houses have they none but tents, which they make of skins of camels and other wild beasts and drink water when they may any get. And they dwell in places where they may have water, as on the Red Sea and other places where they find any water. And oft times it falls that, where men find water a [one] time of the year, another time there is none found; and therefore make they no house in a certain place, but now here, now there, as they may find water. This folk that I speak of travail not about tilling of land, for they eat no bread commonly, but if it be any that dwell near some good town, that they may go to for to get them bread. They roast all their flesh and the fish that they eat upon stone through the heat of the sun."

However, Mandeville noted that they were "strong men" and good fighters: "and not-for-they [nevertheless] they are strong men and well fighting; and great multitude there is of them." Also there is a mention of their independence and resentment of outside authority: "They do nought else but chase wild beasts, to take them for their sustenance. And they set not by their lives; and therefore they dread not the Sultan ne none other prince of all the world, that ne they will fight with them, and they do them any grievance. They have oft-times fought with the Sultan, and namely

At Alisaundre he was whan it was wonne...
In Gernade at the seege eek hadde he be
Of Algezir, and riden in Belmarye.
At Lyeys was he and at Satalye,
Whan they were wonne; and in the Grete See

The Knight, from Chaucer's *Canterbury Tales*, c. 1390.

Alisaundre: Alexandria; *Gernade:* Granada; *Algezir:* Algeciras;
Belmarye: Benmarin (Morocco); *Lyeys:* Ayas (Turkey); *Satalye:* Attalia
(Turkey); *the Grete See:* The Mediterranean

Wel knew he the olde Esculapius,
And Deyscorides, and eek Rufvs,
Olde Ypocras, Haly, and Galyen,
Serapion, Razis, and Avycen,
Averrois, Damascien, and Constantyn,
Bernard, and Gatesden, and Gilbertyn.

The Physician, from Chaucer's *Canterbury Tales*, c. 1390.

Many of the doctors whom the Physician used as authorities were Arabs: *Haly:* Hali ibn al Abbas; *Serapion:* an Arab of the 12th or 13th century; *Razis:* Rhazes of Baghdad, 9th or 10th century; *Avycen:* Avicenna, 11th century; *Averrois:* Averroes, 12th century; *Damascien:* (probably) Yuhanna ibn Masawiah; *Constantin:* Constantinus Afer of Carthage

An illustration from Spenser's *Faerie Queene*, c. 1590: the Red Cross Knight, a pattern of Christian chivalry, overcomes the faithless "Paynim", a representative of the Islamic power

A drawing, made in 1595, of a scene in Shakepeare's *Titus Andronicus*.
The figure on the extreme right is Aaron, the Moor

A scene from *The Empress of Morocco*, written by an inferior but quite popular dramatist, Elkanah Settle. The play was presented in the Dorset Garden Theatre in London, in 1673

that same time that I dwelt with him. Armour have they none to defend them with, but only a shield and a spear. They wind their heads and their necks in a white linen cloth." It is interesting here to note that many of the qualities mentioned by Mandeville were seized upon and incorporated into the image of the Arab in England. At different times, as we shall see, various of these qualities were admired by subsequent English travellers.

In subsequent centuries these two main themes, namely the superior Arab thought and the dangerous desert dweller, appeared over and over again in accounts of English men of letters, merchants and travellers, such as Hakluyt, Pitts and Fitch.

Merchants

An important source of information about Arabs reaching the ears of England, beginning in the fifteenth century, came with the English merchants who sailed in quest of trade as far as the Levant. One of the earliest English vessels to reach the port of Jaffa in Palestine was the *Cog Anne*. The ship was commanded by the "Fulnotable Worshipful Merchant" Robert Sturmy of Bristol. It carried a group of pilgrims and a cargo of wool, tin and other commodities. On the way back to England the vessel sank off the coast of Greece and thus never reached home, although Sturmy survived the disaster and carried news of his travels to England. Another attempt was made by him in 1457 on the vessel the *Katherine Sturmy*, with a cargo of lead, tin, wool and cloth to "divers parts of the Levant", the ship carrying back "pepper and other spices". This vessel was also sunk near Malta by the Genoese, who considered the English merchants to be intruding on their own trade. In 1511 the famous Hakluyt recorded that "divers tall ships of London . . . and of Southampton and Bristow" sailing to Crete, Cyprus and Syria carrying woollen manufactures, carried on their way back commodities such as "silks, chamlets, rubarbe, malmesies, muskadels and other wines, sweet oyles, cotton, woole, twilsie, carpets, galles, pepper, cinamon and some other spices". Hakluyt also speaks of several English ships travelling to the Levant in the intervening years between 1512 and 1535.[4]

In the meanwhile the Turks had conquered the Arab lands. These lands which came under the Turkish rule included Syria (Lebanon, Syria and Palestine), Arabia, Iraq, Egypt and North Africa (Tunisia, Algeria and Morocco). The people who lived in these areas were referred to by Europeans as Arabs, Bedouin, Saracens, Moors, Muslims, and later were confused with the Turks.

When the English merchants first obtained permission to trade in the Turkish dominions in 1553, the Arabs were, as pointed out, subjects of the Ottoman Empire. Those Arab territories which were of special significance to the early merchants included Syria, Palestine, Tunis, Algeria, Tripoli, and Arabia; Aleppo, in the North of Syria, was described by Alfred C. Wood as "the terminus of the great caravan routes from Persia and Mesopotamia," and also had an important factory which stood almost "on an equality with that of Constantinople, and in point of trade probably surpassed it." Palestine was of special concern for its holy places, many pilgrims undertaking pilgrimages to Jerusalem. Tunis, Algeria and Tripoli posed a special threat to English trade on the Barbary Coast. Wood describes them as "the three pirate states" and he describes the population as "a people who lived by plunder and rapine". The Barbary pirates (including English pirates), posed a great threat to English vessels, "enslaving all Christian captives".[5]

Accounts of the Barbary pirates appeared as early as 1566. Bodenham, who commanded a ship loaded with a cargo of goods bound for Spain, described a battle which took place between English merchants and the pirates: "I was bownde even at home at myne owne dores, being calm without brethe of wynd, I was besett with seven gallies of Tourkes of Argell [Algiers]." He describes how he and his men put up a fight from "morning tyll noon", but finally they were "taken and stripped nakyd, and put in too the gallies." Voyages to the Barbary Coast by English vessels were first recorded in 1551. One such trip had two Moors as passengers, these "being noble men" on a "tall ship called the Lion of London".[6]

Syria, on the other hand, was said to be much more hospitable than the Barbary Coast to the early English merchants. It was a haven for travellers who went as pilgrims or to search for the trade route by land to India (the sea routes were still under Portuguese control). One Master Robert Newberry, who embarked on a second trip to Syria with Ralph Fitch and a company of fellow-travellers, left England for Tripoli on *The Tiger* of London, a vessel which attained fame by the mention of its voyage "to Aleppo" in the witches' scene in Macbeth:

> Her husband's to Aleppo gone, master o' the Tiger:
>   But in a sieve I'll thither sail,
>   And, like a rat without a tail,
>   I'll do, I'll do, and I'll do.[7]

While still in London Newberry apparently had been asked to search in Syria for a book of "Cosmographie" written by one Abilfada Ismail. On 28 May 1583 Newberry wrote from Tripoli to Richard Hakluyt describing the various stages of the long journey: "We remained upon our coast untill the 11 day of March, and that day we set saile from Falmouth, and never ankered till wee arrived in the road of Tripolie Syria, which was the last day of Aprill last past, where we stayed 14 days. . . . Since my comming to Tripolis I have made very earnest inquire both there and here, for the books of Cosmographie of Abilfada Ismail, but by no means can here of it."[8]

English traders apparently prospered in the Levant. In 1580 the Levant Company was officially established with its headquarters in Constantinople and a main centre in Aleppo. Two consuls were appointed in Arab lands: Harvey Millers in "Cayro, Alexandria, Egypt and other parts adjacent", and Richard Forester in "Aleppo, Damascus, Amman, Tripolis and Jerusalem", with his headquarters in Tripoli. Two years later (1585) John Tipton was appointed Consul in Algiers, Tunis and Tripoli (Libya). Although a Company Consul was appointed in Egypt, trade within the country was "neither very prosperous nor very popular". John Sanderson, who had investigated the possibilities of trade with Egypt in various markets, reported back discouragingly of little chance of commerce due to the low prices of English wool and the high prices of spices. It was not until very much later, in the nineteenth century, that English trade flourished in Egypt.

In the sixteenth century trade began to acquire an increasingly special importance in England. In the first half of the century there were only two trading companies in England; in the second half of the same century the number increased to six. Each company traded with one area, and merchants who wanted to trade in more areas were obliged to join several companies. The sixteenth century merchants were primarily motivated by self-interest. They believed in all sincerity that commerce was in the best interest of the country and thus began to promote it to the public as "the lifeblood of the nation". Dudley North, a Levant merchant, wrote that "wherever the traders thrive the public of which they are a part thrives also." The Elizabethan merchants acquired prestige and power. Many were knighted, others became Lord Mayors and financial advisors to the Crown. "Trade is now become the Lady, which in this present age is more courted and celebrated than in any former," said the ever-astute Roger Coke. With this vital importance attached to trade, the news and views of English traders operating overseas became of great interest in England.

From the original explorers and encouraged by merchant journeys, a new spirit for travel emerged in England. Veryard wrote about "an insatiable desire for liberty, of giving [men's] thoughts a larger field to expatiate in and an occasion of actually viewing and contemplating such things in the original as they had often admired in the bare copy." Flecker's Court poet in *Hassan* sang as he set out from Baghdad for Samarkand "for lust of knowing what should not be known".[9] However, many of those who travelled reported "superficial" and strange experiences. These were ridiculed and condemned by Samuel Purchas as returning home with "a few smattering terms, flattering garbes, Apish cringes, foppish fancies, foolish guises and disguises, the vanities of Neighbour Nations . . . without furthering of their knowledge of God, the world or themselves."[10]

Remarking about English merchants in the Near East, Lady Mary Montagu said as late as the eighteenth century that the area was "seldom visited but by merchants, who mind but their own affairs, or travellers, who make too short a stay to be able to report anything exactly of their own knowledge," and she added, "they can give no better idea of the ways here than a French refugee, lodging in a garret in Greek Street, could write of the Court of England."[11]

It was from the accounts of such travellers who lacked knowledge of the Arabic language and did not have the vaguest notion of the people and their customs that many ideas about Arabs began to reach England. Daniel suggests that most writers in that period "depended largely on the myths of their own creating."[12]

At the end of the sixteenth century new ideas began to appear in the accounts of English merchants. Ralph Fitch and John Eldred, who left Aleppo, where they found "good company", to see "the countreys of East India", spoke of travel on camels with a "carovan" to the River Euphrates. Eldred describes the city of Hammah as "fallen and falleth more and more of decay." He spoke of the Turks who had earlier stormed the city and were desirous to let the town remain in ruins. "[The Turks] hath written in the Arabian tongue over the castle gate, which standeth in the midst of the Towne, these words: Cursed be the father and the sonne that shall lay their hands to the repairing hereof." However, Eldred was impressed with Aleppo, "greatest place of traffique". On the journey down the Euphrates Eldred came across "troops" of "Arabians" on the river banks of whom "we bought milk, butter, eggs and lambs and gave them in barter (for they care not for money) glasses, combes, corall, amber, to hang about their armes and necks." He remarked that their hair, clothing and colour resembled "those vagabond Egyptians which heretofor have gone about in England." He presumably referred to gypsies, who at that time were supposed by many to come from Egypt.

Eldred described Arab women as heavily jewelled: "all without exception weare a great round ring in one of their nostrels, of golde, silver, or iorn, according to their ability, and about their armes and smalles of their legs they have loops of golde, silver or iorn." Arab women, children and men were said to be "great swimmers", but Eldred goes on to say that these people are "very Theevish", and relates how the Arabs stole his "casket . . . with things of good value" from under the head of one of his sleeping men. He concludes by warning travellers to take heed while passing down the Euphrates.[13] The theme of "thieving" also appears in Ralph Fitch's account of the river journey: "For the Arabians that bee theeves, will come swimming and steale your goods and flee away . . . you should have much a doe to save your goods from the Arabians which be always there abouts robbing." Those Arabs were said to be terrified of guns, "a gunne is very good, for they doe feare it very much." Fitch also spoke of the customs that travellers had to pay to the "sonnes of Aborise, which is Lord of the Arabians." It should be remembered that European traders, such as the Venetians and the Genoese, were established long before the advent of the English merchants. Some of the accounts of the European merchants were translated into English and, according to William Lithgow, the Venetian travellers circulated many stories warning travellers of the dangers of the "Wilde Arabs".

Fitch's account of the Arabs down the Euphrates was almost identical (with minor alterations of merely a few words) to that of the Venetian merchant Caesar Frederick, who reported of them about twenty years earlier. Whether Fitch did actually experience first hand what he narrated, or whether it is a second-hand report, is not crucial to this study. The important fact is that Arabs at the end of the sixteenth century were portrayed in travellers' accounts as a hostile and dangerous element and part of the harsh and unfriendly environment surrounding travellers in those areas.[14]

Scholars and Travellers

In the seventeenth century information about Arabs continued to emanate from two sources; from scholars and from travellers. Many of the earlier pre-conceptions of the Arabs survived and developed and new themes evolved throughout the century.

At the time when unfavourable information about the Arabs was reaching England from English merchants, scholars were engaged in unravelling the wealth of Arabic thought and its contribution to knowledge. Men such as William Bedwell, Edmund Castell, John Greaves and Edward Pococke were among the scholars who established Arabic studies in the two great Universities of England. Bedwell (1561–1632) became known as the "father of Arabic studies" in England. He emphasised the value of Arabic as the "only language of religion and the chief language of diplomacy and business from the Fortunate Isles and the China Seas." His chief work is an Arabic Lexicon, *The Arabian Trudgman*, in which he explained Arabic terms used by European writers and travellers. The primary motive of the early English scholars in studying Arabic was biblical research. Bedwell knew Arabic and was in general favourably disposed to the Arabs. However, this did not immediately lead him to an understanding of the people, their religion and their society. His missionary involvements as a Christian led him to the general biased attitude towards Islam, thus referring to Muhammad as "the name of that famous imposter and seducer of the Arabians or Saracens . . . and inventor of the Alkoran and laws of that superstitious faction." Apart from the study of the Arabic language for religious motives, Arabic texts were beginning to be translated in this century. Among the works of Edmund Castell (1606–85), the first Cambridge Professor of Arabic, was a translation of original Arabic poems, which he dedicated to King Charles II.[15]

Castell's work also included a dictionary of the Semitic languages, considered then to be of "great importance", and a long essay on the value of Arabic studies. John Greaves, an English mathematician, travelled extensively in the area, especially Egypt, and acquired a large collection of Arabic manuscripts, coins and gems. Greaves also spent some time in 1638 measuring the Pyramids. However, his careful mathematical and astronomical computations failed to solve the puzzle of the Pyramids. But the greatest Arabist of the seventeenth century was Edward Pococke (1604–1691). Pococke, a missionary, worked as a chaplain with the Levant Company. He travelled extensively in the area and lived in Aleppo for five years. He made many Arab friends, and especially important was his friendship with Sheikh Fathallah, a Syrian who remained his life-long friend. On his return to England Pococke was appointed Professor of Arabic at Oxford.

It is said that while at Oxford he spent much of his time under the shade of a fig tree which he had brought back with him from Syria. Pococke's work greatly enhanced Arabic studies in England and in Europe. He produced many important works; among them *Specimen of the History of the Arabs*, printed in Oxford in 1649, in which he made a detailed study of various aspects of Arab culture and history; *Lamiyat al-Ajam*, a study of the classical poem *Tughra'i*; and *Al-Mukhtasar fi-d-Duwal*, a history of Abu'l Faraj. Pococke left behind a very impressive list of works, which were later deposited in the Bodleian Library in Oxford. One of his sons, Edward Pococke (1648–1727) followed in his father's footsteps and became interested in Arabic studies.[16]

The number of English scholars specialising in Arabic studies increased in the seventeenth century, as did the number of merchants and travellers who dispatched information about the area and its peoples. Traveller's accounts became popular in England, especially those dealing with the "Islamic World". Daniel remarks that "there was a large public for accounts of the Islamic World. Proportionately to the books in circulation there must have been more travellers' tales even than today."[17] William Lithgow, an English tourist, travelled around the area in the first part of the seventeenth century. In his *Peregrination*,[18] he makes many allusions to the "wilde and savage Arabs", on his journeys in the Near East. Lithgow tells us that he was warned about Arabs by the Venetian Consul in Aleppo, who had told him of reports of "Arabs that lay for them in the deserts". From then on the "incrusive" and "blood thirsty "Arab was portrayed as lurking in the "bush" waiting to rob and plunder. To Lithgow the Arabs were part of the hostile environment: "Every one of these [Arab] savages, according to his power, dealt with men uncivilly and cruelly, even like a wilderness full of wilde beasts, living all upon rapine and robbery wanting all sense of humanity," he wrote.

Lithgow's account of the Arabs is reminiscent of what the first American settlers reported of the Red Indians. In one story the Arabs were said to use "bows and arrows" against their foes. The story in Lithgow's words was as follows: "Scarcely were wee well advanced in our way, till wee were beset with more than three hundred Arabs, who sent us from shrubby heights an unexpected shower of arrowes," he wrote, and when the soldiers accompanying the group fired their guns, the Arabs scampered to safety. "For when any of them hear the shot of a Harquebuse, they presently turne backe with such speed, as if the fiends of the infernall Court were broken loose at their heeles."

Lithgow distrusted Turks, Moors and Arabs because they were infidels who hated Christians. Therefore he hired a Christian guide on a journey to Lidda because the way was difficult, "roky, and hard to knowe and perilous Arabs". However, to his disappointment and amazement, the Christian guide turned out to be in collusion with the Arabs; he "had sent a privie messenger before us, to warn three hundred Arabs . . . to meet him at such a place as he had appointed; giving them to know, wee were rich and well provided." Lithgow warns all travellers who journeyed to that part of the world to refrain from "whoredome, drunkeness, and too much familiarity with strangers," for it is "impossible he can return in safety from danger of Turkes, Arabs, Moores, wilde beasts and . . . the extremities of heat, hunger, thirst and cold."

Lithgow classified the "infidels" into two groups: the tolerable and the intolerable. Turks and Moors seem to fit in the first category; the Arabs in the second: "The Arabians are for the most part theeves and robbers; the Moores cruell and uncivill . . . the Turkes are ill best of all the three, yet all sworne enemies of Christ." The Arabs were said to hate all strangers. They were seen as a "wilde" and unmanageable group who even "annoyed the Turkes". In his own words Lithgow describes the Arabs as people who "cannot be possibly brought to a quiet and well formed manner of living but are continuall spoilers of these parts of Turkes Dominions."

Lithgow's travel narratives evoked interest and admiration: one admirer, introducing one of his early travel accounts, marvels at his adventures:

> Thou durst go like no man else that lives;
> By sea and land alone in cold and raine,
> Through Bandits, Pirates, and Arabian Theeves.

The felonious and evil nature of Arabs became a pronounced theme in the accounts of early English travellers.

In the same year in which Lithgow journeyed to the Levant (1610), another Englishman, George Sandy, made a similar journey to the area, visiting Egypt and Palestine. In his *Relation of a Journey*,[19] Sandy described the Arabs as the inhabitants of deserts who dwell in tents, "They dwell in tents, which they move like walking cities, for opportunities of prey, and benefit of pasturage." He follows Mandeville in pointing out that they are "independent" and proud people. The concept of "nation" is first and significantly introduced in Sandy's accounts, who thus perceives them as a separate entity from the rest of the subjects of the Ottoman Empire. Another quality which appears in Sandy's description is worthwhile noting, and that is of "Nobilitie". Although he himself did not describe them as noble, he infers that because this "Nation from the beginning unmixed with others", therefore they boast of "their Nobilitie". Sandy seems to imply that their sense of nobility emanated from their pure stock. Nonetheless, in keeping with the tradition of early accounts, he portrays them as robbers "of meane stature", "raw-boned" and "tawnie", who have "feminine voyces" and creep "behind you ere aware of them." Sandy concludes: "Their Religion Mahonetanisme, glorying in that the Imposter was their countriman; their language extending as farre as that Religion extendeth."

Sandy spoke of the Arabs as "merchants" selling camels and horses in the desert. "It seemeth strange to mee, how these merchants can get by their wares so far fetcht." Nonetheless Sandy had something good to say about Arabs. "If one of these Arabians undertake your conduct hee will performe it faithfully: neither will any of the nation molest you," he wrote. "They will lead you by unknowne neererways; and farther in four dayes, than you can travell by caravan in fourteen."

Sandy describes the camel as "a creature created for burthen . . . a beast gentle and tractable, but in the time of his venery: then, as if remembering his former hard usage, he will bite his keeper, throw him downe and kick him, forty dayes continuing in that fury, and then returning to his former meekness." He calls the camel a "ship" and the desert a "sea"; "These [camels] are the ships of Arabia, their seas are the desarts." Sandy makes a distinction between Arabia "Felix" and Arabia "desart". Arabia, he wrote, is "a barren and desolate country being neither grasse nor trees, save only here and there a few palmes which will not forsake those forsaken places."

Henry Blount, who was celebrated in a poem:

> Mongst a lawless straggling crew
> Made up of Arab, Saracen and Jew . . .

toured the Levant, especially Egypt. In his *Voyage into the Levant*[20] in 1638, he reports his experiences and makes allusions to the "wild" Arabs. On a journey down the River Nile, Blount describes the Turkish houses on the river banks and compares them to the

"Arabish" and "Egyptians". These houses, he wrote, "which if Turkish they were high built, of bricks or other firme stone, but if Arabish or Egyptian, the houses were most of mud, just in forme of Bee-hives." At the end of the boat journey he saw "six of the wild Arabs, five on horse-backe, one a foot, each with a launce, which they can use in hand." The Arabs ran away after the boatmen fired gunshots.

Blount spoke of the city of Cairo as being guarded by "eight and twenty thousand men", against the "sudden incrusions of Arabs" who came from the wilderness.

Blount's apparent hatred of Arabs and "Egyptians" is in contrast to his appreciation of the Turks. At one point, he glowingly describes the "civilitie" and sweetness of Turkish sailors in the following terms: "The strongest thing I found among the (Turks) was their incredible civilitie; I who had often proved the Barbarisme of other nations . . . and above all others, of our owne, supposed my selfe amongst Bears, till by experience, I found the contrary; and that only in ordinary civilitie, but with so ready service, such patience, so sweet and gentle a way. . . ."

His praise of the Turks went further than that. "He who would behold these times seen then in Turkey," he wrote, and went on to say that the Turks "are the only moderne people, great in action . . . whose Empire both so suddenly invaded the world and fixt itselfe such firm foundations as no other ever did."

Against this testimony of the greatness of the Ottoman Empire, Blount tells us that the Turks have to rule the Arabs and the inhabitants of Egypt with an iron fist because the Turks know "them to be malicious, trecherous and effeminate". He then proceeds to justify the many tortures the Turks practised against them because it was not possible to rule them by a "sweet hand". Blount mentions several methods of torture used by the Turks, "impaling, gaunching, flaying alive, cutting off the waist, hanging by the foot, planting in burning lime and the like." He then, almost with glee, speaks of two torturing sessions which he witnessed. The first was of a man accused of burning his neighbour's house. "He was first flayed alive, with such art, as he was more than three hours a dying; then was his skinne stuffed with chaffe, and borne stradling upon an ass up and downe the Town." The second incident involved "three Arabs" who had robbed in the wilderness; they were taken and executed in the following manner. "They were laid naked upon the ground, their face downeward their hands and legs tyed abroad to stakes," he writes, and proceeds to describe the grotesque manner in which they were executed: "then came the Hangman, who putting their owne half pikes in at the fundament did with a beetle, drive them up leisurely, till they came out at the head, or shoulder." Two of the men died suddenly, the third took some time longer until his brains were "dasht out". Blount remarks that the Turks have committed such atrocities to "break the spirits of this people."

Sandy, Lithgow and Blount were among many English travellers who reported on Arabs and Arab lands in the seventeenth century. Take for example, Fynes Moryson, who had travelled with his brother Henry Moryson (who died later of a nose bleed) by sea to Palestine and who portrays Arabs as robbers and a sinister people. In his *Itinerary*,[21] published in 1617, he makes a reference to a journey he wanted to take to the Jordan Valley, but was discouraged because of fear of "Arabians and Moores".

Henry Mundrell, in the latter part of the century, describes the Jordan Valley as "a most miserable dry barren place it is . . . consisting of high rocky mountains, so torn and disordered as if the earth here had suffered some great convulsion, in which its bound had been turned outwards." Of the Arabs, who lurked in caves in mountains, Mundrell wrote, "In most of these grots we found certain Arabs quartered with five Arabs who obstructed our ascent, demanding two hundred dollors for leave to go up the mountain."[22]

Piracy and Slavery

In the latter part of the seventeenth century two themes of the image of Arabs became particularly popular in England, namely piracy and slavery. Piracy, as mentioned earlier in this chapter, was a major headache to the English merchants. Slavery was related to it, since it was believed that pirates captured Christian travellers and took them to the Barbary Coast on the promise of freedom for ransom.

The Englishman who contributed most to the popularisation of the themes of slavery and piracy was Joseph Pitts. Pitts, an Exeter boy, claimed to have been captured by Algerian pirates in 1678 when he was fifteen years of age. It is also said that the boy was sold as a slave twice over and ended up in Tunis. Whilst he was there, the English Consul and two other merchants were said to have tried to free him, but these efforts failed because "the price demanded proved too high". Eventually, the story asserts, the boy was taken back to Algiers, where his master determined to force him to become a Muslim. English accounts describe the boy's dilemma:

"For a considerable period Pitts withstood manfully blows, hard fare, and other cruelties, but at last, utterly exhausted and hopeless, he gave way and pronounced the required formula, although with a troubled conscience."[23] Pitts' experience and eventual escape excited much interest. The story was published in his *Faithful Account of the Religion and Manners of the Mahometans, with an Account of the Author's having been taken by his Master on the Pilgrimage to Mecca.*[24] This work attracted considerable attention, for several reasons. The first was that Pitts was the first Englishman (with possible exception of an unknown renegade) to enter Arabia, and secondly, he was a Christian slave who authenticated the accounts of Christian slaves in the Barbary states. Pitts in his book describes the *Haj* and speaks of the people of Arab lands. In his narrative he describes the Algerian slave traders as "extremely addicted to cozening and cheating". Of his capture and later beatings he wrote that "I being then but young" could no longer endure the tortures inflicted upon him and turned Muslim, "God be merciful to me a sinner," he added. Of his pilgrimage to Mecca Pitts described the desert caravan, the sea trip and an encounter with a ship laden with slaves; and he was once in Alexandria, a city which was "a very famous city in former times" and now "lies in ruins". He was impressed with the Nile, but stated that it was infested with robbers who "rob in boats". The inhabitants of Egypt are a "mixture of Moors, Turks, Jews, Greeks and Copties". All wear turbans, "the Moors turbants being all white and the Copties white striped with blue." However, all speak one language. He noted that Egypt has an abundance of "East India commodities, as silks, muslins, callicoes, spices, coffee etc. and also of milk, butter, cheese, oil, olives, etc." Egypt, Pitts claimed, is full of whores. "There is in no part of the world, I am apt to think, greater encouragement given to whoredom than in Egypt," he wrote. These whores are "very rich" and "use to sit at the door, or walk in the streets unveiled."

In his accounts of the people of the area he travelled in, Pitts generalises that homosexuality is widely practised. "'Tis common for men there to fall in love with boys as 'tis in England to be in love with women," he wrote.

Pitts proceeds to speak about the city life of "Grand Cairo, a place eminent in history". He paints a picture of many mosques with wells in them. "If I mistake not, it is reported that in this city there are five or six thousand public and private Mosques," he declares.

He also spoke of Christian slaves in a slave market "held twice a week for the selling of Christian slaves". Pitts portrays a pitiful picture of these slaves: "The boys, whose heads are shaved, when they stand in the market have a lock of hair, one part under their caps, the other hanging down their cheeks, to signify they are newly taken and are yet Christians," he wrote. Then he described Christian women slaves as being inspected and fondled by buyers: "and altho' the women and maidens are veil'd, yet the chapmen have liberty to view their faces and to put their fingers into their teeth, and also to feel their breasts. Nay, further, as I have been informed, they are sometimes permitted by the sellers in a modest way to be searched whether they are virgins or no."

Pitts tells us that there are no Turks in Cairo except soldiers. The people of Cairo are "very rugged and much given to passion. They'll scold like whores, but seldom care to fight." The people are also described as robbers "addicted to cozening and cheating", and hate strangers. The city of Cairo has a multitude of beggars, especially Thursday evenings, "the evening before the Sabbath". Well-to-do-people in Cairo keep eunuchs in their houses to guard their wives. Pitts then proceeds to describe the Holy City of Mecca and the *Haj*. The inhabitants of Arabia he describes as a "poor sort of people, very thin, lean and swarthy". He speaks of "dervishes" who constantly travel with a "sheep or goatskin on their back and to lie on, and a long staff in their hand." There are also the "effendies" who are "masters of learning, who daily expound out the Alcoran, sitting in high chairs."

Pitt describes travel in the deserts in caravans: "They travel four camels in a breast which are all tied one after the other, like as in teams. The whole body is called a caravan; which is divided into several cottors, or companies, each of which hath its name and consists (it may be) of several thousand camels; and they move one cottor after another, like distinct troops."

Pitts, whilst travelling back through the desert, does not overlook the lurking Arab thieves. "In this journey many times the skulking, thievish Arabs do much mischief," he writes.

Pitts' accounts of his experiences became popular in England at the beginning of the eighteenth century. His reference to Arabs was not always clear. At times Pitts would call them Algerians, Moors, Arabs, and at other times he would refer to them as Egyptians and Turks. In general he portrayed the Arabs as pirates, slavers, beggars, homosexuals and robbers.

Images, Poetic and Otherwise

Throughout the sixteenth and seventeenth centuries, the reports of the English merchants and travellers did not concern themselves with making a clear distinction between Arabs and Turks. In addition, Arabs were also referred to as Saracens, Moors and Mamelukes: all these were described as "dark", "tawny", "black", and of "swarthy complexion". In general, however, the term Arab was used to refer to the desert Arabs (Bedouin); Saracens were the city Arabs who lived in Syria and Palestine; Moors, the Arab inhabitants of North Africa; and Mamelukes were generally the Arabs of Egypt. In these two centuries the Arabs of the desert were portrayed as a separate entity, as Sandy called them, a "nation". They were described as "wild", "incrusive", "blood thirsty" and "savage". Their main occupation was said to be thievery and looting. This group was perceived as a dangerous element that threatened the safety of travellers and the stability of the Ottoman Empire. The Saracens were described as cruel enemies of Christians, those who fought the Crusaders and later added to the sufferings of Christian pilgrims. It has been noted that in Elizabethan England there were many inns (some can still be found today) called *The Saracen's Head*, with the head pictured as "grotesque in features and of a red or garnish colour". Joseph Hall wrote:

> His angry eyes look all so glaring bright
> . . . like a painted staring Saracen.[25]

Moors were generally spoken of as the pirates in the Barbary States. They were portrayed primarily as the cruel slavers of Christians, "that fiend, that damn'd Moor, that devil, that Lucifer", was the description of Eleazar, a character in William Rowley's *All's Lost by Lust*.

Samuel Chew, describing the image of Moors during the Renaissance in England, wrote: "From Spanish hatred of the Moors, reinforced by the general Christian hatred of Mohammedans and by experiences of piratical depredations, came the Elizabethan emphasis upon the cruelty of these people—and upon their blackness."[26]

The Mamelukes were generally portrayed as residing in Egypt and possessing the same qualities as Arabs, Saracens and Moors.

Arab lands also began to acquire certain reputations in the works of the sixteenth and seventeenth century travellers, and of some writers who had never left England; Arabia, Syria, Egypt, Pales-

tine and North Africa were often mentioned and became stereotyped.

Arabia was often spoken of as being divided into two parts;
Arabia "Deserta" and Arabia "Felix". Arabia the desert was described as "barren" and "rocky". Sandy and Lithgow characterised
it as a "forsaken" place. Spenser, the Elizabethan poet, wrote:

> A silly man, in simple weeds forworne,
> And soild with dust of the long dried way;
> His sandles were with toilsome travell torne
> And face all tand with scorching sunny ray,
> As he had traveiled many a sommers day
> Through boyling sands of Arabie and Ynde.[27]

Arabia "Felix" on the other hand was watered and fertile; it
was associated with wealth and luxury. This land evoked a colourful aura of sweetness, perfume and "Sabaean spices". Marlowe's
Barabas in *The Jew of Malta* says:

> Well fare the Arabians who so richly pay
> The things they traffic for with wedge of gold![28]

Fletcher exclaims:

> The sweetness of the Arabian wind, still blowing
> Upon the treasures of perfume and spices.[29]

Then comes the well known passage which Milton wrote in
Paradise Lost:

> . . . off at sea North-East winds blow
> Sabaean odours from the spicy shore
> Of Araby the Blest; with such delay
> Well pleas'd they slack their course, and many a League
> Cheer'd with the grateful smell old Ocean smiles.[30]

The "robbers" of Arabia, Damascus, Egypt and the Arab lands
were brought together in an English play in 1639. The play, a
tragedy, was called *The Phoenix in Her Flames*,[31] by William Lower.
The plot is thought to have been derived from the works of Helio-
dorus. The work involves an Egyptian Princess and a Prince of
Damascus. Both were captured by "Arab robbers" in the desert,
the Princess whilst on her way to marry a Persian Prince and the
Prince having fled his country in the face of an invasion by the
Tartars. An Arab desert outlaw falls in love with the Princess, but

is killed by the Prince of Damascus. The grateful Princess falls in love with him, but he does not love her. When the Prince of Persia hears that the "Marauding Arabs" have taken his bride-to-be as prisoner, he invades them with his followers. This territorial incursion surprises the King of Arabia, who is unaware of the happenings. The Prince of Damascus, who had won the confidence of the Arab tribes in the deserts, fights against the Persians and brings their Prince as a prisoner to the King of the Arabs. Both the Prince of Damascus and the Prince of Persia fall in love with the daughter of the Arab King, Phaenicia. Later both are urged to a duel in which the Prince of Damascus kills the Prince of Persia, but is slain by the treachery of a Persian Duke. In grief for the Prince of Damascus, Phaenicia kills herself in "clouds of incense", while the Egyptian Princess returns sadly home, having lost both her faithless betrothed and her rescuer.

Egypt was portrayed as a land of mystery. The country evoked to the Elizabethans associations with the River Nile and the Pyramids. The Nile attracted the curiosity of many: its rise and fall, its source and the fertility of the river valley. The construction and description of the Pyramids fascinated English mystical and mathematical thought. Egypt was also associated in Elizabethan literature with the captivity of the Israelites and with the plagues inflicted upon Egyptians. Cairo was perceived as a city of mosques with slave markets, beggars and whores and "multitudes" of people. Lithgow described it as "this incorporate world . . . the most admirable and greatest city seene upon the earth", where "all sorts of Christians" and an "infinite number of infidels" meet. Syria, with Damascus and Aleppo, was a haven for English travellers. The land was known as a "Garden of God" and, as Lithgow put it, an "Earthly Paradise". There were also the Biblical associations revolving around Saint Paul's journey into the city of Damascus. Also there was the ancient legend that Adam was created near that city and that Cain slew Abel at Damascus.

> This be Damascus, be thou cursed Caine,
> To slay thy brother Abel, if thou wilt.[32]

Palestine, the Holy Land, naturally captured the imagination of many writers in the sixteenth and seventeenth centuries. Biblical associations with the "Holy Family", the cities of Jerusalem and Bethlehem, the Jordan Valley and River Jordan, were described in detail and allusions were often made to the "infidels" who controlled them and the dangers of Arab robbers who threatened travellers. The Sinai Desert was often described as infested with Arab "robbers" and pointed out to be a dangerous crossing.

Algeria, Tunis and Libya, the "Barbary States", were primarily associated with piracy and slavery. The "pirates of Algiers" and "pirates of Tripoli" became popular terms in the two centuries. Algeria, according to Francis Knight, was a "citie fatall to all Christians and the butchery of all mankind".[33]

Chapter Three

The Arabian Nights

The Effects of a Legend

The power and might of the Turkish Empire seem to have fascinated and at the same time frightened the Englishmen who were
travelling in the area in the sixteenth and seventeenth centuries.
The Arabs, although spoken of as a nation, were for the most part
ignored and dismissed as thieves and savages, who harassed the
great Empire of the Turks. Simon Ockley, an eighteenth century
Arabist, took note of this fact in a letter to his daughter in which he
was telling her of the difficulties in redressing a "great many mis-
takes" concerning Arabs made by travellers who passing through
the area "without the necessary knowledge of the history and
ancient customs . . . pick up little pieces of tradition from the
present inhabitants and deliver them as obscurely as they receive
them." Ockley also provides us with insight into the then prevalent

attitudes of the English towards Arabs. He thought that many English people "entertain too mean an opinion of them, looking upon them as mere barbarians; and this mistaken notion hindered all further inquiry,"[1] he wrote.

In the eighteenth century a new inquisitiveness about the Middle East, especially Egypt, began to develop in England. This growing curiosity marked a shift from earlier concern about Turks to new interest in Arabs. The change in emphasis occurred as a result of several factors: firstly, the publication of the *Arabian Nights*; secondly, the Arabic studies which were earlier used for Biblical research and which had now led to genuine interest in the literature and history of the Arabs. A third factor was the growing appreciation of and interest in antiquities. Finally, and of great importance for political reasons, this change was especially due to the Napoleonic military expedition into Egypt.

The eighteenth century might even be called the century of the *Arabian Nights* in England. After its publication, the book made a deep and lasting impression on English literature and sensibilities. The *Arabian Nights* appeared in the English language in England in 1712, having been translated from Galland's French version. Soon it governed the form of a surprisingly large output of English fiction. Martha Conant states that it is impossible to study the oriental tale in England without the highlights falling upon the *Arabian Nights*.[2]

Throughout the eighteenth century and subsequent generations the *Nights* exercised a substantial influence, not only on English literature, but also on English attitudes towards Arabs and the Middle East in general. The tales acquired a sense of reality for the English reader who was also reading the "true accounts" of English travellers. The image of Arabs portrayed in travel books complemented that of the *Arabian Nights*.

The fantasy world of the Arabian Tales, with its genies, magic, flying horses and supernatural birds, reinforced earlier accounts of English travellers: for example, Mandeville's "desert monester" in Egypt who was half goat, half man, and Lithgow's birds that flew over the Dead Sea and died from its fumes; and the disintegrating apples in the Jordan Valley, which crumbled when bitten. Pitts' travel narratives, which attained popularity at the time the *Nights* appeared in England, of the mysterious East with the city of Cairo having slave markets, veiled women, whores, dervishes, eunuchs and people who were "much given to passion" complemented the

Nights' exotic and picturesque scenes of harems, princesses, slaves, eunuchs and romance.

Thus, in the eighteenth century, the image of Arabs in England began to acquire new themes of exotic and erotic qualities. These new qualities became part of the general attitude of travellers towards Arabs in particular and the Middle East in general. Alexander Pope called the Middle East the "free region of adultery", in a letter to Mary Montagu, who was travelling to the Near East. Pope wrote:

"I doubt not I shall be told (when I come to follow you thro' those countries) in how pretty a manner you accommodated yourself to the customs of the True Believers. At this Town they will say, she practised to sit on the sofa; at the village she learnt to fold the Turbant; here she was bathed and anointed; and there she parted with her black Fullbottome. . . . Lastly I shall hear how the very first night you lay in Pera, you had a vision of Mahomet's paradise, and happily awaked without a soul. From which blessed instant the beautiful Body was left at full liberty to perform all the agreeable functions it was made for."[3]

Mary Montagu in a letter to her sister describing her meeting with one "Sultana" in Constantinople wrote: "Now do I fancy that you imagine I have entertain'd you all this while with a relation that has (at least) receiv'd many embellishments from my hand. This is but too like (says you) the Arabian Tales; these embroider'd napkins and a jewell as large as a Turkey's egg!—You forget dear sister, those very tales were writ by an author of this country and (excepting the Enchantments) are a real representation of the manners here."[4]

Until the publication of the *Arabian Nights*, there was no clear distinction made between the various people of the Middle East, as mentioned earlier; all were lumped together. However, with the association of the Arabians with the Tales, an autonomous identity of Arabs began to acquire a distinct place in the thinking of the English people. This distinction between Arabs and others was further manifested in the appearance in England of the *Persian Tales* and the *Turkish Tales*.

England's discovery of the Arabs, which had earlier begun with obscure accounts of travellers and scholars, reached a new stage in the eighteenth century with the *Arabian Nights*. Harun El Rashid, the Caliph of Baghdad, Ali Baba with his Forty Thieves, and Sinbad the Sailor were some of the adventurers who attained popularity in England. Cairo and Baghdad became the colourful settings of the plots and plotters. As a result, the Arabs and their lands became irrevocably associated with this satirical, exotic and romantic, but nonetheless unrealistic, world. The old images were synthesised into real and unreal characters from the world of the tales.

Scholars and their Works

In the meanwhile English scholars of the eighteenth century were hard at work unravelling the wealth of works of theology, as well as medicine and mathematics, written in Arabic. Arabic studies had then far outpassed public interest in Arabs. Among the numerous English Arabists of that period was Simon Ockley, who was a pupil of the Oxford Arabist Edward Pococke. Ockley, mentioned above, who later became Professor of Arabic in Cambridge, had initially studied theology. His interest in Arabic led him, despite many personal difficulties, to write a cultural and political history of the Arabs in English in three volumes, entitled *The History of the Saracens*,[5] which was then considered to be a major contribution towards knowledge of the Arabs. Ockley's work "represents the first attempt ever made to present to the English reader in popular and understandable form, a general account of the achievements of Arab civilization." In his preface, Ockley presents the Arabs as people with a book and a sword. "[They] rendered themselves universally remarkable, both by their arms and learning." He held Arabic in high esteem and described it as "that learned copious and elegant language".

However, it seems that what Ockley had to say about the achievements of Arabs shocked and surprised many Englishmen. Ockley mentions this attitude in his introduction to the second edition, where he alludes to the reception of his first volume, stating that the critics received his narrative of Arab history as "the strangest story they had ever heard since they were born!" He continued to describe the attitude of bewilderment: "They never met with such folks in their lives as these Arabians! They never heard too, they said, of these things before, which they of course must have done it, if anybody else had." He wrote, "A reverend dignitary asked me, if, when I wrote that book, I had not lately been reading the history of Oliver Cromwell! They say that the Arabians are given to romance; and for that reason I suppose they are not to be believed (according to Aristotle) when they speak truth."

Ockley's statement clearly explains the popular general attitude towards Arabs in England in the eighteenth century, namely an obscure, marauding people who are, despite the romantic influence of the *Arabian Nights*, still given to passion and incapable of any significant achievements.

Against the background of such ignorance, Ockley was obliged to introduce the Arabs to his readers. He described Arabs before Muhammad as "idolators" and "warlike". He divided them into two classes: the city Arabs who lived in towns and villages, and the tent dwellers who roamed the deserts. According to Ockley, the occupations of these Bedouin included horse breeding, the use of weapons, and poetry: "Their chief excellence, consisted in breeding and managing horses, and the use of bows, swords, and lances. Their learning lay wholly in their poetry, to which their genius greatly inclined them." Ockley could not emancipate himself from his orthodox Christian theological training, however. He subscribed to the general attitude of animosity English scholars held towards Islam, so that his views of Islam and of Muhammad reflected hostility and resentment. Although on the one hand Ockley praised Arabs for their learning and achievements, on the other he condemned them on the grounds that "they were the first ruin of the Eastern church." He called Islam "that new superstition", which Muhammad "pretended to have received by inspiration from God." Nonetheless, Ockley believed that Islam and Muhammad succeeded in uniting "those jarring tribes" and rooted out idolatry. For two hundred years hence, "little else was cared for but war," he wrote. Although Ockley resented Muhammad and Islam on religious grounds we see him transcending his religious prejudice when dealing with one of Muhammad's successors, Al Mamoun, whom he calls "that noble Caliph", for cultivating learning and knowledge. Our scholar did not make any distinction between Arabs, Saracens and Moors. To him they were all "Arabians", with Saracens inhabiting the East and the Moors being the Arabs of Africa. Ockley highly praised Arabs for their love of knowledge, for their insight and practical wisdom: "the sagacity and application of that ingenious, penetrating people," he wrote, to learning, "after they had once entered upon it, seeming no less wonderful than that of their conquests." However, Ockley had two main criticisms of Arab scholars: the first, that they did not, he claimed, study Greek historians as much as they did Greek philosophers; the second was against those Arabs who did not study other languages, such as Greek, considering their Arabic language to be superior. This, according to Ockley, led Arab authors to "tell things, after a careless manner, often stuffing their work with many trifling matters, at other times jingling upon words and, to show the copiousness of their language and variety of expression, spinning out a trifling incident into a long story." Ockley's other works included a general introduction to the study of oriental languages and an English translation of Edward Pococke's (Junior) Latin version of *Hai Ibn Yaqthan*, a philosophical romance by Ibn Tufail. On this translation, Defoe is said to have depended to some extent for *Robinson Crusoe*.

Two other notable English scholars of the eighteenth century who contributed towards the development of Arabic studies in England were George Sale and William Jones. Sale, described as "half a Muslim", was initially a lawyer. He had studied Arabic on his own and collected many Arabic manuscripts. Sale is best known for his translation of the Koran, published in 1734, with explanations of many of the passages and an introduction on Islam. Many English and European scholars used his book as a reference, including Voltaire, who quoted it in his *Philosophic Dictionary*. In his introduction entitled *Preliminary Discourse to the Koran*,[6] Sale gave an account of the "Religion, learning and customs" of the Arabs. He pointed out that for several centuries Christian writers spoke of them "under the appellation of Saracens; the most certain derivation of which word is from *shark*, the East." Sale stated that Arabia, the original habitat of the Arabs, was not as rich as ancient legends had us believe, "yet, in reality," he wrote, "great part of the riches which the ancients imagined were the produce of Arabia, came from the Indies and the coasts of Africa." According to Sale, Arabs, from time immemorial, had lived in groups called tribes. Each tribe valued itself for its traditions and thus fought against other tribes to maintain its identity. Although tribes often waged war against each other, they succeeded in keeping intruders out of their country. Thus Sale reinforced the theme mentioned by earlier English travellers, namely that Arabs treasured their independence and liberty. Even the Turks could not claim sovereignty over them: "Thus have the Arabs preserved their liberty, of which few nations can produce so ancient monuments, with very little interruption, from the very Deluge; for though very great armies have been sent against them, all attempts to subdue them were unsuccessful." Sale was one of the first English writers to state that not all Arabs were Muslims, but there are Christian Arabs and Jewish Arabs. He praised Arabs for their hospitality and for being "exact to their words".

Sale also praised the Arabic language as being "very harmonious and expressive". However, although he spoke of Arab "excellencies", he mentioned "defects and vices" of Arabs. He considered, for example, that Arabs have a natural disposition for war and a reputation for thieving. Apparently the accusations of thieving levelled against Arabs in the accounts of early travellers and merchants became an important part of their image in Europe. Sale wrote:

"The frequent robberies committed by these people on merchants and travellers have rendered the name of an Arab almost infamous in Europe."

In spite of this reputation, a special attraction towards the Arabs began to develop in England. This appeal is reflected in Sale's works when he states that Arabs have always been celebrated for their quickness of apprehension and penetration and for the vivacity of their wit, "especially those of the desert". Thus a romantic theme begins to appear in the works of serious English writers, especially towards the desert Arab.

One other point must be mentioned before we leave Sale's account. He believed that it was only the Arabs' tribal warfare that enabled the Turks to invade Arabia. He was of the opinion that because Arabs were united in "one faith and under one prince" they were able to achieve "those conquests which extended the Mohammadan faith over so great a part of the world."

In the eighteenth century the *Mu'allaqat* (*The Hanging Poems*), which were said to have been written in gold and hung in the Kabah in Mecca in pre-Islamic Arabia, were made available to English readers through William Jones' translation. Jones had earlier learned Arabic at the hands of an Arab from Aleppo, whom he had, at his own expense, brought from London to Oxford. The *Mu'allaqat* represented to the Arabs a miraculous achievement by Arab poets.

The importance of the connection between the Middle East and England became more apparent in the eighteenth century. The conquest of India during this period and the growing French interest and influence in the Levant gave the English the added impetus to understand more fully the Middle East and its inhabitants, especially the Arab race. The English travellers' accounts in this century reflect a more serious approach to Arabs in general. Among those who journeyed and interacted with the normal customs of life of the Arabs were Richard Pococke from 1737 to 1740, Charles Perry in 1739 and 1740, Alexander Russell from 1745 to 1753, James Bruce from 1768 to 1773, and William Eton in 1799.

Richard Pococke, a wealthy clergyman, spent three years, 1737 to 1740, studying the Middle East. In his book, *Description of the East*,[7] he reiterates the old themes about Arabs previously described in this and in earlier chapters, and he makes many references to their "avarice and disposition to thefts and robberies". However, he also introduces some new concepts. On his expeditions he often met Arabs who, he claimed, threatened his life upon non-payment of ransom. In several instances he discovered that the Arabs were, in fact, bluffing and, according to him, if he handled them properly, the traveller could call their bluff with success. There is one incident he mentions in which Arabs on horseback offered to guard him in return for "small gratitude", but when he was "satisfied there was no danger," he wrote, "I signified to them they need not give themselves trouble, on which they always went quietly away." On another occasion, when he was travelling in a caravan, Arabs stopped the company and demanded money, threatening to take Pococke away, but apparently by this time he knew what tactics to adopt. "I treated them with coffee," he wrote, "made them my friends, and refused to pay anything." (The offering of coffee was, and is, a sign of hospitality and courtesy.) The Arabs are easily dissuaded, according to Pococke, who cautions travellers not to give money under threat. "So dangerous a thing is it to give the Arabs money on any account whatsoever." Pococke does not condemn all Arabs, explaining that there are both good and bad Arabs, according to Western ethics. The good ones are hospitable, brave and honest; the bad are robbers, thieves, and haters of foreigners.

He makes a further distinction between Arabs: between those from the East and those from the West, the latter called "mughrabi", who are "rather worse". Pococke also specifies the "Bedoui" as those who "live in tents . . . subsisting mostly by the cattle they graze."

Pococke did not have any respect for the natives of Egypt, who are composed of Arabs and "Filaws": he describes them as "melicious and envious" and condemns them for their laziness and idleness. "The natives of Egypt are now a slothful people," he wrote. "They delight in sitting still hearing tales and indeed seem always to have been more fit for the quiet life." This indolence, he continued, "may be owing to the great heat of the country."

To Pococke Arab women were allowed more freedom than the Turkish females. On one occasion he was entertained by Arab men and their wives. This is how he describes the event: "I sat around a fire in the tent with his (Arab) wife and others," he wrote, "for Arabs are not so scrupulous as the Turks about their women."

Pococke was one of the first English travellers to attempt to explore that great enigma of the period and of the nineteenth century, the source of the Nile, a subject of increasing interest to Europeans. This attempt was later followed by the adventures of James Bruce.

Travellers' Tales

In the meantime, travellers began to report a number of feats performed by the Arabs. One such was described by Charles Perry, a doctor, who journeyed into the area in 1739 and 1740. In his narrative *View of the Levant*,[8] Perry remarked, "we are really sick and surfeited" of the Pyramids, and, so sickened, proceeded to venture into the interior of Egypt. He was impressed by the Arabs who knew how to cure certain diseases, especially the "stone and gravel" illness (gall-stones). "Here are likewise several amongst the Arabs, who make it their profession to cure such as are inflicted with the stone and gravel by Inflation." He then describes the method used by Arabs to blow in the urethra and succeed in extracting the stones and gravel from the bladder. "We have seen one very recent and signal instance of its success, of which we think it worth our pains to give the public a circumstantial account," he wrote.

Another doctor who worked with the Levant Company and wrote an account of the area was Alexander Russell. In his book *Natural History of Aleppo*[9] (described by Sarah Searight as a "delightful and exhaustive survey of the society, flora, fauna and particularly the plague" of the city of Aleppo) Russell described the Muhammadan inhabitants of Aleppo, making fine distinctions between them. Unlike his predecessors, and of importance for this reason alone, he did not lump all the people of the area together into one entity, such as either all Muhammadans or all Turks, but spoke of various groups, such as Osmanli, Turks, Agas and Arabs. Furthermore, he made a distinction between the "Sonnites" and "Shites", the two Moslem sects still existing. Russell described the population of Aleppo as being dominated by Turks. He classified the inhabitants in socio-economic terms and spoke of "Bashaw" and "Effendees". "The Bashaw with his retinue, and all other immediately in the service of the Porte are called Osmanli, and either speak or affect to speak the Turkish language. The Effendees compose the body of the Ullama, or learned men. Their common language is the Arabic, for most of them being natives of Aleppo, but few can speak the Turkish with tolerable purity. The Agas or (in a restricted sense) those who rent the lands, have still some influence in the Divan, or Council of the city, but their power and splendour have been long on the decline, and most of the old families are now extinct."

From the above classifications, the Arabs are the "learned men", the "Effendees", although Russell implied this, rather than making it a specific point. However, later in his narrative, the author clearly identified Arabs and stated that a "considerable number of Arabs dwell within the city and suburbs . . . in small, mean houses." The Arabs, who were also referred to as "Bidoweens", were described as belonging to the lower classes. Arab men were labourers and their women worked as servants. "The men are employed in various kinds of manual labour and the women are often attached to the Harems of the great, as servants, or nurses." Arabs were reported as refusing to marry from outside their own ethnic group, thus retaining their manners and national dress (usually composed of Kunbaz, black sash and Arab abbai). Russell's description of the dress and jewels worn by Arab women is similar to the sixteenth century account of John Eldred. Russell wrote: "Their women, by means of a needle and a certain powder, give a dark blue colour to the lips, and in the same manner make blue marks, or imitations of flowers, on their cheeks, breasts and arms, they prick the parts with a needle, and then rub the powder into the punctures. The mark remains indelible, like what may be seen among sailors, and some of the common people in England." He stated, "They wear a large ring of gold or silver, pendant from the nose, the cartilage on one side being pierced for that purpose: it is usually the external cartilage of the right nostril." Russell further adds, "I have seen some of the rings of at least an inch and a half diameter. La Roque describes them as made not only of gold and silver but of tin, lead, or copper, and of a size so large as to encompass the mouth; he adds that it is a piece of gallantry among the Arabs, to kiss their women through them."

Although Arabs kept their identity distinct from the rest of the inhabitants of the city, they were described as being "insensibly led" and as borrowers of something "from the more polished people among whom they dwell".

Not only did Russell make distinctions between the various peoples, their customs and occupations, but he also differentiated between the various groups of Arabs. He divided them into two principal divisions: those "who live in cities and villages", and "those who live constantly in tents". The latter group, the

Bedouin, are called the "true Arabs" and were said to despise the "Moors", the city dwellers. "The true Arabs hold them [the Moors] in contempt, considering them as a dishonourable people who by dwelling in towns, living as traders, or applying themselves to agriculture (employment altogether unworthy of the nobility of the pure Arabs), have degenerated from the virtues of their ancestors." Russell also refers to the *Arabian Nights*, stating that it was a "scarce book at Aleppo"; and after much inquiry "I found only two volumes, containing two hundred and eighty nights, and with difficulty obtained liberty to have a copy taken." Throughout his book, Russell used Arabic words in his footnotes, an indication that he was certainly more than slightly conversant with the language.

In the second half of the century, another traveller, James Bruce, journeyed in the area with the aim of discovering the source of the Nile, now assuming increasing interest in England, which he claimed to have reached, having traced its course from Lake Tana in Ethiopia to the sea. Bruce's experiences are described in a biography called simply *Travels*.[10] At an early age Bruce studied Arabic in the Escorial in Spain, and later was appointed British Consul in Algiers. Whilst there he began to plan an exploration to discover the source of the Nile. From Algiers he travelled along the North African coast: from there he visited the ruins of Baalbek in Lebanon, and remarked that the temple there "far surpassed anything of the kind at Palmyra." In his eventful travels Bruce had many encounters with Arabs. As an example of one mishap, he was shipwrecked and almost drowned. However, after an arduous struggle he found himself breathless on the beach. Having survived the ordeal, he did not escape the marauding "Arabs who had come down to the shore to plunder the vessel". The Arabs were said to have "stripped him of the little clothing he had and after bestowing many blows, kicks and curses," left him in a state "semblence to death". It was stated that for a long time he bore the marks inflicted on him by the Arabs.

Bruce was later aided by some Arabs who asked whether he was a Turk. To this Bruce says that he replied in Arabic "that he was not a Turk, but a poor Christian; a dervish, who was going about the world seeking to do good for God's sake . . . He said this in a tone of such affliction, that the Arab entertained no doubt of the truth of the circumstance." The Arabs then covered him with "a ragged, dirty baracan" and took him to their tent.

In 1768 he arrived in Cairo dressed as a dervish, accompanied by his Italian secretary, Luigi Balugani by name. Bruce describes the luxurious French quarter in Cairo as "exceedingly commodious", but he felt sad for the "natives" who, although their "situation be ever so bad", did not fail to put on "a cheerful face before a stranger". Bruce also sympathised with the Egyptians for the surprising tolerance shown to their rulers, the "Beys", of whom he said that "a more tyrannical and oppressive set of miscreants is not on earth, than are the members of the government of Cairo."

On his way from Cairo to Ethiopia, Bruce travelled into the interior of Egypt, which was little known at that date to the outside world. On his way he describes the Pyramids and the Nile and all kinds of plant growth and animals, these latter including crocodiles and an eagle "about six feet ten inches from wing to wing", which he claimed to have killed. He portrays the people living in the villages as sickly and dirty. "The inhabitants are a yellow, unhealthy appearance," he wrote, "probably owing to the bad air, occasioned by a very dirty calish that passes through the town." Bruce remarks that women marry before reaching sixteen years of age. "They are little better coloured than a corpse, and look older at sixteen than many English women at sixty," he wrote.

In the meanwhile antiquarianism had become the great eighteenth century hobby in England for that section of the population of good means, social position, and, of course, interest and knowledge. Naturally, a good number with neither knowledge nor interest took up the subject, simply because it was the latest thing. Several societies were formed to study and preserve antiquities. Egypt with its Pyramids, mummies and tombs attracted the attention of many an Englishman. For example, the Earl of Sandwich and William Stukeley, both of whom had earlier visited the Middle East, formed a special Egyptian Club, "to enquire into Egyptian antiquities". Sandwich became the first President and became known as "The Sheick". In the same century antiquarian literature began to appear in England. One of the best-known publications was Robert Wood's *Palmyra*, a description of the desert city to the East of Aleppo, discovered by two English merchants at the end of the seventeenth century. Later Wood also published a similar edition on Baalbek, the famous ruins in Lebanon. These two publications, illustrated by drawings and engravings, moved even Horace Walpole to write, "Of all works that distinguish this age, none perhaps excel these beautiful editions of Baalbek and Palmyra ... The pomp of the buildings has not a nobler air than the simplicity of the narration."[11] These two publications aroused general interest in Graeco-Roman art and architecture in eighteenth century England, within the upper classes and sections of the middle classes.

Political Influences

The Napoleonic expedition to Egypt at the end of the eighteenth century signalled the beginning of a chain of events which eventually pushed the Arabs into the limelight of British and European interest in the political sphere.

The French army's victory over the Egyptians in 1798 took place after Napoleon had adequately acquainted himself with the Arabs and their way of life. French interest and knowledge of Arabs had already been established; Frenchmen such as Volney and Savary had visited the Arabs at the end of the eighteenth century and found in them a group who could be used against the Turks.

The British presence in Egypt was regarded as a mere minority influence when compared with the growing French community there. British and French rivalry for the Middle East had already reached a critical point. The primary concern of Britain with the area then was to safeguard its trade routes with India. The two problems the British faced at the close of the eighteenth century were the growing influence and power of France, and the weakened ability of the Ottoman Empire to maintain the *status quo*. Charles Perry commented in 1743 on the "present weak, feeble condition of the Turkish Empire". Perry's view gained credence in the following century. A sense of disenchantment with the Turks reflected itself in English accounts. Canning, the diplomat in Constantinople at that time, wrote to his sister that the Turkish capital was "not fit place for a gentleman to live in . . . and did not political circumstances make it at this moment more interesting than usual it would be quite intolerable." Canning was of the opinion that the Ottoman Empire would crumble from within. "Destruction will not come upon the Empire either from the North or from the South; it is rotten at the heart; the seat of corruption is in the government itself," he wrote.[12]

Negative British attitudes towards both the Turks and the French were best exemplified in William Eton's remarks: "They (the Turks) are enemies still and ever will be to Christians: they think all Christians are equally enemies to Mahomedans. I would answer a Turk: I was your enemy as long as you were friends of the French: now you are their enemies I, as an Englishman, am your friend."

Eton, who wrote a book called *A Survey of the Turkish Empire*,[13] had resided both in Turkey and in Russia. He despised the Turks for their "conceit of superiority" and for their being "Mahomadans". His observations of the Turkish dominions led him to believe that the Ottoman Empire was disintegrating and losing much of its power and authority over its provinces.

He saw the Arabs as a nation who despised and defied the Turks. "Whenever there is a war with an European power, and the Pasha of Baghdad is called on to furnish his quota of troops, he pretends the necessity of keeping them all at home, to defend the province against the attacks of the Arabs and finds means to provoke some Arab nation to war," he wrote, "or in connivance with the prince of the Montefiks (an Arab nation on the bank of the Euphrates) carries on a sham war." In short Eton believed that "the Sultan is the nominal sovereign of Baghdad, but the Pasha has the real sovereign independent power in his hands."

Eton portrayed Arabs very favourably in comparison with the Turks. He wrote, "The Arabs, who had been as great enemies of the sciences as Turks, now cultivated them with great success, and had acquired a considerable portion of knowledge and politeness, while the rest of Europe was degraded by ignorance and barbarism. But the haughty Turk is not merely exalted above his subject Greek as a conqueror; he considers himself still more highly elevated as the favourite of heaven, and the greater part of his ferocity as a tyrant is owing the arrogant and barbarous dictates of his religion."

Eton saw the Arabs who lived in the Ottoman Empire as possessing both the ability and the genius which could have benefited humanity, had it not been for the backward state of affairs of the Turks. According to Eton, an Arab inventor who resided in Constantinople discovered the secret of casting iron. "A remarkable instance occurred to my knowledge of an individual fact," Eton testified, "which might have been of the utmost use to society, but which, owing to the state of knowledge and government in Turkey, was wholly lost to the world. An Arabian at Constantinople had discovered the secret of casting iron, which, when it came out of the mould, was malleable as hammered iron." Eton continued, "This man, whose art in Christendom would have insured him a splendid fortune, had died poor and unknown and his secret has perished with him."

Eton, curiously enough, absolves the Arabs from the Christian sin of being Muslims, and tenderly insinuates that they exercised good influence on Islam. "The lively manners and ardent minds of the Arabs tempered the influence of a religion fundamentally barbarous and gloomy; but the Turks have not only given to superstition its full sway, but have even augmented its influence by circumstances of additional barbarism."

English opinion of Arabs seems to have turned full circle since the time of Blount, who hailed the Turks and denigrated the Arabs.

It appears to have been Eton who set the stage and rehearsed a role for the Arabs to play in the eyes of the English, for he later wrote to London to persuade the Government to send an agent to keep an eye on the French in Egypt and at the same time to woo the Arabs, who "do not acknowledge the sovereignty of the Sultan." Eton perceived that such an agent should "be acquainted with the manners and way of thinking of the Arabs and have such a command of temper and pliancy of character as to adopt his language to their prejudices."[14] In other words Eton believed that the Arabs were a simple enough race to be manipulated by a smart Englishman who could succeed in playing a role of a friend to attain political objectives. It must be remembered that during the eighteenth and nineteenth centuries English diplomacy can be said to have been at its most egotistical.

Thus began the political involvement of the British in Arab affairs. About a century later, Eton's agent was personified in T. E. Lawrence, better known as Lawrence of Arabia.

The eighteenth century marked a turning point in English accounts of Arabs. Not only was more attention given to Arabs, but the portrayal of them became more realistic. The scholars of this century wrote histories and accounts of Arabs in the English language, not in Latin, the language hitherto used by earlier scholars, thus making them available to more readers. This, of course, like the translation of the Bible from Latin in an earlier era, was of incalculable importance, enabling texts to be read which formerly could not be understood except by the very small educated class.

Furthermore, English scholars no longer studied the Arabs solely for theological purposes but showed genuine interest in their language, history and literature for its own sake. This was also reflected in the accounts of eighteenth century travellers, who spent more time in the area and produced far more serious and accurate accounts than their predecessors had done. This century also saw the publication of the *Arabian Nights*, which was destined to leave a lasting impression on the image of Arabs in Britain.

Chapter Four

The Romantic Image

The Nineteenth Century

Ideas acquired about Arabs before the nineteenth century had gradually defined them as a distinct group in the Ottoman Empire: a people proud of their identity and heritage. They were represented as resenting outside authority and control, thus hating their masters the Turks in particular and all foreigners in general. Characteristics assigned to them included thievishness, a warring spirit, and a wild and unruly temper. Yet favourable qualities were also ascribed to them, such as a pleasant exoticism, hospitality and fidelity. Furthermore, the Arabs were generally portrayed as two distinct groups: the desert Arabs and the city Arabs. Scholars were now depicting Arab civilisation as being "superior".

In addition to these ideas, the sources which influenced the portrayal of the Arabs in the nineteenth century included the *Arabian Nights*, the scholarly works of learned men, experiences

53

as related by travellers and soldiers, and reports of the undertakings of diplomats.

The tales of the *Arabian Nights*, published in the previous century, became exceedingly popular in nineteenth century England; it had "attained a popularity such as few books have. It would not be easy to find a person who had never read the tales in his youth and who does not gladly remember them still." Thus wrote Marie E. de Meester in her *Oriental Influences in the English Literature of the Nineteenth Century*. The author confirms the fact that the tales provided the West in general with a source of information which gave "a faithful picture of the Orient, its life and customs, that many people who afterwards happen to visit these countries seem to be quite familiar with them already," she wrote. "The best authorities to oriental conditions and manners have attested the veracity of the scenes described in the *Nights*."[1]

Many translations of the *Arabian Nights* had been made since Galland, a Frenchman, first introduced it in his native tongue in 1704. Among the better known authors to translate the book was first, in 1840, Edward William Lane, *The Thousand and One Nights*, known in England as *The Arabian Nights Entertainments*. Lane's translation was from the Arabic, and he included copious notes. Secondly there was John Payne's translation, written in English prose and verse and called *The Book of the Thousand Nights and One Night*. Then there was Sir Richard F. Burton's translation, in 1885–8, entitled *Thousand Nights and a Night*, with an introduction on the manners and customs of Muslims and a history of the *Nights*.

Henry Reeve, the editor of the *Edinburgh Review*, and incidentally an old enemy of Burton, attacked Burton's translation of the *Arabian Nights* in 1886 in the following manner: "Probably no European has ever gathered such an appalling collection of degrading customs and statistics of vice," he stated. "It is a work which no decent gentleman will long permit to stand upon his shelves . . . Galland is for the nursery, Lane for the Library, Payne for the study, and Burton for the sewers."[2]

English and Western travellers to the Middle East in the nineteenth century never forgot the subtle pervasive quality of romance of the Arabian Nights. Thackeray in his *Journey from Cornhill to Grand Cairo* wrote, "Some men may read this who are in want of a sensation. If they love the odd and picturesque, if they loved the Arabian Nights in their youth, let them book themselves on board of the Peninsular and Oriental vessels, and try one dip into Constantinople or Smyrna. Walk into the bazaar and the East is un-veiled to you: how often and often have you tried to fancy this lying out on a summer holiday at school! It is wonderful too, how like it is: you may imagine that you have been in the place before, you seem to know it so well."[3]

Disraeli, who had visited the Middle East in 1831, wrote to his father, "The meanest merchant in the bazaar looks like a Sultan in an Eastern fairy tale." He regretted the loss of a Greek servant because "he wore a Mameluke dress of crimson and gold, with a white turban thirty yards long, and a sabre glittering like a rain-bow." He wrote, "I must now content myself with an Arab attendant in a blue shirt and slipperless."[4]

The spell of the Arabian tales coloured, to a very great extent, Western visions of Arabs and of the Middle East. However, a definite sense of deflation fell upon many a Western traveller, apart from those yet under the *Arabian Nights'* spell, when dis-covering that the realities of the Middle East were far removed from the exotic world of the *Nights*. A *Times* correspondent dis-appointed his readers while describing a Pasha sitting upon a divan: "In the height of his splendours, led away by reminiscences of *Tales of the Geni* and the *Arabian Nights*, the readers must not imagine that this divan was covered with cloth of gold, or glittering with precious stones. It was clad in a garment of honest Manches-ter print."[5] The American writer, Mark Twain, whose writings are almost as well known in England as in the States, wrote after a tour in Egypt, "When I think how I have been swindled by books of oriental travel, I want a tourist for breakfast." He did not hide his disappointment when the reality of the land of the *Tales* did not conform to what he imagined. "The Narghili, the dervishes, the aromatic coffee, the Turkish bath—those are the things I have accepted and believed in, with simple, unquestion-ing faith, from boyhood; and, behold, they are the poorest sickest wretchedest humbugs the world can furnish. . . . The great slave marts we have all read so much about—where tender young girls were stripped for inspection, and criticised and discussed just as if they were horses at an agricultural fair—no longer exist."[6]

In spite of the fact that the fictitious world of the Arabian Nights bore, for many travellers, no relation to the realities of Arab lands, there were some writers who thought otherwise. John Payne, in his publication *The Book of the Thousand Nights and One Night: its History and Character*, insisted that the life described in the Tales "is mainly that of the people, those Arabs so essentially brave, sober, hospitable and kindly, almost hysterically sensitive to emotions of love and pity, as well as to artistic impressions, yet susceptible of being aroused to strange excesses of ferocity and brutality, to be soon followed by bitter and unavailing repentance —a people whom extreme sensibility of the nervous tissue inclines to excess of sensuous enjoyment yet who are capable of enduring without a murmur the severest hardships and of suffering patiently the most cruel vicissitudes of fortune without other complaint than that implied in the utterance of the Koranic formula: 'There is no power and no virtue but in God the most High, the Supreme.'" Payne's testimony reflects the extent to which people went in identifying the fictitious world of the *Nights* with Arabs. The attestation is also one more example of the romantic portrayal of Arabs as a consequence to these tales.[7] Exotic names and places had become familiar: Harun El Rashid and the city of Baghdad with its gardens on the banks of the Tigris; the colourful bazaars of Cairo and Damascus, filled with harems, dervishes, water-carriers, story tellers and eunuchs. All fantastic aspects of imagery mingled with cities of brass and black marble, Jinns, Efreets, flying horses and magic carpets. This became the world of Arabs in the eyes of readers.

Harun El Rashid "the wise Caliph of Bagdad" was celebrated in a poem by Longfellow:

> One day, Haroun al Raschid read
> A book wherein the poet said:
> Where are the kings, and where the rest
> Of those who once the world possessed?
> They're gone with all their pomp and show,
> They're gone the way that thou shalt go.
> O thou who choosest for thy share
> The world, and what the world calls fair,
> Take all that it can give or lend,
> But know that death is at the end!
> Haroun al Raschid bowed his head:
> Tears fell upon the page he read.[8]

The *Arabian Nights* became an important document for nineteenth century writers, poets and students, who utilised it in their attempt at describing and understanding the Arab and his world. The book also inspired many English writers to imitate, adopt and adapt the tales. W. F. Kirby mentions a number of such important works: *The Orientalist, or Letters of a Rabbi*; *Oriental Fairy Tales*;

Tales of the Caliph; *The Adventures of Caliph Haroun al-Raschid* and *New Arabian Nights*.[9] Furthermore, many of the important nineteenth century writers were to a greater or lesser degree influenced by the *Arabian Nights*. They borrowed from the Tales and made use of the stories in their works. Southey in his poems *Thalaba the Destroyer* and *The Curse of Kehama* borrows from the Arabian Nights; Moore in his *Lalla Rookh* includes in his fairy tale much of the exoticism and splendour of the *Nights*. Tennyson dedicates to them his *Recollections of the Arabian Nights*; Byron's many works show that he was influenced by the Tales, and much of Scott's knowledge of the East came from them. Coleridge's famous *Kubla Khan* reflects, through that fantasy of Coleridge's mind, the magic, mystery and spell-bound quality of the Orient. Indeed the book he was reading when he fell asleep and dreamed the poem was *Purchas His Pilgrims*. Charles Dickens in *A Christmas Carol* has Scrooge exclaim when seeing himself as a little school-boy, "Why, it's Ali Baba!" and continues later, "And what's his name, who was put down in his drawers, asleep, at the gate of Damascus; don't you see him! And the Sultan's groom, turned upside down by the Genii; there he is upon his head! Serve him right. I am glad of it. What business had he to be married to the Princess!"

In *The Old Curiosity Shop*, Dickens had one of his characters, Richard Swiveller say, "If this is not a dream, I have woke up, by mistake, in an Arabian Night, instead of London one," and later, "It's an Arabian night; that's what it is . . . I am in Damascus or Grand Cairo. The Marchioness is a Genie and having had a wager with another Genie about who is the handsomest young man alive. . . ."[10] Carlyle in his *Sartor Resartus* has one of his characters (the Professor) say, "To my Horse, again, who unhappily is still more unscientific [than the Dutch King of Siam,] do not I work a miracle, a magical *open sesame*! every time I please to pay twopence, and open for him an impassable *schlagbaum*, or shut Turnpike?"[11]

Burckhardt

Perhaps it was only a minority of the nineteenth-century English authors who were not impressed and influenced by the *Arabian Nights*. Traces of the *Tales* are also obvious in the works of American authors read in England, such as Washington Irving, Edgar Allan Poe and Mark Twain. In addition, the nineteenth century saw a long list of scholars and travellers who used a more scientific approach to learning about the Arabs than their predecessors. Among those who combined scholarly interest with travel and adventure was John Lewis Burckhardt. Burckhardt was born in Switzerland at the end of the eighteenth century, but was educated in England, of which he became a citizen. After spending two years at Cambridge studying Arabic, he was commissioned by the African Association to explore the Sahara Desert. It is said that Burckhardt prepared himself for the journey by walking barefoot, sleeping in the open and subsisting on water and vegetables. In 1809 Burckhardt travelled to Aleppo in Syria, where he spent two years studying Arabic and familiarising himself with the manners and customs of the people and with the area. Burckhardt was one of the first few Europeans to assume the identity of an Arab and adopt the name of Sheikh Ibrahim Ibn Abdullah. Apparently his disguise was successful enough to escape the detection of Arabs and Englishmen alike; for while in Egypt Burckhardt met two Englishmen, Thomas Legh, a Member of Parliament, and the Reverend Charles Smelt (whose experiences were published in a book entitled, *Narrative of a Journey in Egypt and the Country Beyond the Cataracts*); Legh and Smelt were said to have failed to recognise him and only learned of his true identity upon their return to England. Burckhardt's travels took him to Syria and Egypt and into Arabia.

He died in Cairo in 1817 at the age of thirty three, known to his friends only as Sheikh Abdullah, and was buried in a Muslim burial site on the Eastern side of the city.

Hogarth says of Burckhardt: "By the word of scholars, and especially by the best of his own successors, no name of an Arab explorer has been held in higher esteem than Burckhardt's, not indeed . . . for the magnitude or moment of his discoveries; for his travels covered a less area even than Neibuhr's."[12]

Burckhardt is thought to be one of the first Europeans to visit Petra, now well known by the description of "rose-red city, half as old as time". He also explored the Nubian country in Egypt. He seems to have admired the Nubians for their sense of independence and their bravery. Thieving, venereal diseases and prostitution did not exist among them. These people, Burckhardt states, often commit highway robberies against travellers: he points out, however, that the Nubians do not consider this as theft, for it is part of their way of life. He claims that they demanded ransom from travellers and if, however, their victim refused to pay they began to dig his grave. Burckhardt relates an incident in which he himself was approached for a ransom, having none to give: ". . . and as soon as he began to construct my tomb, I alighted, and making another, told him that it was intended for his own sepulture . . . At this, he began to laugh; we then mutually destroyed each other's labours."[13]

In his book *Bedouins and Wahabys* Burckhardt maintained that all events were based on first-hand experience. In it he gives a detailed account of the life of the Bedouin, and a history of the Wahabys, the people who were described by William Ouseley as "those Mohammedan sectaries and fierce enthusiasts".

Burckhardt presents a description of the social, economic and political institutions of the Bedouin. He begins by classifying the Bedouin tribes, especially those of the Syrian Desert. He describes the tent, furniture and dress of the people, proceeds then to elaborate upon their diet, arts (especially poetry), industry, customs and manners. He portrays the Bedouin as independent, freedom-loving and hospitable. He wrote of his first impressions of the Bedouin and of how his European image of them changed, in spite of all their faults: "My first view of the Bedouin in their own habitations on the Desert was recently after my arrival from Europe, while the impressions which I brought with me were still very strong. Whatever preference I might give in general to the European character, yet I was soon obliged to acknowledge, on seeing the Bedouin, that, with all their faults, they are one of the noblest nations with which I ever had an opportunity of becoming acquainted."

Burckhardt concedes that robbery and theft are a pronounced characteristic in Bedouin behaviour, nevertheless explaining this in terms of the social structure and the value system of the Arabs. "The Arabs may be styled a nation of robbers, whose principal occupation is plunder, the constant subject of their thoughts. But we must not attach to this practice the same notions of criminality that we entertain respecting highwaymen, house-breakers, and thieves, in Europe. The Arabian robber considers his profession as honourable; and the term *haramy* (robber) is one of the most flattering titles that could be conferred on a youthful hero."

Burckhardt, a perceptive traveller, cautions against rash condemnation and accusation of the Arabs as a result of defining their cultural values in terms of European modes. He furthermore attempts to explain the motive for thievery as being prevalent only among the tribes who constantly are at feud with each other (*ghazw*). Other tribes, who are less exposed to attacks from others, seldom practised robbery. "Among the Arabs of Sinai," he wrote, "robberies are wholly unknown: any articles of dress, or of furniture, may be left upon a rock without the least risk of being taken away." Indeed in some instances the punishment for robbery among such Arabs is legendary. "Some years ago, an Arab Sowaleha laid hold of his son, carried him bound to the summit of a mountain, and precipitated him, because he had been convicted of stealing corn from a friend."

Burckhardt depicts the Arab male as displaying his "manly character" when he defends his guest "at the peril of his own life". He also portrays him as being jealous of his women, but yet allowing them to laugh and talk with strangers. Arab women are described as being fond of jewellery which consists of an array of rings, ear-rings, nose rings, finger rings, ankle rings and bracelets. He adds, "In the absence of males, women entertain their guests."

Burckhardt speaks of the Bedoui as the true Arab who is not corrupted by city life. He is a lover of poetry, of oratory and of eloquence. "A Sheikh, however renowned he may be for bravery or skill in war, can never expect to possess great influence over his Arabs without the talent of oratory." "A Bedouin," he wrote, "will not submit to any command, but readily yields to persuasion." The Bedouin lead a democratic life. "The Sheikh has no fixed authority, but endeavours to maintain his influence by the means which wealth, talents, courage and noble birth afford. Although the Sheikh can alone decide in minor matters, yet when it comes to major problems the opinion of every distinguished individual in the tribe must be ascertained."

According to Burckhardt, the principal feature in the Levantine character is "an inordinate love of gain and money". This characteristic, he noted, is a basic and pervasive quality in the behaviour pattern of all people of the area: "it pervades all classes, from the *Pasha* to the wandering Arab." In this, of course, the West was an equal, if not greater culprit, although the "modus operandi" was of a subtler kind.

Burckhardt portrays Arabs much more favourably than Turks, whom he despises. "The Turk is cruel, the Arab of a more kind temper . . . the Arab is free, sprightly, jocose, and decent . . . The Turk is insinuating, grave, cautious."[14]

Thus Burckhardt, in his favourable accounts of the Bedouin, adds to the growing attractions of Arabs for the English in the nineteenth century.

Lane

In the meanwhile Arabic studies in England became of major concern to all those who wished to study Muslim culture. A new chair of Arabic was set up at the University of London. The number of English Arabists increased, especially since the Arab World had entered the sphere of European politics.

Among the better known English Arabists in the nineteenth century were men such as J. H. Hindley, whose work included a biography and study of the Arab poet Abu Tayyib al Mutanabbi, and M. Lumsden, a professor of Arabic who compiled a book of Arabic grammar.

But by far, wrote Bernard Lewis, the "greatest figure in England, and perhaps in Europe", in that century was Edward William Lane (1801–76).[15]

While only a child Lane developed a passionate interest in Egypt. In 1825 he embarked on his first journey to Alexandria. In his diaries he described his feelings upon arriving, exclaiming, "On my first landing I was filled with emotion like an Eastern bridegroom about to lift the veil of his as yet unseen bride." Lane's chief purpose in visiting Egypt was to study the Arabic language "in its most famous school". Though he had also intended to study the ancient Egyptians, he found that the people of the time and the things he saw were more interesting. Thus, during the three years he spent in Egypt, he made a study of the country, its people, their customs and manners. "I devoted much of my attention," he wrote, "to the manners and customs of the Arab inhabitants."

Upon his return to England in 1828, Lane refused to publish his work on Egyptian life, insisting on a second visit to Egypt, because, as he stated, his aim was "correctness". He was adamant in his wish for this, and succeeded.

His second visit took place between 1833 and 1835. He devoted most of his time to the study of life in Cairo. He persisted in wearing native dress and kept exclusively Arab company. He lived in a house of his own in the city of Cairo and tried to emulate the way of life of an Egyptian, assuming the role of a participant observer. He wrote, "I have associated, almost exclusively, with Muslims, of various ranks in society: I have lived as they live, conforming with their general habits; and, in order to make them familiar and unreserved towards me on every subject, have always avowed my agreement with them in opinion whenever my conscience would allow me, and in most other cases refrained from the expression of my dissent, as well as from every action which might give them disgust, abstaining from eating food forbidden by their religion, and drinking wine, etc.; and even from habits merely disagreeable to them, such as the use of knives and forks at meals."

Lane, who was known in Egypt as Mansour Effendi, gave to his readers descriptions of some of his Arab friends. One such acquaintance, as portrayed by Lane with unintentional humour, was a one-eyed character called Sheykh Ahmed, "one of the numerous class of 'Shereefs' or descendants of the prophet", who made his living as a bookseller. Lane said that this man belonged to the "Order of the Saadeeyeh darweeshes" and at one time was a serpent-eater. "One night," Lane related, "during a meeting of a party of darweeshes of his Order, at which their Sheykh was present, my friend became affected with religious frenzy, seized a tall glass shade which surrounded a candle placed on the floor, and ate a large portion of it. The Sheykh and other darweeshes, looking at him with astonishment, upbraided him with having broken the institutes of his Order, since the eating of glass was not among the miracles which they were allowed to perform; and they immediately expelled him." According to Lane, his friend later joined another Order of the "Ahmedeeyeh", and vowed that he would not eat glass again. "However, soon after, at a meeting of some brethren of this Order, when several Saadeeyeh also were present, he again was seized with frenzy, and, jumping up to a chandelier, caught hold of one of the small glass lamps attached to it, and devoured about half of it, swallowing also the oil and water which it contained." Lane tells of further misadventures of his friend and of how he reiterated his weird promise but could not stop himself eating glass, or of how he tried to atone when brought to trial by reciting some verses from the Quran: "I repent again: repentance is good: for He whose name be exalted hath said, in the Excellent Book, 'verily God loveth the repentant.'"

Curiously enough, Lane portrays the Arab people among whom he lived as resembling the characters in the *Arabian Nights*, which were then at their height of popularity in England.

On his return to England for the second time he published his book, *An Account of the Manners and Customs of the Modern Egyptians*, which attained wide popularity and was even referred to as a masterpiece. Bernard Lewis described it in 1941 as "an historical document of the first importance, and still indispensable to all students of Egypt".[16] Lane, in his preface, stated that the English reader's knowledge of Arabs was primarily based on Alexander Russell's book *Natural History of Aleppo*. He claimed, however, that Russell's book contained several deficiencies: the publication was "upon the whole, rather an account of the Turkish than of Arab manners," and the author, according to Lane, was not "sufficiently acquainted with the Arabic language".

What Burckhardt did earlier in his book *Bedouins and Wahabys*, Lane set out to do for the inhabitants of Cairo. Lane's book is a detailed description of the country and the people. The city of Cairo was the main object of his study. Its population, which consisted of Muslims, Copts and Jews, was then estimated to be about 240,000. "Muslims, in a great degree of Arabian origin, have for many centuries, mainly composed the population of Egypt," he wrote. "They have changed its language, laws, and general manners; and its Metropolis they have made the principal seat of Arabian learning and arts." Lane perceived Cairo as an Arab city whose inhabitants represented a cross-section of Arabs in other parts. "In every point of view Masr (or Cairo) must be regarded as the first Arab city of our age; and the manners and customs of its inhabitants are particularly interesting, as they are a combination of those which prevail most generally in the towns of Arabia, Syria and the whole of Northern Africa," he wrote, and added that the city is the only place that can serve as a basis to study the city Arabs. "There is no other place in which we can obtain so complete a knowledge of the most civilized classes of Arabs."

Lane depicted the climate of Egypt as "being remarkably salubrious" and after describing the houses and the city of Cairo he portrayed the people of Egypt, distinguishing two types: the city dwellers and "El-Fellaheen", the country people. The Turks, he said, often used the term "Egyptians" in an abusive sense as meaning boors, or clowns, and improperly stigmatized them with the appellation of "Al-Far'oon", or "the people of Pharaoh", whereas the Egyptians referred to the hated Turks as "Ahl Nemrood" or "the people of Nimrod".

The people, according to Lane, are generally thin: "the men muscular and robust; the women very beautifully formed, and plump; and neither sex is too fat." The middle and higher class men wear "a pair of full drawers of linen or cotton, tied round the body by a running string or band, the ends of which are embroidered with coloured silk, though concealed by the outer dress. In addition to this they wear a shirt and a coat called "gibbeh"; their head-dress consists of a cap, a "Tarboosh", and a turban. Lower class men wear simply drawers and a long shirt. On the other hand, the women's attire consists of colourful robes with a veil to conceal the face. Lane describes the form and features of the Egyptian women and states that women begin to develop early at the age of nine or ten years, and by the time they are fifteen or sixteen they "generally attain their highest degree of perfection." Although the Egyptian woman's physical maturity begins to take place early in life, they soon degenerate in appearance, Lane wrote. "From the age of about fourteen to that of eighteen or twenty, they are generally models of beauty in body and limbs . . . but soon after they have attained their perfect growth, they rapidly decline." By the age of forty, Lane continues, "it renders many, who in earlier years possessed considerable attractions, absolutely ugly." Women generally are fond of cosmetics. The material used to decorate their bodies includes kohl, henna and tattooing.

Socialisation of children, according to Lane, begins as soon as the child is born, when his parents recite the "Adan", or call of prayer, in the baby's right ear. This ceremony, he claimed, should be performed by a male. The reason for this custom is to "preserve the infant from the influence of the 'ginn' or genii". The child of the upper classes is indulged and over-protected; yet the less fortunate children receive little attention or care. The children of Cairo are depicted as dirty and shabby. Lane wrote, "The young children in Egypt, though objects of so much solicitude, are generally very dirty, and shabbily clad. The stranger here is disgusted by the sight of them, and at once condemns the modern Egyptians as a very filthy people." Lane expressed his astonishment and amazement to have seen meticulously dressed mothers with very dirty children. However, he stated that he learned that this is done purposely in order to protect the child "from fear of the evil eye", this being the fear of envy, perhaps leading to harm. Some mothers go so far as dressing their sons in girls' garments so as to make them less "obnoxious to envy", a boy-child being infinitely preferable to a girl-child. However, Lane narrated that Arab children, although shabbily dressed, are considered the "greatest blessings". All Muslim male children are said to be circumcized. They also do not receive proper education, with the exception of some religious teaching. The girls "are seldom taught to read or write," this being considered of little use for wives and mothers.

The Egyptians are portrayed by Lane as being very religious.

In fact the most important aspect of their education and "the main foundation of their manners and customs" is based upon religion.

"The Arabs are a very superstitious people," Lane declared, "and none of them are more so than those of Egypt." He claimed that much of their superstition is part of their religion and the most prominent of these is the belief in "ginn," or genii. Lane describes at length the "ginn", which is in Arabic variously called "Efreet", "Sheytan" and "Iblees". He quotes a verse from the Qur'an as a testimony that the belief in their existence is mentioned in their religion. He also spoke of "Ghools", considered by people to be a kind of ginn, and of Saints and "Darweeshes". Other superstitions of the people of Egypt were described, such as their trust in written charms, which are said to be based on magic and used primarily as a guard against every "rebellious devil". The Arabs are also said to believe in magic, fortune-telling, and in the seance.

They are furthermore generally depicted as indolent, excessively obstinate, submissive to authority, and sensual. Lane described Egyptian women as "being the most licentious in their feelings of all females who lay any claim to be considered as members of a civilized nation". This he attributed partly to the climate and partly to the lack of proper instructions and "of innocent pastimes and employment".

In addition, the Egyptians are said to indulge in the practice of swearing in God's name and are easily excited into quarrels. They are defined as having a sense of humour and "often display considerable wit in their jeers and jests," he wrote.

The people of Egypt are also portrayed as loving and appreciative of dancing. In Egypt, Lane claims, there are public dancers, who give performances at weddings and other festive occasions. Men as well as women engage in various forms of dancing both in the streets and also privately. The "Ghazeeyeh" (plural Ghawazee) is the woman dancer, and a man is called "Ghazee". Lane described the Ghawazee as the "most abandoned of the courtesans of Egypt". He pictures them in the main as prostitutes, whose performances, especially in private courts, are "lascivious" and their dancing is appreciated by both men and women. The dance which is performed is a "very rapid vibrating motion of the hips, from side to side". Lane asserts that the Ghawazee call themselves "Baramikeh", being descendants of the family which was closely associated with Harun El Rashid, of whom we read in several of the tales of the *Arabian Nights*. The Ghawazee are

65

favourably portrayed in Lane's narratives: "Many of them are extremely handsome; and most of them are richly dressed," he wrote. "Upon the whole, I think they are the finest women in Egypt." So Lane was certainly no prude respecting these women and his knowledge of their trade.[17]

Lane presented the society of Egypt of the nineteenth century as a world not far removed from the setting of the fables of the *Arabian Nights*. His selection of the people and customs he described generally reflects the strange and the exotic.

Nonetheless, despite this closeness to the *Arabian Nights*, Lane's book became an important document in early nineteenth-century England for knowledge and information about the city Arabs; whereas Burckhardt's accounts were consulted for information about the desert Arabs.

Lane's obvious preoccupation with the *Arabian Nights* prompted him, immediately after his return to England, to devote himself to an English translation of the *Thousand and One Nights*. His translation was accompanied by notes and essays on mediaeval Arab customs, entitled *Arabian Life in the Middle Ages*, and later reprinted separately.

In 1842, Lane yet again, for the third time, journeyed to Egypt, this time to work on compiling his own Lexicon, based on the classical dictionaries such as *Taj al-Arus*. He had undertaken a tremendous task and spent about two years in Egypt, working "usually from twelve to fourteen hours a day". When he had gathered his material, he returned to England and devoted the remaining years of his life to the completion of his Lexicon. However, his work was unfinished when he died in 1876. Towards the end of his life, Lane was hailed in England and Europe as the "Grand Master of Arabic studies".

Palmer

The English scholars who had earlier travelled to the Arab lands in order to learn and observe were unlike Lane, who took a special interest in the Arabs and their culture. Whether his reasons were motivated by scholarly interest, personal attraction, or a combination of both, is not of much concern. However, it is of some consequence to note that a new breed of learned Englishmen as a result of Lane's work began to develop a keen interest in Arab influences, these revealing themselves in their lives and work.

Lane's book, *Arabian Society in the Middle Ages*, was dedicated by Lane and Poole the editors in 1883: "To the Memory of E. H.

Palmer, the true Successor of Edward William Lane, in his insight into Eastern Character and Thought and his Genius for the Arabic language, this book is sorrowfully dedicated."[18] Edward Henry Palmer, sometimes known as Sheikh Abdullah, was another English figure who developed an interest in the Arabs. He was born in Cambridge in 1840, and studied several languages such as Urdu, Persian and Arabic. At an early age he was translating English poetry into Arabic, "my favourite language." He was attracted to the Arab community in England and befriended a Syrian Arab named Rizallah Hassan al-Halabi. After completing his education at Cambridge University, he made two trips to the Middle East on behalf of the Palestine Exploration Society. Among his many publications were: a critical edition of the full Arabic text of the poetry of Baha-ad-Din Zuhair; a grammar of the Arabic language in English, and a biography of Harun El Rashid the Abbasid Caliph. In addition, he published an account of his travels in the Sinai Peninsula, into which he also ventured.

Palmer was a linguist, and on his first visit to the Middle East he went with Tyrwhitt Drake on an exploratory mission as the man best suited to the collection of place names for the Palestine survey. It is claimed that Palmer and Drake made the trip back from Sinai to Jerusalem on foot. Palmer was apparently used by the British Government for political and military purposes. In 1882 he was sent by Gladstone into Sinai to persuade Arab tribes to refrain from supporting Arabi Pasha, who was then leading a revolution in Egypt. It is said that Palmer was killed whilst attempting to secure the allegiance of the Arab tribes of the Peninsula to Britain.

In his book *Desert of the Exodus*, Palmer reported his experiences as an explorer in Palestine. "The Palestine Exploration Fund, ever anxious to promote a better knowledge of the Holy Land, had entrusted to me the task of exploring that wide and comparatively unknown tract of desert which lies between Judea and the Sinaitic Peninsula," he wrote. He described the area he was to explore as "the great and terrible wilderness", which was infested with Arabs. He perceived the natives of his "field of exploration" as primitive and evil. Palmer did not have any love for the Bedouin. He called them a "terrible scourge", and suggested that they ought to be removed: "I would put an end to their existence *qua* Bedawin." He noted that his attitude towards the Bedouin was at odds with their romantic image then prevailing in England, and remarked: "I cannot expect respectable and tax-paying Englishmen to enter with much appreciation into the Bedawin question, and I know the prejudice that exists, in this country particularly, against the extinction of a romantic and interesting race." The Bedoui was depicted as a renegade and uncivilized robber, who brought with him "ruin, violence and neglect"; furthermore, Palmer insisted that "robbery is not regarded by the Bedawin as in the least a disgraceful thing."

He wrote about "the ancient Arabs" who "prided themselves upon three things, above all: eloquence, hospitality and the honour of plundering." The first two qualities, according to Palmer, have gradually disappeared, and what remained was "their daring and persistence in making raids". To call the Bedouin "son of the desert" was a misnomer, Palmer stated. He likened the Bedouin to the American Red Indians; but he considered the latter inferior to the former, who possessed independence and dignity.

"The sympathy already wasted on the Red man of North America warns me that I am treading on delicate ground, but I must nevertheless state my belief that the 'noble savage' is a simple and unmitigated nuisance. To the Bedawin this applies even more forcibly still ..."[19]

Palmer hated the desert and the Bedouin, and thus stood aloof from the generally favourable picture which was being painted of them by some of his countrymen, such as Richard Burton, who will be discussed in depth.

Burton

The second half of the nineteenth century saw several other scholars who added to the image of the Arabs in England. William Wright, who was born in India, where his father was an English Army Officer, was said to have been encouraged by his mother to study Arabic, she herself being interested in oriental languages. Eventually, Wright became successively Professor of Arabic in London, Dublin and Cambridge. His major contributions to Arabic studies included an edition of the travels of Ibn Jubair, an Arabic Grammar in two volumes, and his collaboration with Dozy in the work concerning the history of Spain of Al-Maqqari.

Robertson Smith was another scholar, a Scot from Aberdeen. Smith, who succeeded Wright in the Arabic chair at Cambridge, travelled extensively in the Middle East, visiting Egypt, Palestine, Syria and Arabia. He provided English readers with a study which he called *Kinship and Marriage in Early Arabia*.

Finally, there was William Muir, an administrator in India and later a scholar at Edinburgh University. He produced, among

Baalbek in Lebanon, 1839 (Roberts)

Ruins of the Temple at Baalbek, 1839 (Roberts)

Encampment of Pilgrims at Jericho (Roberts)

Fortress of Ibrim, Nubia (Roberts)

Gate of Mosque, Cairo (Roberts)

The Citadel, Cairo, 1856 (Roberts)

The Citadel, Jerusalem, 1841 (Roberts)

other works, a history of the Caliphate, which was considered by Bernard Lewis of London University to be the best work on the subject in English.[20]

These were some of the English figures in academic circles who contributed to the portrayal in England of the Arabs during the nineteenth century.

However, during the same century, three Englishmen of differing backgrounds and outlook proved to be greatly instrumental in adding to the growing conglomeration of ideas and impressions of Arabs. These men, all three Victorian travellers and explorers, were Sir Richard Burton (1821–90), Wilfred Scawen Blunt (1840–1922), and Charles Doughty (1843–1926).

Of the three men, perhaps Burton contributed the most to the image of the Arabs in England. He was often referred to as Burton of Arabia and was known as a flamboyant figure in the annals of English travellers to the Arab World. Burton first studied Arabic whilst at Oxford. Before completing his course he left to serve in the British Army in India, where he studied both Arabic and Persian and of choice lived in Muslim districts. In 1853 he visited Egypt and from there he set out on a journey by camel to Suez. A sea voyage took him to Yanbu, a seaport in Arabia; once there he travelled to Hijaz and visited the Muslim Holy cities of Mecca and Medina. Upon his return to England, via Jedda and Egypt, he published a narrative of his travels which was used widely in England as a source of information about the area and the people he visited.

Burton's adventures were not confined to Arab lands. Among the areas he explored in depth was Abyssinia, where he was often disguised as an Arab merchant. He also ventured into Central and West Africa. In 1855 he joined the British forces in the Crimea.

In 1869 Burton returned to the Arab World with his wife, Isabel, whom he had met in England and who was basically both reticent and conservative. His post was that of British Consul in Damascus. During his stay there, he explored Syria in the company of his wife and Edward Henry Palmer. About 1877 Burton returned to Egypt from England, having taken a further period of leave. He explored the interior regions of Egypt, little known to Europeans, and conducted geological surveys in these parts.

Although his portrayal of the Arabs and their world was romantically rendered, his general attitude towards them was that of ambivalence. The deserts represented a colourful and exciting landscape to Burton, the adventurer. He portrayed the wide and wild deserts as a land in which man felt free and emancipated from the hypocritical and servile aspects of civilisation. In his book *Pilgrimage to Al-Madinah and Meccah*, Burton was full of fascination when describing the desert where "the senses are sharpened, and the perceptive faculties, prone to sleep over a confused mass of natural objects, act vigorously when excited by the capability of embracing each detail." His attraction to the desert drove him to eulogize: "Moreover, desert views are eminently suggestive; they appeal to the future, not to the past: they arouse because they are by no means memorial. To the solitary wayfarer there is an interest in the wilderness unknown to Cape seas and Alpine glaciers, and even to the rolling prairie—the effect of continued excitement on the mind, stimulating its powers to their pitch. Above, through a sky terrible in its stainless beauty, and the splendours of a pitiless blinding glare, the Samun caresses you like a lion with flaming breath. Around lie drifted sand heaps, upon which each puff of wind leaves its trace in solid waves, flayed rocks, the very skeletons of mountains, and hard unbroken plains, over which he who rides is spurred by the idea that the bursting of a water-skin, or the pricking of a camel's hoof, would be a certain death of torture—a haggard land infested with wild beasts, and wilder men—a region whose very fountains murmur the warning words 'Drink and away!' What can be more exciting? What more sublime? Man's heart bounds in his breast at the thought of measuring his force with nature's might, and of emerging triumphant from the trial. This explains the Arab's proverb, 'voyaging is victory'. In the desert even more than upon the ocean, there is present death: hardship is there, and piracies, and shipwreck, solitary, not in crowds, where, as the Persians say, 'Death is a Festival';—and this sense of danger, never absent, invests the scene of travel with an interest not its own."

"The mere animal existence" of the desert appealed to Burton, as he wrote: "Though your mouth glows, and your skin is parched, yet you feel no languor, the effect of humid heat; your lungs are lightened, your sight brightens, your memory recovers its tone, and your spirits become exuberant, your fancy and imagination are powerfully aroused, and the wildness and sublimity of the scenes around you stir up all the energies of your soul—whether for exertion, danger, or strife. Your morale improves; you become frank and cordial, hospitable and single-minded: the hypocritical politeness and the slavery of civilization are left behind you in the city. Your senses are quickened: they require no stimulants but air and exercise,—in the desert spirituous liquors excite only disgust. There is a keen enjoyment in mere animal existence."[21]

Captured by his surroundings, Burton saw the desert as a haven, an escape from the drudgery of Europe. "At last!" he remarked with ardour in the opening sentence of his book, *The Gold-Mines of Midian.* "Once more it is my fate to escape the prison-life of civilized Europe, and to refresh body and mind by studying nature in her noblest and most admirable form—the nude. Again I am to enjoy a glimpse of the glorious desert; to inhale the sweet pure breath of translucent skies that show the red stars burning upon the very edge and verge of the horizon; and to strengthen myself by a short visit to the Wild Man and his old home."[22]

It is not difficult to imagine that many an Englishman would have been pleasantly attracted to the Arabs and their way of life upon reading such eloquent and evocative descriptions. Furthermore, it is safe to assume that some, especially the well-to-do people in Britain, would have been moved to escape the drudgery of their city life and journey to the Arabs and their deserts in search of the "Wild Man and his old home".

Burton portrayed the Arabs of the desert more favourably than the city Arabs. He was impressed with the nomadic life, the freedom, cleanliness and manliness of the Bedouin, as compared to the degraded city dweller, of whom he wrote, "There is degradation, moral and physical, in handiwork compared with the freedom of the Desert," and continued to insist, "The loom and the file do not conserve courtesy and chivalry like the sword and the spear." To Burton the desert nomads were the noble Arabs who possessed the "quality of mercy", whereas the urban Arabs were untrustworthy and unattractive. They were, Burton remarked, "rancorous and revengeful as camels."

As he despised the life of the city, so, on the contrary, the Arab of the desert symbolized for Burton the embodiment of chivalry. He observed that "from ancient periods of the Arab's history we find him practising knight-errantry, the wildest form of chivalry." He saw in the Arabs the origin of love: "I should attribute the origin of 'love' to the influence of the Arabs' poetry and chivalry upon European ideas rather than the medieval Christianity," he asserted. "Certain 'Fathers of the Church', it must be remembered, did not believe that women have souls. The Moslems never went . so far."

In one of his footnotes, and as a matter of interest, Burton attributed the origin of the name "Trafalgar" to an Arabic word;

he wrote, "Trafalgar is nothing but a corruption of Tarf al-Gharb —the side or skirt of the west; it being the most occidental point then reached by Arab conquest."

Burton described the "Kayf" of the Arabs, which, he insisted, is untranslatable into English. It should be remembered that earlier English travellers depicted this pattern of behaviour to mean laziness, idleness and indolence. Burton, however, defined it as the way Arabs enjoy life. He wrote, with enthusiasm and evocative beauty: "And this is the Arab's Kayf. The savouring of animal existence; the passive enjoyment of mere sense; the pleasant langour, the dreamy tranquillity, the airy castle-building, which in Asia stand in lieu of the vigorous, intensive, passionate life of Europe. It is the result of a lively, impressible, excitable nature, and exquisite sensibility of nerve; it argues a facility for voluptuousness unknown to Northern regions, where happiness is placed in the exertion of mental and physical powers; where *Ernst ist das Leben*; where niggard earth commands ceaseless sweat of face, and damp chill air demands perpetual excitement, exercise, or change, or adventure, or dissipation, for want of something better. In the East, man wants but rest and shade; upon the banks of a bubbling stream, or under the cool shelter of a perfumed tree, he is perfectly happy, smoking a pipe, or sipping a cup of coffee, or drinking a glass of sherbet, but above all things deranging body and mind as little as possible; the trouble of conversations, the displeasures of memory, and the vanity of thought being the most unpleasant interruptions to his Kayf. No wonder that 'Kayf' is a word untranslatable in our mother-tongue."

It is understandable in the circumstances that Burton became entranced by this concept.

On numerous instances Burton came to the defence of Arabs in an attempt through his writings to correct European misunderstanding of their way of life. At the same time the Victorian traveller provided insight into the prejudiced attitudes of some of his English contemporaries towards the Arabs. In one such example, Burton, in defence of the Arabs, stated, "I lament to see so many intelligent travellers misjudging the Arab after a superficial experience of a few debased Syrians or Sinaites. The true children of Antar," he exclaimed, "have not 'ceased to be gentlemen'."

On another occasion, Burton, travelling with John Speke, the perfect English Officer, in search of the source of the Nile, commented on Speke's attitude towards the Arabs and stated that the

English Speke, like the Anglo-Indians he had met, "expected civility as their due and treat all skins a shade darker than their own as 'niggers'."

As can be sensed from his work, Burton felt a certain kinship towards the Arabs. Of all the people of the area he visited in the East, the Arabs, particularly the nomads, attracted him the most. After an arduous journey, Burton and Speke finally reached an Arab settlement and were warmly greeted by the tribe's Chief, Snay bin Amir who, according to Burton, possessed a "wonderful memory, fine perceptions and passing power of language". Their host had ordered two goats and two bullocks to be slaughtered for his guests. "Striking indeed," Burton remarked, "was the contrast between the open-handed hospitality and hearty goodwill of this truly noble race and the niggardness of the savage and selfish African—it was heart of flesh after heart of stone."[23]

Burton was, furthermore, impressed by the absolute independence of the Arab. This desire for independence was acceptable to Burton, as long as it agitated against the Turks, but it had to be submissive to British rule. Here we see where Burton's allegiance was basically directed. We notice Burton's ambivalence: on the one hand he praised and romanticised the Arabs, but on the other, he viewed them as children of simplicity, easily placated. "The best character of the Badawi is a truly noble compound of determination, gentleness and generosity. Usually they are a mixture of worldly cunning and great simplicity, sensitive to touchiness, good tempered souls, solemn and dignified withal, fond of a jest, yet of a grave turn of mind, easily managed by a laugh and a soft word, and placable after passion, though madly revengeful after injury," he wrote.

The Arab, according to Burton, can easily be manipulated: "nothing is easier for a man who knows them than to work upon their good feelings." Probably this impression of the Arabs moved Burton to impersonate them. Burton's disguise as an Arab dervish and merchant reminds us of the established tradition of European travellers who assumed Arab identity—such men as Pitts and Burckhardt.

Burton related, with apparent satisfaction, how he was successful in misleading the Arabs as to his true identity when, "with a beard and a shaven head", he was approached by a beggar who asked for a "Bakhshish" to which he obtained a reply from Burton of "Mafish". Burton exclaimed that this incident "convinced the bystanders that the sheep-skin covered a real sheep."

Fawn Brodie, in his biography of Burton *The Devil Drives*, stated that Burton's primary aim was the "penetration into the mysteries of the Arab family life. To assure this goal he chose to play the role of combination dervish and doctor."[24]

Despite Burton's admiration for the Arab, his culture and religion, to the end of his life, he never forgot that he was an Englishman and must act in the interest of his country. He urged the English to occupy the Middle East: "It requires not the ken of a prophet to foresee the day when political necessity . . . will compel us to occupy the fountain head of al-Islam," he wrote in his *Pilgrimage*. He criticised the English preoccupation with the study of Hindu and Sanskrit literature, because he believed that it led the English away from the Semitic studies which are necessary to qualify English scholars, travellers and diplomats in dealing with the Muslims, "a race more powerful than any pagans". Moreover, Burton observed that England was ignorant of the many aspects of Arabic culture and manners. He suggested that his country would do well to understand the Arabs in order to be equipped with the "means of dispelling her ignorance concerning the Eastern races with whom she is constantly in contact."

In his accounts Burton proposed numerous ways for the proper treatment of the Arabs. In *The Gold Mines of Midian*, he divides the Arabs into two categories; the Bedouin, and the city Arab, whom he identifies with the "Fellah"—the peasant Arab. Concerning the former, he described him as "still a gentleman in his native wilds. Easy and quiet, courteous and mild-mannered, he expects you to respect him, and upon that condition he respects you—still without a shade of obsequiousness or servility." Moreover, "the Bedawi never tells a lie, and when told one, never forgets it. His confidence is gone forever, and all the suspiciousness of his nature is aroused." Burton finds these qualities very useful, for "should we find it necessary to raise regiments of these men, nothing would be easier," he wrote. "Pay them regularly, arm them well, work them hard, and treat them with evenhanded justice—there is nothing else to do." He believed that Arabs "respect manly measures, not the hysterical philanthropic pseudo-humanitarianism of our modern Government, which is really the cruellest of all."

A further proposal which Burton put forward to ensure the management of the Egyptians was: "They are to be managed, as Sir Charles Napier governed Sind—by keeping a watchful eye upon them, a free administration of Military Law, disarming the

population, and forbidding large bodies of men to assemble."
Burton's ambivalence which betrayed this attitude of superiority
towards the Arabs is clearly reflected in seeing noble traits in the
desert Arab and, on the other hand, also seeing him as a "nuisance". Of this he wrote: "I agree with Professor Palmer that the
Bedawi, the 'father', not the 'son of the desert', is, like the noble
savage generally, a nuisance to be abated by civilisation. Yet the
race has high and noble qualities which, as the old phrase is, the
world would not willingly see die; and perhaps the pure blood of
the wilderness may be infused to good purpose into burgher-men,
as into their horses."

Burton's general portrayal of Islam, the religion of the Arabs,
was favourable when compared with the views of earlier travellers.
He compared Islam with Christianity and stated that Islam
"systematically exalts human nature, which Christianity takes
infinite trouble to degrade and debase."

In his accounts, Burton described his pleasure in Arab women.
"I have often lain awake for hours listening to the conversation of
the Bedawin girls, whose accents sounded in my ears rather like
music." He praised the fair sex and wrote, "Women in troubled
times throwing off their accustomed feebleness and frivolity, became helpmates meet for a man . . . Here, between the extremes of
fierceness and sensibility, the weaker sex, remedying its great want,
power, raises itself by courage, physical as well as moral."

Burton's perceptions of the Arabs seem to have been influenced
by several factors. First, it must be remembered that as a boy he
was fascinated with the fables of the *Arabian Nights*. "He had
learned to tell them himself in Arabic, with all the gusto and brav-
ura of the Moslem storyteller," remarked Brodie. Burton himself
admitted that he found the tales, "an unfailing source of solace
and satisfaction . . . a charm, a talisman against ennui and des-
pondency." A second factor was his fascination with travelling,
accompanied by its attendant dangers. Arabia was then almost an
unexplored and unknown region as far as the Europeans were concerned. This land seems to have appealed to the sensibilities of the
restless and ardent Burton, the explorer.

Thirdly, the Middle East with its "mere animal existence"
provided an escape and a haven for the Victorian traveller from
the conventions and morality of nineteenth-century English
society, whose conventions were kept to rigidly and without
question.

In October 1890 Burton died, his indefatigable enthusiasms and ardour not yet spent. His wife Isabel, remembering that her husband had once told her, "I should like us both to lie in a tent side by side" designed an exotic tomb in the shape of an Arab tent. Today both Richard Burton and his wife Isabel are buried in the tomb fashioned after an Arab tent at Mortlake. A sonnet by Justin Huntly M'Carthy is inscribed on a marble plaque at the grave:

> Oh last and noblest of the Errant Knights
> The English soldier and the Arab Sheik,
> O Singer of the East . . .

Tragically and ironically, an unknown amount of Burton's work was destroyed by Isabel, after his death, since she considered it immoral and unfit for publication.

Blunt

Another well-known traveller in the annals of English voyagers to the Middle East was Wilfred Scawen Blunt (1840–1922). Blunt began his career as a diplomat. His first visit to Egypt was on a holiday in 1875–76. He was particularly interested in the oppressed people of that area and soon developed an attachment to Egypt and the Arabs. With his wife, Lady Anne (granddaughter of Byron), an Arabist in her own right and a constant and valuable companion, they journeyed through the Arab countries of the Middle East and North Africa. In 1878 they visited Nejd in Arabia and the Arab Emir presented them with his choicest brood mares. During Blunt's stay in Egypt he became friends with Arabi Pasha, the Nationalist Egyptian leader. In 1881 Blunt purchased an estate near Cairo, which became known as Sheyk Obeyd. He lived there a life of an Arab, wearing native clothes and speaking only Arabic.

Blunt was attracted to the Arabs for two main reasons: first, he admired them as a sensitive and emotional race of people who possessed human qualities which appealed to him; secondly, he found them to be oppressed people in need of help in their fight against foreign domination, especially against the spread of British imperialism.

As a young attaché at the British Embassy in Buenos Aires, Blunt had met Burton in Argentina. In a recollection of that meeting, Blunt wrote thirty-eight years later: "His dress and appearance were those suggesting a released convict, rather than anything of more repute. He wore, habitually, a rusty black coat with a crumpled black silk stock, his throat destitute of collar, a costume which his muscular frame and immense chest made singularly and incongruously hideous, above it a countenance the most sinister I have ever seen, dark, cruel, treacherous, with eyes like a wild beast's . . . If I had submitted to his gaze for any length of time— and he held me by my thumbs—I have no doubt he would have succeeded in dominating me," he wrote, "but my will also is strong; and when I had met his eyes of a wild beast for a couple of minutes I broke away and would have no more."[25]

Although Blunt admired Burton for his adventures in Arab lands, he criticised him on several counts. He believed that Burton made his journey to Arabia seem more difficult than it actually was. He thought that Burton was a glory-seeker.

Furthermore, Blunt suspected that Burton's love for the Arabs was not genuine, believing his loyalty to be first and foremost to his own country. He asserted that Burton had shown "little true sympathy with the Arabs he had come to know so well". "He would at any time, I am sure, have willingly betrayed them to further English, or his own professional interests."[26] Upon first meeting Burton's wife, Isabel, Blunt described her as a "sociable and very talkative woman, clever, but at the same time foolish, overflowing with stories of which her husband was always the hero. Her devotion to him was very real, and she was indeed entirely under his domination, an hypnotic domination Burton used to boast of."[27]

Blunt and his wife journeyed to the Middle East in 1873 as tourists, "to escape a late Spring in England", and also because Blunt was in indifferent health. After visiting Constantinople, the Blunts crossed into Algeria in early 1874. It was in North Africa that they first came in contact with the Arabs. Blunt disapproved of "an Eastern people in violent subjection to a Western". Although he had great admiration for the French, he resented the fact that the indigenous people of the country were made servants to the Frankish "Lords".

While in Algeria, Blunt first encountered the Arab tribes of the Sahara. He was impressed with their deep sense of independence, "their noble pastoral life", and their "life of high tradition filled with the memory of heroic deeds".[28]

In 1875 the Blunts arrived back in Egypt with no other thought "than that of another pleasant travelling adventure in Eastern lands". However, once in Egypt, Blunt developed a deep sympathy for the Fellahin, the grossly impoverished and overtaxed peasants of the country, and spent the rest of his life championing their cause in particular and that of the Arabs in general.

In 1876 the Blunts made their first trip to the interior of Arabia, but because they were not familiar with the language, their visit was of little significance. Nonetheless, they later visited the Bedouin in the Syrian Desert and, by then being more familiar with the language and the people, their trip proved to be successful. As a result of this visit, Lady Anne Blunt wrote her book *Bedouin Tribes of the Euphrates*.

In 1878 they made their second trip to Arabia, "to penetrate into Central Arabia and visit Nejd, the original home and birthplace of the Arabian horse." By this time Blunt was wholly committed to the Arab cause. He described his attitude towards the Arabs as "enthusiastic feelings of love and admiration". He remarked that he had gradually developed towards the Arabs "a political 'first love', a romance which more and more absorbed me, and determined me to do what I could to help them preserve their precious gift of independence."[29]

Blunt desired first and foremost to help the Arabs attain their freedom from the Ottoman Empire. Initially, he believed that England would espouse the Arab cause. However, he soon realised the contrary, that British Imperialism was a major force which inhibited Arab National movements. In his book, *Secret History of the English Occupation of Egypt*, Blunt remarked that he looked up to England to act as a friend of the Fellahin, "in their actual condition of beggary, robbed and beaten and perishing of hunger". But disappointed in his country, he exclaimed, "They (Egyptians) did not suspect the immense commercial selfishness which had led us, collectively as a nation, to so many aggressions on the weak races of the world." Blunt sympathised deeply with the common man of Egypt. "The Egyptians," he wrote, "are a good, honest people as any in the world—all, that is, who do not sit in the high places, of these I know nothing."

Perhaps the people who evoked in Blunt most compassion and pity were the Fellahin of Egypt, of whom he wrote, "But the peasants, the Fellahin, have every virtue which would make a happy, well-to-do-society. They are cheerful, industrious, obedient to law, and pre-eminently sober, not only in the matter of drink, but of the other indulgences to which human nature is prone. They are neither gamblers nor brawlers, nor licentious livers; they love their homes, their wives, their children. They are good sons and fathers, kind to dumb animals, old men, beggars, and idiots. They are absolutely without prejudice of race, and perhaps even of religion." Along with this praise, however, Blunt described the Fellahin as materialistic. "Their chief fault is love

of money," but he quickly explains, "but that is one political econo-
mists will readily pardon . . . It would be difficult to find anywhere
a population better fitted to attain the economical end of the
greatest happiness for the greatest number."

He portrayed the Egyptian peasants as lacking political aspirations except for the simple axiom of "to live and let live". Blunt
observed the Egyptian character as being marked by submissive-
ness. He justified this in terms of their goodness and the absence
of political prejudice. "They have been ill-treated for ages without
losing thereby their goodness of heart; they have few of the
picturesque virtues; they are neither patriotic nor fanatical nor
romantically generous. But they are free from the picturesque vices.
Each man works for himself—at most for his family. The idea of
self-sacrifice for the public good they do not understand, but they
are innocent of plots to enslave their fellows. . . . In spite of the
monstrous oppression of which they are the victims, we have heard
no word of revolt, this not from any superstitious regard for their
rulers, for they are without political prejudice, but because revolt
is no more in their nature than it is in a flock of sheep. They would
hail the Queen of England, or the Pope, or the King of Ashantee
with equal eagerness if these came with the gift for them of a penny
less taxation in the pound."[30]

It is apposite at this juncture to clarify the context by providing
a brief outline of the position of the British Government in Egypt
during the nineteenth century.

The British Government became politically, diplomatically and
economically aware of Egypt's strategic importance at the time of
Napoleon's Egyptian conquests in 1798. Although the French
occupation of Egypt lasted only three years, numerous technicians
were put to work establishing schools and hospitals and commenc-
ing various other projects.

In 1801 the French army were driven out of Egypt by the allied
forces of the British and Egyptian armies. Mohammad Ali, an
officer in the Albanian contingent in the Ottoman Army, seized
power in 1805. He embarked on numerous reforms in an attempt
to modernise the country. One of his accomplishments was the
creation of a well-disciplined and well-equipped army for Egypt.

In 1831 he successfully invaded Syria. Nine years later he
relinquished his occupation in return for international recognition
of hereditary rule in Egypt.

However, Mohammad Ali and his successors involved Egypt
in heavy financial losses, especially over the expense of the Suez

Canal, built under the supervision of the French engineer de Lesseps in 1869, which was added to the mounting expenses. This exploit, though a tremendous achievement, was a cumbersome monetary burden.

To remedy this grave financial problem, the rulers of Egypt imposed heavy taxation on the Egyptians. Despite this attempted solution, financially the country became almost wholly dependent on the European powers. As a result of internal discontent, Arabi Pasha, an Egyptian army officer, led an Army revolution against the Khedive, the Ruler of Egypt, in 1881.

In full knowledge of these facts, British forces invaded and occupied Egypt in 1882, in order to protect the growing British interests in the area, especially since the Suez Canal had become an important trade route to the East, and especially to India. During the invasion, the British bombarded Alexandria and landed at Ismailia. The Egyptian Army was defeated at Tel el-Kebir, and Arabi was exiled to Ceylon.

Sir Evelyn Baring (later Lord Cromer) governed Egypt for the British from 1883 until 1907. In addition, Charles Gordon, considered by one admirer "one of our National treasures", was dispatched to Khartoum in 1884 to contain the power of the Mahdi, who was leading a rebellious religious movement in the Sudan. Gordon was killed in battle at Khartoum, an act considered by the British to be monstrous. Kitchener replaced him and achieved victory, largely due to the Egyptian troops he employed.

It was against this background of warfare and politics that Blunt perceived the Egyptians and their country.

He disapproved of the British occupation of Egypt, and particularly of the methods that were being adopted by Cromer in his treatment of the Egyptians as the conquered people.

During one incident in 1906, a group of British officers embarked upon a hunting party in the Delta. They apparently began shooting down domestic pigeons which belonged to a nearby village called Denshawi. When the villagers saw what was happening to their birds, they were enraged and chased the officers away. One of the British officers fell by the roadside whilst running away and the next day was found dead. An Arab boy who was standing nearby at the time was kicked and beaten to death by the British soldiers, although later it was discovered that the officer had died of sunstroke. Four of the village elders were sentenced to death and executed the next day in Denshawi.

This incident caused an uproar in both Egypt and England. The

Egyptians, already discontented with British domination, cited this incident as an example of British tyranny over Egypt, whilst on the contrary the whole matter was justified by the English newspapers as a necessary measure. *The Times*, in an editorial, exonerated the authorities and believed that the event was a "revolt upon a small scale on the part of the lowest and most fanatical of the Mussulman population . . ." It thundered on: ". . . The severe sentences passed upon the ringleaders are not only justified but imperatively demanded by the circumstances."[31]

Cromer, who was out of the country at the time, later admitted that the sentences, "though just, were, I may now readily admit, unduly severe." Blunt wrote in protest to the *Manchester Guardian* and to the *Tribune* about the "abominable Denshawi affair", but the executions were carried out. The day after the hangings Blunt wrote in his diary, "I have worried myself all day about the Egyptian villagers, and I see now that they were hanged yesterday under circumstances of revolting barbarity. All day I have been writing, and the thing is weighing on me like a nightmare still."[32]

Blunt and Cromer were in constant disagreement about the British occupation of Egypt. Cromer on the one hand criticised Blunt's romantic idealism, "he appears to have believed in the possibility of a regeneration of Islam on Islamic principles." Blunt, who was in fierce opposition to his country's Imperialism, retorted with "the world would be a poor misshapen deformity were it planted from pole to pole with a single crop of wheat; and how valueless will it have become, according to any concern of beauty, when the Anglo-Saxon rule of law and order shall have overspread both hemispheres—which may God forbid—and established over them its debased industrialism, its crude cookery and its flavourless religious creed."

Blunt believed that he could help the Arabs attain their political aspirations through the revitalisation of Islam. In his book *The Future of Islam*, he appealed to his countrymen in particular and the West in general to view Islam as a positive force which had contributed to human knowledge and values. Christians, he argued, should not fear Islam since "Christendom has pretty well abandoned her hopeless task of converting Islam, as Islam has abandoned hers of conquering Europe; and it is surely time that moral sympathy should unite the two great bodies of men who believe in and worship the same God."[33]

Although Blunt espoused Egypt's political cause, he was also intensely enthusiastic about the history, values and aspirations of Arabs in general.

He seems to have been pleasantly attracted to the traditions of the Bedouin and to their mode of living.

Blunt believed that the city Arabs generally were a degenerate people due to the tyranny of their foreign rulers. Although noting that the Arabs of the city belonged to the same race of people as the Bedouin, he found the former "a race demoralised, impoverished and brutalised by Ottoman rule!"

Nevertheless, Blunt presented the Arabs who lived in the "heart of Arabia" and away from Turkish influences as a most civilised and contented group: "In Nejd above all the countries of the world I have visited, either East or West, the three great blessings of which we in Europe make our boast, though we do not in truth possess them, are a living reality: 'Liberty, Equality, Brotherhood', names only even in France, where they are written up on every wall, but here practically enjoyed by every free man," he asserted. He depicted the Arab community as enjoying true democracy and real fraternity. "Here was a community living as our idealists have dreamed, without taxes, without police, without conscription, without compulsion of any kind, whose only law was public opinion, and whose only order a principle of honour," he wrote. In addition to his involvement with the Arabs and their political problems, Blunt also admired pre-Islamic Arabic poetry. Assad, the author of *Three Victorian Travellers*, stated that "the impact of Arabic culture is evident in Blunt as a poet," and emphasised that Blunt "admired Arabic poetry of pre-Islamic times because it was naive in its display of emotion, uninhibited, and hedonistic."[34] Blunt, a recognised poet, turned into English verse his wife's translation of the *Mu'allakat* and *The Stealing of the Mare*.

Blunt spent part of his time in the Arab World collecting Arab horses and taking them to a stud in Sussex, in order to breed them in England. In ironical order of priority, Blunt announced, "If I can introduce a pure Arab breed of horses into England, and help see Arabia free of the Turks, I shall not have lived in vain."

Towards the end of his life Blunt wrote that the view of Egypt from the desert, with its walls and minarets and the Nile, brought tears to his eyes, "as sudden wonders are apt to do."

In general, Blunt depicted the Arabs as a noble race with a superior culture, who were not "contaminated" by western civilisation. He sympathised with their aspirations for freedom from foreign domination and, furthermore, he commiserated with the poor common man.

Doughty

The third Victorian explorer was Charles M. Doughty (1843–1926), who had journed through the Arab World after "having spent the best part of ten years of early manhood, sojourning in succession in most of the continental countries."

His interest in the Bible and in oriental antiquities produced the urge in him to travel to the Middle East. He visited Syria, Palestine, Egypt, the ancient city of Petra (which had now become popular among European travellers) and the Maan Bedouin settlement in Jordan. Doughty, in his preface to his book, *Travels in Arabia Deserta*,[35] describes his difficulties and the harshness of travel in Sinai, writing that "with Beduin guides, I wandered on, through the most of that vast mountainous labyrinthine solitude of rainless valleys; with their sand-wind burnished rocks and stones and in some of them, often strangely scribbled Nabatean cliff-inscriptions (the names, the saws and salutations of ancient wayfarers)." At a place called Ayn Mussa in Jordan, he heard some Arabs talking about other monuments bearing inscriptions at Medain Salih, a watering place for pilgrims' caravans travelling to the holy cities of Mecca and Medina. He decided to visit the place, "interested as I was, in all that pertains to Biblical research," he wrote. Moreover, Medain Salih, "cities of their (Arab) reputed prophet Salih," according to him, "was at that time not known to Europeans." A year later Doughty arrived at the monuments after a long and tedious journey on a pilgrims' caravan from Damascus. He found the place "an old ruinous sand-plain, with sand rock cliffs; where our encampment was pitched by a great cistern, defended from the interference of Beduins, by a rude-built Turkish fort of Kella." After two months of examining and carefully impressing their formal superscriptions, which he found to be "sepulchral and Nabatean", he departed with a "friendly Sheykh of the district Beduins, to live with them awhile in the high desert." Once with Bedouin, Doughty sets out his purpose for further travels in Arabia, explaining: "I might thus, I hoped, visit the next Arabian uplands and view those vast waterless marches of the nomad Arabs; tent-dwellers, inhabiting, from the beginning, as it were beyond the world." In addition, he states, "I might find moreover, in so doing, to add something to the common fund of Western knowledge." For two years Doughty lived and journeyed with the Bedouin. In the preface of his book, he later described his travels, which he termed an "adventure": "In the adventure thus begun, there passed over me, amongst the thinly scattered, generally hostile and suspicious inhabitants of that land of wilderness, nearly two long and partly weary years; but not without happy turns, in the not seldom finding, as I went forth, of human fellowship amongst Arabians and even some very true and helpful friendships."

Doughty, unlike many of his predecessors, had disdained concealing his nationality or religion. "The name of Engleysy [Englishman] might stand me at first in some stead," he wrote, "besides the bitterness and blight of a fanatical religion, in every place."

In his travels Doughty took on the name of Khalil because, according to him, it sounded similar to "Carl", or "Charles". However, he was often referred to by Arabs as "Nasrany" (Christian).

Doughty reported his experiences in his book *Travels in Arabia Deserta*, of which he wrote, "I have set down that which I saw with my eyes, and heard with my ears and thought in my heart; neither more or less."

On publication, Doughty's book was widely acclaimed in Britain. T. E. Lawrence called it "the first and indispensable work upon the Arabs of the desert", and was confident that "every student of Arabia wants a copy".[36] Barker Fairley, in his publication *Charles M. Doughty: a critical study*, maintained that Doughty's work on Arabia differed from his predecessors' works in not seeing Arabia "as exotic writers do, a land of dream". Fairley believed that "Arabia of all countries has been the happy hunting-ground of romantic poets. It has become the chosen land of exotic romance." But for Doughty, Fairley asserted, "Arabia had not and could never have the faintest tincture of the picturesque, because he did not approach it with that part of his nature in which the picturesque could exist."[37] Richard Burton, a contrasting character in both his impressions of and beliefs in the Arabs, in a review of *Arabia Deserta*, described it as a "twice told tale writ large . . . which, despite its affectations and eccentricities, its prejudices and misjudgments is right well told."[38] Blunt, upon reading Doughty's book, wrote in his diary on 5 March, 1897, that it was "certainly the best prose written in the last two centuries." Doughty, stressing his factual reporting, stated, "I pray that nothing be looked for in this book but the seeing of an hungry man and the telling of a most weary man; for the rest the sun made me an Arab, but never wrapped me to Orientalism."

Although Doughty's work on Arabia was considered objective and dispassionate and Lawrence had once remarked that "Doughty went among these people, dispassionately looked at their life, and wrote it down word for word," yet we find Doughty's description of the Damascus Caravan quite colourful and even evocative. He describes the scene: "Upon the bearing harness of the Takht Camels are shields of scarlet, full of mirrors, with crests of Ostrich plumes, and beset with ranks of little bells, which at each slow camel's foot gingle, sinking together, with a strange solemnity: it is the sound of the Haj religion wonderfully quaint and very little grateful in my hearing."

In his book Doughty describes his experiences while travelling; the places he saw, but more important, the life and culture of the Bedouin. Doughty often refers to the places and people of Arabia by Biblical names. For example, he calls Arabia "the land of Ishmael" and the Arab "the Ishmaelite". Moreover, his book is strewn with Biblical verses explaining what he saw by reference to what Christians believed according to the Holy Bible.

According to Doughty the desert is a desolate and silent place. "No sweet chittering of birds greets the coming of the desert light, besides man there is no voice in this waste drought," he wrote. Travel in the desert, he reports, is beset with three dangers; famine, fanaticism and robbery. "Two chiefly are the perils in Arabia: famine and the dreadful-faced harpy of their religion, a third is the rash weapon of every Ishmaelite robber," he declared. Doughty calls the desert a "dead land" and the Arab who inhabits it, according to him, is "like a man sitting in a cloaca to the eyes, and whose brows touch heaven." In order to understand the desert Arabs, the adventurer, he noted, must "make his peace with them, so he knows the Arabs." According to Doughty, the harshness of the desert is the ally of the Arabs, as a safeguard for them against the many armies who tried in the past to subdue them. "The Arabian deserts may be passed by armies strong enough to disperse the resistance of the frantic but unwarlike inhabitants; but they should not be soldiers who cannot endure much and live of a little," he concluded.

Doughty then tells of how the Egyptians invaded Arabia but failed to retain it due to the "great cost to possess so poor a country". The Romans under Aelius Callus entered Arabia in quest of its riches. The Arabs fought the well-equipped Roman army with "slings, swords and lances and two edged hatchets". Although "many thousands of the Arabs" fell dead in the battle and only a few Roman soldiers were killed, the Romans finally found it impossible to remain.

Doughty describes their retreat: "In returning upwards the General led the feeble remnant of his soldiery, in no more than sixty marches, to the port of el-Hejr. The rest perished of misery in the long and terrible way of the wilderness: only seven Romans had fallen in battle!"

Doughty makes allusions to the ideas and impressions retained by the Romans of the Arabs, stating that "The Roman General found the inhabitants of the land 'A people unwarlike, half of them helping their living by merchandise, and half of them by robbing'." And he adds "such they are now." Doughty mentions Strabo's description of the Arabian desert: "It is a sandy waste, with only a few palms and pits of water: the thorn (Acacia) and the Tamarisk grow there; the wandering Arabs lodge in tents and are camel graziers." To Doughty the Roman image of the Arabs seemed to agree with his own. He concludes by saying, "Europeans, deceived by the Arabs' loquacity, have in every age a fantastic opinion of this unknown calamitous country." Despite this utterance Doughty nonetheless depicted the Arabs of the desert as possessing nobler qualities than the city dwellers, whom he termed malicious and deceitful. Yet as a whole Doughty thought of the Arab race in general as evil and ill-tempered, worshipping a religion he considered disdainful:

"To speak of the Arabs at the worst", he remarked, "in one word, the mouth of the Arabs is full of cursing and his prayers: their heart is a deceitful labyrinth—we have seen their urbanity; gall and venom is in their least ill-humour; disdainful, cruel, outrageous is their malediction."

Nonetheless and somewhat ambiguously he detected in them "antique humanity" and hospitality, "all the souls of a tribe or oasis are accounted *eyyal amm* 'brother's children', and reputed brethren of a common ancestry." Doughty seems to have been impressed with this closely knit social structure of the Arabs: "Full of humanity is that gentle persuasion of theirs from their hearts, for thy good *ana abuk*, 'my word is faithful, I am thy father', or *ana akhuk*, 'I am thy brother', *akhtak*, 'thy sister', *ummak*, 'thy mother': and akin to these is a sublime word in Moses, which follows the divine commandments, 'I am the Lord thy God'." The welcome proffered to the visitor by the Arabs also impressed Doughty. "In the hospitality of the Arabs is kin-ship and assurance, in their insecure countries," he wrote, adding, "This is the piety of the Arab life, this is the sanctity of the Arab-ian religion, where we may not look for other."

He relates incidents of Arab generosity: "Returning one day, in Syria, from a journey, I enquired the way of a countryman in the road. It was noon; the young man, who went by eating bread and cheese, paused and cut a piece of his griddle-cake, with a pleasant look, and presented it to the stranger: when I shook the head, he cut a rasher of cheese and put it silently to my mouth; and only then he thought it a time to speak." Doughty also tells us of an amusing fable concerning Arab generosity. According to him the "merry tale" is told in the mountains in Syria, the haunt of bears (Doughty mentions hunting them in "Helbon", in Syria). This is how he describes the scene: "The Syrian villagers sleep out in their orchards to keep night-watch in the warmer months. A husband-man hearing a bear rout in the dark, lifted himself hastily into the boughs of the next tree, which was an almond. The sweet-toothed brute came and climbed into that tree where the trembling man sat; and put out his paw to gather the delicate green nuts to his mouth. When the Arab saw this bear would become his guest, he cried before his thought, *Kul!* 'Eat, and welcome!' The bear, that had not perceived him, hearing man's voice, gave back; the branch snapt under his weight!—the brute tumbled on his head, and broke his neck bone. After an hour or two the good man, who saw this bear lie still as stone, in the starlight! took heart to come down;.and finding the brute dead, he cut his throat and plucked the fell over his ears; which on the morrow he sold to the cobbler for sole-leather."

Doughty also describes the dress and diet of the Arabs. Clothing of the males consists of a long robe with a *mandil* (kerchief) cover-ing the head. Women wear a *thob* (a long dress). "The nomad ker-chief, cast loosely upon their heads, is not girded with the circlet-band (*agal*),—which is the dignity of Arab clothing."

The diet of the Arabs consists primarily of camel's milk and of meat, often sun-dried. The locust is considered a delicacy among desert and city-dweller Arabs. "This early locust, toasted, is reckoned a sweet-meat in town and in desert." Doughty also ex-plained the "Keyif" (*kayf*), which was earlier mentioned by Burton. He translated this concept as meaning "pleasance" and "solace", and described it as "all that is genial solace to the soul and to the sense is *keyif*,—the quietness after trouble, repose from labour, a

beautiful mare or *thelul*, the amiable beauty of a fair woman."
Doughty depicts the Nomads as the "noblemen of the desert,
men of ripe moderation, peacemakers of a certain erudite judgment." But conversely he points out that the Bedouin "mind is
ever in the *Ghrazzu* [raid]; the knave would win, and by whose
loss he recks not, neither with what improbity; men in that squalid
ignorance and extreme living, become wild." The form of government of the tribe he describes as moderate and humane. "The
nomad Sheykhs", he wrote "govern with a homely-wise moderation and providence; they are the peace-makers in the *menzil*
(tribal meetings), and arbiters betwixt tribesmen."

As to family life Doughty describes the status of the female as
inferior to that of the male. Arab women, according to him, out-
number men. In the desert and in the city, women are "in bond-
age". He considers "the woman's lot is here unequal concubinage,
and in this necessitous life a weary servitude." Doughty describes
Arab women as being veiled and not allowed to show their faces
except to their husbands. Furthermore, they are at the mercy of
their husbands, who are dictators. The woman is used as a sexual
object and is cast away once "she withers". A woman's only
salvation is to bear many sons, thus ensuring her proper place in
the family. Arab women are portrayed by Doughty as good
mothers and "will suckle the babe very long at their meagre
breasts." Children are depicted as lacking proper socialisation
from the family, as they "grow up without instruction of the
parents." Their learning is incidental, gleaned primarily from what
they see and hear from adults, and "their only censor is public
opinion."

All Arabs, men and women, bedouin and city dwellers, use
kohl as a cosmetic, something which makes Arab males look like
women, according to the unaccustomed eye of Doughty. He wrote,
"In all Arabia both men and women, townsfolk and Beduins where
they come by it, paint the whites of their eyes blue, with *Kahl* or
antimony . . . not only they be more love-looking, in the sight of
their women, who have painted them, and that braid their long
manly side-locks; but they hold that this sharpens too and will
preserve their vision. With long hair shed in the midst, and hanging down at either side in braided horns, and false eyes painted
blue, the Arabian man's long head under the coloured kerchief,
is in our eyes more than half-feminine; and in much they resemble
women."

Doughty did not hold any sympathetic views of the religion of the Arabs. He states, "The Arabian religion of the sword must be tempered by the sword: and were the daughter of Mecca and Medina led captive, the Moslemin should become as Jews."

Doughty seems to have come to the Arab World with a Bible tucked under his arm. His explicit aim was to search for ancient inscriptions to validate his belief in the Holy Book. However, it looks as if Doughty had an unconscious need to probe into the meaning of life and the place of man on earth. Whilst with the Arabs he apparently stumbled on a group of people who seemed to him to have retained some of the basic values which gave man a purpose in life; namely their humanity and hospitality. Doughty, in his portrayal, praised the Arabs for these qualities and identified and sympathised with them to a certain extent. Nonetheless, on the other hand, he found the Arabs to be an "outgroup", whose religion, norms and mores differed from his own. Being religious and ethnocentric, Doughty condemned them for being different from the expectations of his own society.

Burton, Blunt and Doughty added considerably to the gathering store of ideas about Arabs in England during the nineteenth century.

Although these three men lived with Arabs and had intimate contacts with them, each traveller presented a different portrayal of the Arabs. Thomas Assad, in his book *Three Victorian Travellers*, describes their views about Arabs as follows: "Burton's view of the Arab was too grotesque; Blunt's too ornate, too sentimental; and Doughty's, too pure, too simple, too harsh."[39]

It is interesting to note that individually each believed his own perception of the Arabs to be the valid one and each was deeply entrenched in his own particular convictions.

However, as Assad points out, all three shared one characteristic, namely believing that the English were *ipso facto* superior to the Arabs "and therefore engendered the respective modes of mastery, condescension and chauvinism."[40]

Nonetheless, their portrayal of Arabs was, taken as a whole, colourful and romantic. Burton perceived the desert Arab as a noble savage, chivalrous, hospitable, revengeful and free. Blunt admired him for his sensitivity, high tradition and aspiration for freedom; whereas Doughty was impressed by the Arab's humanity and hospitality.

Curzon

The Arabs were also described to the English readers by other

Victorian travellers. Throughout the nineteenth century many journeyed to Arab lands, some motivated by a love of adventure or search for romance, others more seriously were driven by missionary zeal or scientific inquiry.

Robert Curzon travelled to the Middle East in search of ancient manuscripts. In his book *Visits to Monasteries of the Levant* (1849),[41] Curzon, who seems to have been under the spell of *Arabian Nights*, related that upon the arrival of their ship at Alexandria, they were hailed by "curious looking" people in a pilot boat. Curzon then describes how he first laid eyes on an Arab; he writes, "The pilot was an old man with a turban and a long grey beard, and sat cross-legged in the stern of his boat. We looked at him with vast interest as the first live specimen we had seen of an Arab sailor. He was just the sort of man that I imagine Sinbad the Sailor must have been." Curzon then describes Alexandria itself and how strange the "oriental city" looked to him. "The picturesque dresses, the buildings, the palm trees, the camels, the people of various nations, with their long beards, their arms, and turbans, all unite to form a picture which is indelibly fixed in the memory."

Curzon's description of the city Arabs in Alexandria impresses upon the reader a page from the *Arabian Nights*. He tells his readers, "Among the first things we noticed was the number of half-naked men who went running about, each with something like a dead pig under his arm, shouting out 'Mother! Mother!' with a doleful voice. These were the sakies or water-carriers, with their goat-skins of the precious element, a bright brass cupful of which they sell for a small coin to the thirsty passengers. An old man with a fan in his hand made of a palm branch, who was crumpled up in the corner of a sort of booth among a heap of dried figs, raisins, and dates, just opposite our window, was an object of much speculation to us how he got in, and how he would ever manage to get out of the niche into which he was so closely wedged. He was the merchant, as the *Arabian Nights* would call him, or the shop-keeper as we should say, who sat there cross-legged among his wares waiting patiently for a customer, and keeping off the flies in the meanwhile, as in due time we discovered that all merchants did in all countries of the East. Soon there came slowly by a long procession of men on horseback with golden bridles and velvet trappings, and women muffled up in black silk wrappers: how they could bear them, hot as it was, astonished us. These ladies sat upon a pile of cushions placed so high above the backs of donkeys on which they rode that their feet rested on the animals' shoulders. Each donkey was led by one man, while another walked by its side with his hand upon the crupper. With the ladies were two little boys covered with diamonds, mounted on huge fat horses, and ensconced in high-backed Mameluke saddles made of silver gilt."

In his accounts Curzon speaks of slave markets, the veiled harem, strange sounds and eerie music. He describes the city inhabitants as "primitive and submissive", being astonished to observe the "tyranny and oppression" of the police who, on horseback, struck people on the head to make way for a "great personage". Curzon notes that if such things were to happen in England then, "What a ferment would it create! what speeches would be made about tyranny and oppression! what a capital thing some high-minded and independent patriot would make of it! how he would call a meeting to defend the rights of the subject! and how he would get his admirers to vote him a piece of plate for his noble and glorious exertions! Here nobody minded the thing; they took no heed of the indignity; and I verily believe my friend and I, who were safe up at the window, were the only persons in the place who felt any annoyance."

Curzon, who like many travelling Englishmen had heard of Arabs but had never seen them prior to his journey, depicts another street scene in the city of Alexandria centred on a "multitude of donkeys". "There were hundreds of them, carrying all sorts of things in panniers; and some of the smallest were ridden by men so tall that they were obliged to hold up their legs that their feet might not touch the ground," he writes. "Donkeys, in short, are the carts of Egypt and the hackney-coaches of Alexandria."

Curzon also provided his readers with a portrayal of the Bedouin. Accompanying a caravan of donkeys and camels, which formed "long strings of ungainly-looking camels . . . generally preceded by a donkey", the nomads were described as "swarthy men clad in a short shirt, with a red and yellow handkerchief tied in a peculiar way over their heads, and wearing sandals; these savage-looking people were Bedouins, or Arabs of the desert," he remarked. "A very truculent set they seemed to be, and all of them were armed with a long crooked knife and a pistol or two, stuck in a red leathern girdle. They were thin, gaunt, and dirty, and strode along looking fierce and independent. There was something very striking in the appearance of these untamed Arabs: I had never pictured to myself that anything so like a wild beast could exist in human form.

The motions of their half-naked bodies were singularly free and light, and they looked as if they could climb, and run, and leap over anything. The appearance of many of the older Arabs, with their long white beard and their ample cloak of camel's hair, called an abba, is majestic and venerable."

As is apparent, Curzon was highly excited and at the same time impressed, when viewing the Bedouins for the first time. He remarked, "It was the first time that I had seen these 'Children of the Desert' and the quickness of their eyes, their apparent freedom from all restraints, and their disregard of any conventional manners, struck me forcibly."

Curzon's obvious astonishment was due to the fact that the Bedouin seemed to him to be so very unlike Englishmen, "an English gentleman in a round hat, and a tight neck-handkerchief and boots, with white gloves and a little cane in his hand, was a style of man so utterly and entirely unlike a Bedouin Arab, that I could hardly conceive the possibility of their being only different species of the same animal," he exclaimed.

Curzon also commented on his impression of the harem, "There is no greater mistake than to suppose that Eastern ladies are prisoners in the harem, and that they are to be pitied for the want of liberty which the jealousy of their husbands condemns them to." He underlines the point that women, behind their veils, "do as they choose, . . . go where they like, and carry on any intrigue [as] the Europeans; for their complete disguise carries them safely everywhere."

Christian Arab women are also described as leading the same life as the "Mohammedan women". Viewing a sixteen-year-old Arab Egyptian girl, Curzon was overwhelmed by her beauty, and described her thus: "She had a beautiful fair complexion, very uncommon in this country, remarkably long hair, which hung down her neck, and her dress, which was all of the same rich material, rose-coloured silk shot with gold, became her so well, that I have rarely seen so graceful and striking a figure."

The idea of women waiting on the men seems to have appalled Curzon. "This custom of being waited upon by the ladies is rather distressing to our European notions of devotion to the fair sex," he stated firmly.

Curzon believed that young Arab women are extremely pretty: however, they become astoundingly ugly when they grow old. The "ugliness of some of the old women is too terrible to describe," he wrote. "In Europe we have nothing half so hideous as these

brown old women. In comparison old men are peculiarly handsome and venerable in the appearance," he wrote. He found the
picturesque scene of an Arab Sheikh sitting in the shade of a tree
with his sons and grandsons around him waiting for his commands
"singularly imposing", and suggested that "painters who are
wishing to illustrate scenes of the patriarchal times of the Old
Testament have only to make careful sketches of such groups as
these."

Palgrave

Another English traveller to Arab lands was William Gifford
Palgrave, of Jewish ancestry. Palgrave became a Jesuit and
travelled to Arabia in 1862 and 1863. However, upon his return to
England he left the Jesuit Order and in 1865 published his book
*Narrative of a Year's Journey Through Central and Eastern
Arabia*.[42] In his preface he says, "The best part of my life indeed,
passed in the East, familiarity with the Arabic language till it
became to me almost a mother tongue, and experience in the ways
and manners of 'Semitic' nations, to give them their general or
symbolic name."

Palgrave travelled in Arabia with a Syrian Arab and assumed the
disguise of Salim Abu Mohumud al-Ays, a Syrian doctor. The
aim of his journey to Arabia is not clear; perhaps he was on a secret
mission for France, since his travel funds, as he stated, were provided by the Emperor Napoleon III. Burton doubted his sincerity
and accused him of hypocrisy.

Palgrave depicted the harshness of travel in the deserts of Arabia.
He described the hot wind of the desert blowing under the un-
clouded sky and the Bedouin wrapped in cloaks covering their faces
and running for cover under small black tents. He related how he
and his friend lay in a tent, covered and almost suffocating, while
the camels prostrated themselves outside on the sand. "We remained thus for about ten minutes, during which a still heat like
that of red-hot iron slowly passing over us was alone to be felt.
Then the tent walls began to flap in the returning gusts, and
announced that the worst of the semoom had gone by. We got up,
half dead with exhaustion, and unmuffled our faces. My comrades
appeared more like corpses than living men, and so, I suppose, did
I. However, I could not forbear, in spite of warnings, to step out and
look at the camels; they were still lying flat as though they had
been shot. The air was yet darkish, but before long it brightened up
to its usual dazzling clearness. During the whole time that the

semoom lasted, the atmosphere was entirely free from sand or dust; so that I hardly know how to account for its singular obscurity."

Palgrave preferred the city Arabs to the Bedouin. His views on the nomads were unfavourable and ran contrary to the accepted ideas of them in his time. He perceived them as treacherous, describing them as ignorant, coarse, and immoral; they were hardly touched by Islam and had debased their Arab race which he called "one of the noblest races of earth".

He was attracted to the city Arabs and marvelled at their sociable and energetic character. He describes the city of Hail in Arabia and presents a colourful and picturesque scene. "The market-place is more crowded from end to end; townsmen, villagers, Bedouins, some seated at the doors of the warehouses and driving a bargain with the owners inside, some gathered in idle groups, gossiping over the news of the hour. For the tongue is here what printed paper is in Europe, and I doubt whether an Arab loses more time in hearing and retailing the occurrences of the day than an Englishman every morning over his *Times*, although the latter has at least the advantage of looking the more studious."

Palgrave favours Arabs rather than Turks, whom he terms "overbearing and despotic". He depicts the city Arabs as kind and gracious. The Arabs were said to despise the corrupt and repugnant Turk because of "that independent high-mindedness which stamps the genuine Arab caste".

Arab townsmen are depicted by him as democratic and civil. "The well dressed chieftain and noble jostles on amid the plebeian crowd on terms of astounding familiarity and elbows or is elbowed by the artisan and the porter; while the court officers themselves meet with that degree of respect alone which indicates deference rather than inferiority in those who pay it."

Palgrave describes the serene pleasantness of the city atmosphere and its inhabitants, "a gay and busy scene; the morning air in the streets yet retains just sufficient coolness to render tolerable the bright rays of the sun, and everywhere is that atmosphere of peace, security, and thriving unknown to the visitors of Inner Arabia, and almost or wholly unknown to the Syrian or Anatolian traveller. Should you listen to the hum of discourse around, you will never hear a curse, an imprecation, or a quarrel, but much business, repartee, and laughter."

Nonetheless Palgrave had no sympathy with the Wahaby movement, and wrote: "Its atmosphere, to speak metaphorically, is sheer despotism, moral, intellectual, religious, and physical . . .

Incapable of true internal progress, hostile to commerce, unfavourable to arts and even to agriculture, and in the highest degree intolerant and aggressive, it can neither better itself nor benefit others."

Although Palgrave's attitude towards the Bedouin was so obviously unfavourable, his attraction to the people in general reinforced (as a result of his outstanding respect for the city dweller) the then prevalent notion, in England, of the nobility of the Arabs.

He reiterated the theme that Arabs are both simple and naive. This stereotype was given prominence in the narratives of some of the more important English figures who contributed to the making of the image of the Arabs in Britain, such as William Eton and Richard Burton.

In his book Palgrave quoted an "Arab proverb" which he described as "a common proverb, and current among all, whether Bedouins or townsmen." According to him the saying "The Arab's understanding is in his eyes" implied that "the Arab judges of things as he sees them present before him, not in their causes or consequences." Palgrave believed that this proverb actually explained the character of the Arabs. He continued to stress the validity of the proverb among the Arabs: "This is eminently true of the Bedouins, though more or less of every Arab whatsoever; it is also true in a measure of all children, even Europeans, who in this resemble not a little the 'gray barbarian'. A huge palace, a few large pieces of artillery, armed men in gay dresses, a copious supper, a great crowd, there are no better arguments for persuading nomads into submission and awe; and one may feel perfectly safe that they will never inquire too deeply whether the cannon are serviceable, the armed men faithful, the income of the treasury sure, or the supper of wholesome digestion."

Assuming that Palgrave in this instance was correct in his interpretation and analysis of the character of the Arabs as set in one of their proverbs, then one must ask whether those Arabs who were able to know and see themselves so objectively and so vividly could be as shallow and as naive as some of the English travellers, including Richard Burton and later T. E. Lawrence, depicted them.

Layard

Austen H. Layard travelled to the Middle East as an archaeologist financed by the Trustees of the British Museum to excavate the site of ancient Nineveh. His second trip, which took place in

1848, saw him travelling in Turkey and the city of Basra (Iraq), Egypt and Syria. Layard's *Discoveries in the Ruins of Nineveh and Babylon*,[43] relates his experiences and makes many allusions to both the Arabs and their countries.

His description depicts vividly and evocatively both the colour and the aspects of the desert. After a "sudden storm" and "whilst incessant lightnings broke the gloom, a raging wind almost drowned the deep roll of the thunder. The united strength of the Arabs could scarcely hold the flapping canvas of the tents. Rain descended in torrents, sparing us no place of shelter. Towards dawn the hurricane had passed away, leaving a still and cloudless sky. When the round clear sun rose from the broad expanse of the desert, a delightful calm and freshness pervaded the air, producing mingled sensations of pleasure and repose."

Layard shows a distinct interest in the Arab horse. He often mentions the animal and stresses its beauty and "pure blood". He describes the beast in glowing terms, remarking, "The Arab horse is more remarkable for its exquisite symmetry and beautiful proportions, united with wonderful powers of endurance, than for extraordinary speed. I doubt whether any Arab of the best blood has ever been brought to England. The difficulty in obtaining them is so great, that they are scarcely ever seen beyond the limits of the desert."

The Arabs of the desert are presented as a hospitable people, both sagacious and honest. They are also depicted as a generous people, willing to share their provisions with strangers and guests.

Describing the generosity of the Arabs, Layard relates: "Almost every traveller who passes the encampment eats bread with the Sheikh, and there are generally many guests dwelling under his canvas. In times of difficulty or scarcity, moreover, the whole tribe frequently expects to be fed by him, and he considers himself bound, even under such circumstances, by the duties of hospitality, to give all that he has to the needy."

Layard sees the Arabs as perceptive and observant, explaining that these traits are encouraged from the earliest age to enable the desert-dweller to survive successfully in a harsh and demanding environment.

On one occasion, while Layard and his companions were on a desert journey, the horses they possessed were stolen. A Bedouin, hearing of this theft, swore an oath to reclaim the animals. After a total of six weeks' searching, the Bedouin did locate the stolen animals and duly brought them back to their owners. Layard commented, "Such instances of honesty and good faith are not uncommon amongst the wandering Arabs, as I can bear witness from personal experience."

It appears from his own writing that Layard had read Burck-hardt's accounts of the desert Arabs, as there are several obvious references to this particular work. As an example, he agrees with Burckhardt that the Bedouin "are, perhaps, the only people of the East that can be entitled true lovers."

Layard provides an imaginative description of Bedouin women, and portrays the young women as graceful, with "large, almond shaped brilliant eyes, and black and luxuriant hair". He does however remark, "But their beauty is only the companion of extreme youth," for late in life they "rapidly change into the most hideous of old hags."

He was highly impressed with the undeniably noble Arab custom of "Dakheel": when a man approaches an Arab and asks for his protection, it becomes a sacred duty of the Arab to defend him, even at the cost of his own life. He expressed a wish that this characteristic would remain an integral part of Arab life, and exclaimed, "a disregard of this sacred obligation is the first symptom of degeneracy in an Arab tribe; and when once it exists, the treachery and vices of the Turk rapidly succeed to the honesty and fidelity of the true Arab character."

Kinglake

Alexander William Kinglake was another traveller who went to the Middle East as a tourist. His accounts are humorously presented in his book *Eothen*[44] (1864). During his journeys through Lebanon, Syria, Palestine and Egypt, he makes numerous references to the Arabs. Apparently he entertained a colourful image of the "wandering tribes", speaking of an intense curiosity, engendered by the various influences already present in England, to see the Bedouin before leaving the East. On one occasion his guide lost the way, yet promised that they would soon arrive at a Bedouin encampment. "I made no question about the road, for I was but too glad to set my horse's hoofs upon the land of the wandering tribes," he exclaimed. When finally they approached an Arab encampment, "The low black tents which I had so long lusted to see were right before me, and they were all teeming with live Arabs—men, women, and children." But, alas, Kinglake was disappointed when "some twenty or thirty of the most uncouth looking fellows imaginable came forward to see me." He remarked with a certain naivety that "they were of many colours, from dingy brown to jet black, and some of these last had much of the negro look about them. They were tall, powerful fellows, but repulsively ugly. They wore nothing but the Arab shirt confined at the waist by leather belts." Kinglake maintained that he found those people a poor and miserable lot, but was told by his guides that they were not real nomads. Later, whilst crossing the Sinai desert on his way into Egypt proper, his party ran into an Arab camp; finally, "I was now amongst the true Bedouins," he exclaimed. However, he seems to have been unimpressed with this experience. "Almost every man of this race closely resembles his brethren; almost every man has large and finely formed features, but his face is so thoroughly stripped of flesh, and the white folds from his head-gear fall down by his haggard cheeks so much in the burial fashion, that he looks quite sad and ghastly; his dark orbs roll slowly and solemnly over the white of his deep-set eyes; his countenance shows painful thought and long suffering—the suffering of one fallen from a high estate. His gait is strangely majestic, and he marches along with his simple blanket, as though he were wearing the purple. His common talk is a series of piercing screams and cries very painful to hear."

Later on his journey to Egypt, which was then reported to be suffering from the plague, Kinglake claimed that he had met *en route* a fellow Englishman then returning from Egypt. When their paths crossed and both men found themselves unable to communicate with each other on any level, their Arab guides stopped and began to converse. This situation seemingly embarrassed the two Englishmen, upon seeing the sociable nature of the Arabs, who although strangers to one another had thus entered immediately into a dialogue. After a long pause, Kinglake and his fellow-countryman hesitantly approached each other. "I dare say you wish to know how the plague is going on at Cairo?" the returning traveller managed to say. Kinglake tried to justify this episode thus, "Of course among civilized people, the not having anything to say is no excuse at all for not speaking; but I was shy, and indolent."

Kinglake reported in his book that whilst in Lebanon he had met Lady Hester Stanhope, the Englishwoman who was then living in an "old convent on the Lebanon range". He claimed that he had, as a child, heard stories about "the Englishwoman ruling over Arabs".

Of the Pyramids, he commented, "When I came, and trod, and touched with my hands, and climbed, in order that by climbing I might come to the top of one single stone, then, and almost suddenly, a cold sense and understanding of the pyramid's enormity came down over-casting my brain."

He described Damascus as being "safer than Oxford", writing of it, "She is a city of hidden palaces, of copses, and gardens and fountains, and bubbling streams. The juice of her life is the gushing and ice-cold torrent that tumbles from the snowy sides of Anti-Lebanon. Close along on the river's edge through seven sweet miles of rustling boughs and deepest shade, the city spreads out her whole length, as a man falls flat, face forward on the brook, that he may drink, and drink again; so Damascus, thirsting for ever, lies down with her lips to the stream, and clings to its rushing waters."

However, it seems that Kinglake's general portrayal of the Arabs and the things he saw lacked real sympathy and deep interest. He seems to have treated his whole journey as part of a farce, as if still contemplating it from England.

Warburton

Eliot Warburton, another English tourist in the second half of the nineteenth century, travelled to the Middle East in 1844, having been attracted by the colourful image of the East acquired from the portrayals of the area and its peoples by adventurers, writers and poets. His experiences were recounted in a book entitled *The Crescent and Cross*.[45]

In the first paragraph of his preface he describes the Middle East as being unchanged from time immemorial. "Immutability is the most striking characteristic of the East: from the ancient strife of Cain and Abel, to the present struggle between the Crescent and the Cross, its people remain in their habits of thought and action less changed than the countries they inhabit. The fertile Vale of Siddim has become the coffin of the Dead Sea and the barriers of the Nile have rolled down from Ethiopia to the Delta; but the patriarch still sits at the door of his tent on the Plain of Mamre, and the Egyptian still cultivates his river-given soil in the manner practised by the subjects of the Pharaohs."

According to Warburton it was not only the "antiquity, piety of scholastic lore" that attracted the European traveller to the Middle East. The area also provided other colourful and exotic compensations. He elaborates on this in these terms: "The variety that strikes upon the senses—the delicious climate, scarcely obtained in our conservatories—the wild animals, only known to our menageries, and the wayside flowers, that rival our most choice exotics—all these are pleasant things. Then, in the cities there is the mystery that envelops woman—the romance of our daily life— the masquerading-looking population—politics and manners of the time of Moses, Saracen society, cloudless days, and Arabian Nights."

Warburton, writing in the mid-nineteenth century, asserts that Egypt has by then become well-established as "our shortest and, therefore, our only path to India", and that the Church of England is obvious in its presence and is "at length represented at Jerusa- lem", and the "brave, industrious, and intelligent tribes of Lebanon have made overtures for our protection and our missionaries' due to the increasing spread of Christianity, particularly the Anglican factor, in Lebanon itself."

During his sea-journey, Warburton describes the places visited during the voyage, noting that Gibraltar was originally named by the Arabs "Gibel Tarik", Mountain of Tarik. The population of the Rock included "the Moors, dusky faces, with white turban wreathed . . ." He also describes the Barbary Coast as "beautiful in the fading light, which harmonized well with that land of old romance and mystery." He refers to the people of North Africa, describing them as "a fierce race of Moors, who believe that their best chance of paradise is to swim thither in Christian blood." But the Moors of bygone days, in his opinion, who had resided in Spain for three hundred years had, "enlightened Europe with the wisdom of the East and the chivalry of the Desert. Under their rule its gardens smiled, its valleys waved with corn, its very rocks were wreathed with vines and the Alhambra rose."

In addition Warburton noted that the French had occupied Algiers, the city "picturesque in shape and colouring", as seen by him in 1830. He also portrayed the Egyptian city of Alexandria and was repelled by it, seeing it as a place whose suburbs "are en- crusted with the wretched hovels of the Arab poor," being built of "filthy lanes, with blank white windowless and doorless walls on either side". He compared it to "the handsome square of tall white houses", of the French quarter of the same city.

Warburton, like many of his English contemporaries, was en- chanted with the Nile and with the antiquities of Egypt.

In both romantic and glowing terms, he exhorts his readers to abandon the "feverish life of Europe" and come away to the majestic Nile:

Henry Austen Layard

Layard's excavations at Nimroud

John Lewis Burckhardt's
tomb at Cairo

BURCKHARDT'S TOMB AT CAIRO.

Edward William Lane

Sir Richard Burton

Alexander William Kinglake

Wilfred and Anne Blunt

Lady Mary Wortley Montagu

A romantic image of the Arabs, late 19th century.
"Far and Wide, or, Songs from Other Lands." An illustration from
The Parlour Song Book, by Michael R. Turner, Pan Books 1974

"Reader! whoever you are, you may one day be induced to change the feverish life of Europe, with all its perplexing enjoyments, its complicated luxuries, and its manifold cares, for the silence, the simplicity, and the freedom of a life on the desert and the river. Has society palled upon you? Have the week-day struggles of the world made you wish for some short sabbath of repose? Has our coarse climate chafed your lungs, and do they require the soothing of balmily breathing breezes?—Come away to the Nile! Has love, or hate, or ambition, or any other ephemeral passion, ruffled up a storm in your butterboat of existence? Here you will find that calm counsellor Egeria—whose name is solitude. Have the marvellous stories of the old world sunk into your soul, and do you seek for their realization? or have mere curiosity and the spirit of unrest driven you forth to wander, *à l'anglais*, as a man takes a walk on a dreary day for the pleasure of returning from it? —come away to the Nile. Here are sunshines that are never clouded, and fragrant airs as gentle as a maiden's whisper, instead of northern gales, that howl round you as if you were an old battlement. Here are nights all a-glow with stars, and a crescent moon, that seems bowing to you by courtesy, not bent double by rheumatism. Here is no money to be lost or gained, no letters to disturb into joy or sorrow, none of the wear and tear, and petty details of life. You never hear the sound of your native tongue, and somehow men don't talk, and therefore don't think, so lightly when they have to translate their thoughts into a strange language. In a word, here is the highest species of monastic retirement. You stand apart from the world; you see its inhabitants so widely differing from yourself in their appearance, their habits, their hopes, and their fears, that you are enabled to look upon man in the abstract, to study his phenomena without prejudice. As you recede from Europe further and further on, towards the silent regions of the past, you live more and more in that past; the river over which you glide, the desert, the forest, the very air you breathe, are calm; the temples, in their awful solitudes, the colossal statues, the tombs, with their guardian sphinxes, all are profoundly calm and, at length, even our island restlessness softens down, and merges into the universal peace around."

Although Warburton depicted the lands of these Arabs as a haven and a pleasant place to escape to from the societies of Europe, he had little regard for the actual inhabitants of the Middle East and for their living conditions. He made several derogatory references on this subject. On one occasion he wrote, "The hyena and the Arab prowl within hearing of the citizen." In another instance, whilst describing the inhabitants of a place outside Cairo, he dismissed it as ". . . only inhabited, or rather haunted, by some outcast Arabs and troops of wild dogs."

In his accounts Warburton makes allusions to the slave markets in Cairo and calls them "human bazaars", where the girls, the "poor things", wait for their prospective purchasers. The women of the city were pictured as being huddled in the harem, "like cage-born birds".

The Egyptian male is described by Warburton, prejudiced strongly by Christianity, as "a sensualist and a slave, and only fit to be a subject in what prophecy long since foretold his country should become—'the basest of kingdoms'." The allusion is of course to the Biblical prophecy.

The Egyptian male's attitude towards his women, according to Warburton, is bestial and cruel. "Thus woman lives and dies, as if she were indeed the mere animal his miserable creed would make her!"

Warburton also held the desert Arabs in little respect. Although he describes them as hospitable, he portrays them in general as wild and fierce. He wrote of them: "This reverence for hospitality is one of the wild virtues that has survived from the days of the patriarchs, and it is singularly contrasted, yet interwoven with other and apparently opposite tendencies. The Arab will rob you, if he is able; he will even murder you, if it suits his purpose; but, once under the shelter of his tribe's black tents, or having eaten of his salt by the way-side, you have as much safety in his company as his heart's blood can purchase for you." He explained that Bedouin possessed some desirable qualities, such as reliability and bravery. "The Bedouin are extortionate to strangers, dishonest to each other, and reckless of human life. On the other hand, they are faithful to their trust, brave after their fashion, temperate, and patient of hardship and privation beyond belief," he commented.

Warburton was more fascinated with the history of the Arabs than with the living people with whom he made contact. "The Arab is the hero of romantic history," he exclaimed. He also noted that during the time of the Crusades, "the name of Saracen was almost exclusively applied to the Arab; and with that name are connected some of the brightest associations that shine over war's dark annals in elder times." Chivalry, he asserted, "was an earnest, solemn, absorbing feeling—almost a religion in itself." He makes allusion to the legend of Saladin, inquiring of his reader, "Who has not heard of Saladin, when he saw the lion-hearted being dismounted, sending his own horse to carry him? 'For,' said he, 'it is not meet that such a *knight* should fight on foot.'"

Warburton also had high praise for the Arabian horses, described by him as "noble animals, . . . no less remarkable for their chivalrous dispositions than their strength and endurance: gallant, yet docile; fiery, yet gentle; full of mettle, yet patient as a camel . . . The head is beautiful; the expansive forehead, the brilliant, prominent eye, and the delicately-shaped ear, would testify to nobleness in any animal; the high withers, and the shoulder well thrown back, the fine, clean limbs, with their bunches of starting muscle, and the silken skin, beneath which all the veins are visible, shew proofs of blood that never can deceive." The author relates a story about a French officer who had once seen a very beautiful horse being ridden by a Bedouin, and had subsequently offered a very large sum of money to "its poor proprietor", but to his surprise his offer was refused by the owner. When the Turkish Governor heard of this, he ordered that the Bedouin relinquish his horse to the Frenchman. "With tears in his eyes, the poor man dismounted from his loved companion, and kissed him on the forehead: then, suddenly exclaiming, 'Thou hast been the friend of the free, thou shalt never be the servant of the slave!' he shot the animal dead."

Warburton describes the city and village dwellers as people who have lost many of the traits of their noble ancestors. "The Fellaheen of Egypt are degenerate Arabs, who have lost almost all the characteristics of their race," he asserts with apparent authority.

In his book, he makes several references to Lady Hester Stanhope and quotes her as saying that the Arabs are the ancestors of the Irish, a very strange assertion.

In his appendix Warburton offers travellers in the East some helpful hints which clearly reflect his sense of English superiority over the Arabs: they should "insist on the most profound respect; preserve your temper and nonchalance as your best title to influence and security." He cautions travellers: "Never join in a row; let your people fight it out: if you must act, do so finely, boldly, and fearlessly of consequences: there are no consequences that can concern a right-minded Frank." Finally, Warburton concludes, "The people of the West are known to the people of Egypt and Syria only as *Frangee*, or Franks, and *Ingeeleez*, or English, and I think I may venture to say that they make a wide difference in favour of the latter, which it behoves every traveller to maintain."

Warburton generally viewed the Arabs and their homelands in terms of the stereotypes he had acquired about them from nineteenth-century English society before leaving for the East. His portrayal provides us with a most interesting insight into the attitudes of many English travellers of this period. First, these travellers carried with them certain preconceived ideas about the Middle East gleaned from former travellers' tales and the *Nights*, and subsequently interpreted what they saw in terms of these notions, usually against a background of the Bible, as Christianity was invariably a strong characteristic in these visitors. Secondly, their attitudes were characterised by a sense of superiority, that of an advanced race, as the English considered themselves, mingling with inferior and backward people. Thirdly, they appeared to consider the East as something akin to an amusement park, where they could recline and observe the natives at their leisure.

Hogarth and the Missionaries

David Hogarth travelled to the East in the latter half of the nineteenth century. In his book *The Wandering Scholar*, first published in 1896, Hogarth reiterates the theme of the profit-loving Arab. On one occasion, comparing some Turks with Arabs, he wrote, "These 'Turks' are honest, too, able, unlike some Arabs, to withstand long temptation of gold." In another instance, whilst describing a Turkish proprietor of an inn, he remarked "[The proprietor] began forthwith, Arabwise, to revolve in his slow mind how the chance might be turned to profit."[46]

Other nineteenth century travellers to the Middle East included a good number of English missionaries. These individuals, with the explorers and travellers, were also instrumental in the gradual formation of the image in England of the Arabs. One of the themes reinforced by missionaries in that period was the representation of Arabs as slave traders. Ironically, slavery and the slave trade existed in Britain and in its colonies until 1806. Thereafter, a group of English people, referred to as "emancipators", who had led the campaign for abolition in Britain, began to crusade against "the evils of slavery" around the world. However, special emphasis was placed on the "curse of the Arab slave-raider". One of the men who participated in depicting the Arabs as slavers was David Livingstone, the famous Scottish missionary teacher and philanthropist.

Livingstone journeyed through Africa between 1853 and 1856 in an attempt to gain converts to Christianity. Apparently meeting little success, he began to make allegations to the British public about "the horrors of Arab slave trade". He claimed that Africa was infested with inhuman Arab slavers, taking Zanzibar as a headquarters. He suggested that the Arabs must be forced out of Africa and replaced by Christian missionaries, in order to redeem the continent. Fisher, in his *History of Europe*, described the prevalent attitude at that time: "From this time a conviction steadily grew that unless the African continent were opened up, settled with farmers and missionaries, and brought under the control of the European powers, the poison of [Arab] slavery would never be fully eliminated."[47]

There were other English missionaries who went to Arab lands with the specific aim of converting Muslims, oriental Christians and Jews, to Anglican Christianity. Michael Alexander, himself a converted Jew, was dispatched to Jerusalem by the London Society to promote Christianity among the inhabitants of Palestine, especially the Jews. The mission failed.

Samual Gobat, who succeeded Alexander, was discouraged by his efforts to convert Muslims and Jews into Anglicans, so he turned to the oriental Christians, but that plan also did not materialise, since the oriental Christians in Palestine resented the intrusion of other denominations and their potential influence. Nonetheless, other English missionaries were more successful in the Lebanon.

One colourful character was a man by the name of Lawrence Oliphant, an eccentric Englishman who journeyed to the Arab world with various projects in mind. Oliphant toured many Arab countries, including Egypt, Lebanon and Palestine, in an attempt to establish a colony in the Holy Land for Eastern European Jews. However, having failed he turned his efforts to gaining converts for his own version of the 'mystical Union with God'. Again he failed in his appeals, and, together with his wife, took residence in Haifa, in Palestine.

The Oliphants' house became a centre for the "practice of a mystical conception of sexual love". Assad commented, "Perhaps we will never know whether or not Alice indeed slept with the Arabs in order to bring about a union of the individual with his spiritual counterpart, as Hannah Whitall Smith charged, or whether Oliphant himself, co-administrator of this new life, considered and practised such acts as consummations of the scheme's mystical rites."[48]

Oliphant went to great pains to have his doctrine as expounded translated into Arabic and other languages. He even cited Quranic verses to substantiate his ideas; but alas, only one Arab was con-verted to his ideology.

There was also Charles Gordon, with "the missionary gleam in his eye", who expounded peculiar theories in his book, *Reflections suggested in Palestine*. One such concept concerned digging a canal from Haifa to Aqaba (in Jordan), which would, according to him, bring the water from the sea into Jordan and thus fulfill a prophecy of Ezekiel's.

Two Novels

In the meantime Arabs were also portrayed in the works of nineteenth century English novelists and poets back in England. Among the most popular novels depicting the Arabs were Dis-raeli's *Tancred*, and Walter Scott's *Talisman*.

Disraeli, as mentioned earlier, had visited the Middle East in 1831. In his novel, which he completed around 1840, Disraeli "propels his hero towards the East—his darling East, still rich with travel memories," wrote Philip Guedalla in a note on *Tancred*.

The novel deals with a young English nobleman, Tancred, the son of the Duke and Duchess of Bellamont. Tancred apparently had everything he wanted in life, except that he did not know what the basis of his belief in life should be. He decided to make a pil-grimage to the Holy Sepulchre in Palestine, as a crusading fore-bear of his had done hundreds of years before.

It is interesting to note that Disraeli takes his hero from England to the Middle East in order to seek a solution for his dilemma. The novel makes many allusions to Arabs and their homelands. In one instance, for example, Tancred, while journeying to the Mount of Olives in Jerusalem, felt the coolness of the air. The author wrote, "It seemed to Tancred that a spicy gale came up the ravines of the wilderness, from the farthest of Arabia."

In another scene, Tancred addresses his beloved Eva: "'Why, thou to me art Arabia,' said Tancred, advancing and kneeling at her side. 'The Angel of Arabia and my life and spirit! Talk not to me of faltering faith. Mine is intense.'"

Although the Arabs and their country were depicted in Disraeli's novel as purely a background to the plot, they nevertheless were pictured both colourfully and romantically and with appreciation.[49]

The novel, *Tancred*, according to Guedalla, was accepted by Lady Blessington "as a revelation". In addition, Isabel Burton asserted that she had kept *Tancred* with her as a constant companion.

Walter Scott's novel, *The Talisman*, was another book which portrayed Arabs favourably and was also widely read. Scott confessed in *The Talisman* that he had never visited the Middle East. He said, "I felt the difficulty of giving a vivid picture of the world with which I was almost totally unacquainted, unless by early recollections of the *Arabian Nights' Entertainments." The Talisman* is a story which romanticizes Richard the Lionheart, the Crusader. The book was described as being written in the "true spirit of old romance. Picture after brilliant picture rises on the eye: the lonely coast of the Dead Sea, accursed solitude, where one Scottish man-at-arms rides unattended through the haunted wilderness; the sudden apparition of the Emir, the unwitnessed tournay, the halt of the Diamond of the Desert . . ."; thus wrote Andrew Lang.

Scott depicted Saladin in a most colourful and complimentary fashion. He was described as the most renowned Sultan of Syria and Egypt, "than whom no greater name is recorded in Eastern History". He referred to him as a "generous and valiant enemy", who is true-hearted and loyal. Scott pictured Saladin as a worthy opponent to Richard in point of chivalry. Both men were presented as noble and each loved and honoured the other "as noble adversaries ever love each other."

Scott's *The Talisman* was widely read and became a favourite, especially with the young. It still remains a popular and well-known novel.[50]

Some Poets

The Arab, the Desert, the Nile and the Pyramids were some of the subjects that evoked colourful pictures for both famous and little-known poets.

Byron, Longfellow, Shelley and Keats, for instance, all made reference to Arabs in their verse.

In *Don Juan*, Byron alludes to Arab hospitality:

> An infant when it gazes on a light,
> A child the moment when it drains the breast,
> A devotee when soars the Host in sight,
> An Arab with a stranger for a guest . . .[51]

Longfellow associates Arabs with tents and mystery:

> And the night shall be filled with music,
> And the cares, that infest the day,
> Shall fold their tents, like the Arabs,
> And as silently steal away.[52]

Egypt with its Nile and its Pyramids evoked an enormous amount of curiosity and interest; Shelley wrote of the Nile:

> Month after month the gathered rains descend
> Drenching yon secret Aethiopian dells,
> And from the desert's ice-girt pinnacles
> Where Frost and Heat in strange embraces blend
> On Atlas, fields of moist snow half depend.
> Girt there with blasts and meteors Tempest dwells
> By Nile's aëreal urn, with rapid spells
> Urging those waters to their mighty end.
> O'er Egypt's land of Memory floods are level
> And they are thine, O Nile—and well thou knowest
> That soul-sustaining airs and blasts of evil
> And fruits and poisons spring where'er thou flowest.
> Beware, O Man—for knowledge must to thee,
> Like the great flood to Egypt, ever be.[53]

Egypt and the city of Cairo were eulogized by Moore and Montgomery. Moore describes the city of Cairo with its gardens and minarets:

> While far as sight can reach, beneath as clear
> And blue a heaven as ever blessed this sphere,
> Gardens, and minarets, and glittering domes,
> And high-built temples, fit to be the homes
> Of mighty gods, and pyramids whose hour
> Outlasts all time, above the waters tower.[54]

James Montgomery wrote:

> Egypt's tall obelisk, still defying Time,
> While cities have been crumbling into sand,
> Scattered by winds beyond the Arab's desert,
> Or melted down into the mud of the Nile.[55]

Syria and Damascus were also depicted in verse. Moore, in a colourful portrayal of Syria, wrote:

> Now upon Syria's land of roses
> Softly the light of eve reposes,
> And, like a glory, the broad sun
> Hangs over sainted Lebanon;
> Whose top in wintry grandeur towers,
> And whitens with eternal sleet,
> While summer, in a vale of flowers,
> Lies sleeping rosy at his feet.[56]

Arabs also played a role in a number of ballads and songs which became popular in England during the nineteenth century. *Abdul Abulbul Amir*, a ballad, with its origins in the United States, was sung in England in the late nineteenth century. Sigmund Spaeth, in his book *Read 'em and Weep*, comments, "One of the first non-stop songs to run between New York and San Francisco was *Abdul Abulbul Amir*. It was the direct and only tangible result of the Crimean War, and started a school of Oriental atmosphere whose influence is still felt in American song literature."[57] Although this is a humorous song, not intended to be taken seriously, it reflects a popular notion of the chivalric pride and the religious fanaticism of the Muslim Arab. It tells of a duel between Abdul and a Russian aristocrat, Count Ivan Skavinski Skavar.

> The sons of the prophet are brave men and bold
>   And quite unaccustom'd to fear,
> But the bravest by far in the ranks of the Shah
>   Was Abdul Abulbul Amir.
>
> If you wanted a man to encourage the van
>   Or harass the foe from the rear,
> Storm fort or redoubt, you had only to shout
>   For Abdul Abulbul Amir.

The fight is provoked thus:

> One day this bold Russian had shouldered his gun,
>   And donned his most truculent sneer,
> Downtown he did go, where he trod on the toe
>   Of Abdul Abulbul Amir.
>
> "Young man," quoth Abdul, "has life grown so dull
>   That you wish to end your career?
> Vile infidel, know, you have trod on the toe
>   Of Abdul Abulbul Amir."

After further mutual threats:

> Then this bold Mameluke drew his trusty skibouk,
>   With a cry of "Allah akbar,"
> And with murderous intent he ferociously went
>   For Ivan Skavinsky Skavar.

At the end of a night-long fight, attended by "huge multitudes", both the Shah and the Tsar arrive to encourage their champions, only to find that each hero has slain the other. Although the song is a parody of the romantic tale, it nevertheless indicates that in the Western mind the East still preserved the follies and the grandeur of mediaeval days.

Such was one of the most popular songs of the era, far reaching in its effect, and in its impression of the Arab upon the ordinary man and woman in the street.

The Ladies

The colourful portrayal of Arabs in England during the nineteenth century fascinated many women, leading them to journey to the Middle East. Lesley Blanch in her book *The Wilder Shores of Love* observes that "many women, particularly Englishwomen, who have been enthralled by the Oriental legend", have followed the "beckoning Eastern star wherever it led." A number of Englishwomen, such as Isabel Burton and Anne Blunt, completely different in character, travelled to the Arab World with their husbands. Many others, however, journeyed alone, and these were described by Lesley Blanch as finding "in the East, glowing horizons of emotion and daring which were for them now vanishing from the West". Lesley Blanch describes the background of the growing romantic image of the Middle East in Europe in the eighteenth and nineteenth centuries. Of this she writes: "It was a time when the West was suddenly aware of the romantic aspects of the East. In the eighteenth century it had been seen as a fabulous backdrop; a stage setting for Mozart's *L'Enlèvement du Serail*, all toppling turbans and giddy goings-on in key with the elegant salons of Versailles or the Hofburg where it was first applauded. But even such tinkling echoes had died away by the time the nineteenth century dawned and Byron's verses were intoxicating an avid public. Now another, more sultry East was seen, although treated with an equal subjectivity. Mock heroics gave place to savage grandeurs. Travellers such as Prince Pückler-Muskau returned with tales of chivalresque Arabs and their splendours. Far away, across the steppes Pushkin luxuriated in the exoticism of Crimean legends, and was to be followed by Lermontov writing of Caucasian bandits. Presently jewelled scimitars adorned even the most prosaic country houses and the *Mameluke's Waltz* lay open on every pianoforte. Ingres and Delacroix were covering huge canvases with voluptuous scenes where beneath the expanses of exoticism and local colour, the most disturbing realities of flesh and blood were apparent."[58]

It was against this background that European and English

women began to view the Arab World, seeking to fulfil romantic needs which apparently went unsatisfied in their orderly and predictable Western lives. Lesley Blanch continues to observe the pleasant influence of the image of Arabs over women in the West. "And some women," she noted, "must have been aware of this, even subconsciously. Instinctively they must have sensed the contracting horizons of their age and seen the cold light of reason dawning like a grey streak across the blue. It was to spread over the whole sky. But the romantic image could still be translated into reality, could still be lived elsewhere; they turned Eastward trustingly."

Among the Englishwomen who journeyed in the Arab World in the early nineteenth century was Lady Hester Stanhope. The product of an unhappy childhood and very much the dreamer, she had left England for the Middle East apparently in search of peace of mind, after the death of her uncle, William Pitt. Kinglake, who visited her in Lebanon, stated that Lady Hester's trip to the East was primarily motivated by a "longing for the East very commonly felt by proud people when goaded by sorrow."

The eccentric and unconventional English lady reached Constantinople in 1811 accompanied by an "expensive retinue". Her party was composed of Michael Bruce, her lover, who was to play a significant part in her life, and the son of a London banker; a personal physician, Dr Meryon, and a maid. Lady Hester was described by Sarah Searight as "one of the most self-centred tourists to visit the Middle East." In England her name became legendary and, according to Kinglake, who participated in inflating her image in England, Hester's name was "almost as familiar to me in my childhood as the name of Robinson Crusoe. Both were associated with the spirit of adventure; but whilst the imagined life of the castaway mariner never failed to seem glaringly real, the true story of the Englishwoman ruling over Arabs always sounded to me like a fable." Lady Hester perceived herself quite sincerely as a "queen and goddess of wild Arabs". In a letter to Canning, she described the manner in which she was met by Mohammad Ali, the ruler of Egypt: "[He] admitted me to the Divan and when at Acre I rode Soliman Pasha's parade horse, having the use of his own sword and khangar [dagger], all over jewels. My visit to the Pasha of Damascus in the night during Ramadan was the finest thing possible. I was mounted on an Arab horse he had given me, my people on foot and he surrounded with two thousand servants and picked guards." While at Palmyra, she described her reception:

"I carried everything before me, and was crowned under the triumphal arch . . . pitched my tent amidst thousands of Arabs and spent a month with these very interesting people."[59]

According to Kinglake, Lady Hester had told him that she had been initially accepted by the Arabs in Syria because "The people of that country . . . had begun to imagine the possibility of their land being occupied by the English." Kinglake continues that "many of them looked upon Lady Hester as a Princess who came to prepare the way for the expected conquest."[60] Nonetheless, Searight believed that Lady Hester's success in evoking Arab attention and curiosity was due to her free spending. "Without spending vast sums," Searight observes, "it is unlikely that she would have achieved her greatest triumph—the revival of Zenobia's splendour."[61] This was a factor in her success that Lady Hester chose to ignore. However, upon the return of her lover, Bruce, to England, Lady Hester could not afford the luxury and extravagant spending she had once enjoyed in the company of her benefactor as well as lover. Eventually the Englishwoman went to live near Sidon, a town in Lebanon, in the Convent of Mar Elias, and later moved to another convent near the village of Jounieh, where she lived almost penniless until her death in 1839. Despite her egotism, however, it cannot be denied that Hester Stanhope was a truly remarkable woman, a daring lover of adventure, despite her overwhelming pride.

Among other English women who travelled to the Middle East and who were instrumental in the portrayal of Arabs in their subsequent accounts, were Isabel Burton, Richard Burton's wife, and Anne Blunt, who also accompanied her husband, Wilfred Scawen Blunt.

Although Isabel Burton went to the Arab World for the first time with her adventurer husband, she had been, as a young girl, pleasantly though romantically affected by the image of the Arabs portrayed in England.

Isabel Arundell came from a conservative Catholic family. It seems that she first became aware of Arabs as a young woman in Essex, where she lived with her family. "At Furze [her family house in Essex] she first began groping towards her lodestar East," Blanch noted. "In the woods, she found the gypsy encampments, and spent her days among them, drawn irresistibly towards the dark, free Romany people. In them she found those first echoes of the exotic, the East which was to be her life's obsession. In the library she discovered *Tancred*, and Disraeli's strange oriental *conte* remained a life-time companion, a bedside book, and one which, with her Bible, went with her everywhere, even in the desert in her saddle pocket." It seems that Disraeli's novel had a gripping hold on Isabel's imagination; it painted for her a romantic picture of the Middle East. Isabel, in her memoirs, confesses that *Tancred* had such a strong hold on her that when she finally saw the Arabs in the Middle East she was not surprised, for Disraeli's novel had brought them alive to her. "I almost knew it by heart," she wrote in her memoirs, "so that when I came to the Lebanon . . . when I found myself in a Bedouin camp or among the Maronite and Druze strongholds . . . nothing surprised me." Although Isabel's love for the Middle East was primarily due to her love for Richard Burton, yet as a young woman she seemed to have craved for "gypsies, Bedouin Arabs and everything Eastern and mystic; and especially a wild and lawless life." The reaction against her upbringing had had a strong and permanent effect.[62]

Although Isabel was married to Richard Burton in 1861, she did not journey to the East until 1869. When finally she embarked on the journey to Damascus to join her husband, who was appointed British Consul in Syria, she wrote "My destination was Damascus, the dream of my childhood. I should follow the footsteps of Lady Mary Wortley Montagu, Lady Hester Stanhope, and the Princesse de la Tour d'Auvergne, that trio of famous European women who lived of their own choice a thoroughly Eastern life, and of whom I look to make a fourth. I am to live among Bedouin Arab chiefs: I shall smell the desert air; I shall have tents, horses, weapons and be free . . . Fortunately my husband has had the same mind from his youth." Blanch commented on Isabel's first journey to the Middle East: "At last," she wrote, "it had all come true, all that she had prayed for, longed for . . . Tancred's East and Richard's arms."[63]

Isabel spent two years in Syria, often dressed in native clothes. Apparently those years were among the happiest of her life. Blanch says "The two years of their life there [Damascus] were something she most treasured, next to her love for Richard." Isabel's attachment to the East is reflected in her book *The Inner Life of Syria*. In the opening of her first chapter, Isabel, in response to the question as to whether she liked Damascus, replied "Like it! My eyes fill, and my heart throbs even at the question."[64] Like her husband, Isabel loved the desert: "I yearn for the desert to recover the purity of my mind and the dignity of human nature—to be regenerated amongst the Arabs." Upon the abrupt recall of her husband from his post in Syria, Isabel was shattered. She waited in torment for the confirmation of the bad news. "A few hours later she received the much-quoted message, *I am superseded, pay, pack and follow*. She sat amid the ruins of her life. It was the expulsion from Eden," observed Blanch.[65] By this time Burton's aptitude for debauchery had long since revolted the prudish Isabel, especially when shades of it appeared in his work. She grew increasingly bitter and one of her first acts after his death was to destroy all available papers written by Richard Burton that she could lay her hands on.

Lady Anne Noel Blunt was the granddaughter of Lord Byron. She journeyed to the Middle East with her husband. Gradually, Lady Anne became interested in the Arab World and especially in Arab culture. It is widely believed that she became better versed in Arabic than her husband. Her numerous works on Arabs and Arab culture included a book on the *Bedouin Tribes of the Euphrates*, a translation of the pre-Islamic "hanging poems", *The Mu'allakat or Seven Golden Odes of Arabia*, and she also wrote a book entitled *A Pilgrimage to Nejd*.

Lady Anne was among the first European women to enter the interior of Arabia. In her journal, she describes the journey of their caravan among the wastes of Arabia: "As soon as it was light we climbed to the top of the crater and looked over the plain. It was a wonderful sight, with its broken tells and strange chaotic wadys, all black with volcanic boulders, looking blacker still against the yellow morning sky. There is always something mysterious about a great plain, and especially such a plain as this where Europeans, one may say, have never been, and which even the people of the Hauran know little of."

Lady Anne was as much interested in the now renowned Arab horse as was her husband. In one section of *A Pilgrimage to Nejd*, she described how Arabs rear their colts: "'If,' said our informant, 'you would make a colt run faster than his fellows, remember the following rules. During the first month of his life let him be content with his mother's milk; it will be sufficient for him. Then during five months add to this natural supply goat's milk, as much as he will drink. For six months more give him the milk of camels, and besides a measure of wheat steeped in water for a quarter of an hour and served in a nose-bag.

"'At a year old the colt will have done with milk; he must be fed on wheat and grass, the wheat dry from a nosebag, the grass green if there is any.

"'At two years old he must work, or he will be worthless. Feed him now, like a full-grown horse, on barley; but in summer let him also have gruel daily at midday. Make the gruel thus: Take a double-handful of flour, and mix it in water well with your hands till the water seems like milk; then strain it, leaving the dregs of the flour, and give what is liquid to the colt to drink.

"'Be careful from the hour he is born to let him stand in the sun; shade hurts horses, but let him have water in plenty when the day is hot.

"'The colt must now be mounted, and taken by his owner everywhere with him, so that he shall see everything and learn courage. He must be kept constantly in exercise, and never remain long at his manger. He should be taken on a journey, for work will fortify his limbs.

"'At three years old he should be trained to gallop. Then, if he be of true blood, he will not be left behind. Yalla!'"[66]

These three English women, Lady Hester Stanhope, Isabel Burton and Lady Anne Blunt, were instrumental in contributing to the portrayal of Arabs in England in the nineteenth century. Although each woman was motivated by a different personal reason into appreciating the Arab world, yet the three of them are representative of the adventurous and romantic spirit of their age.

Separate Countries

In the nineteenth century Arab countries as individual lands acquired specific reputations in England.

Egypt had been depicted by early writers as a strange land inhabited by mysterious creatures, and in subsequent centuries as a land of bizarre cities with slave markets, various types of animals and an *Arabian Nights* atmosphere, the River Nile and the Pyramids evoking most interest and being described in great detail and at length. In the nineteenth century the search for the source of the Nile caused great geographical debate in England.

The Pyramids had been portrayed at length by numerous travellers, such as Edward Webb, who wrote: "Seven mountains builded on the outside, like unto the point of a Diamond, which mountains were builded in King Pharaoh's time to keep corne in, and they are mountains of greatest strength." Other early writers explained them in terms of the Bible; Veryard, for instance, believed that the Israelites built them "to keep them out of Idleness, the Nurse of all Sedition". Closer to the truth, other travellers saw them as representing tombs for the Pharaohs.

Mummies had also been a subject of intense interest to the English. John Sanderson, an employee of the Levant Company, describing a cave full of mummies, wrote of his experience, at the end of the sixteenth century, "We were lett downe by ropes as into a well, with waxe candles burning in our hands, and so waulked upon bodies of all sorts and sizes, great and smaule, and some are embaulmed in little earthen pots. . . . I broke off all parts of the bodies to see how the flesh was turned to drugge, and brought home divers heads, hands, arms and feete for a showe." Mummy powder became a medicinal commodity with magical properties supposed to cure certain illnesses.

In the nineteenth century, Egypt became popular with antique collectors. Visitors returned to England with various mementos. Gradually, however, Egypt became more a centre for archaeological enthusiasts. A new and expanding group of specialists known as Egyptologists began to appear. John Gardiner Wilkinson travelled to Egypt in 1821 and spent about twelve years excavating tombs and deciphering ancient Egyptian hieroglyphics.

Egyptology developed further into a new field of knowledge. Scholars became seriously interested in developing the practical as well as the theoretical study of Egyptology. Several societies were established to encourage and promote research in this field. Erasmus Wilson, a wealthy Egyptologist, paid personally for the removal of Cleopatra's Needle, which was re-erected on the banks of the River Thames in London.

Palestine had always held the interest and attention of Christians. The country was known and referred to as the "Holy Land". Many English pilgrims journeyed to Palestine to visit the land of Christ and of the Bible. Palestine was also envisaged as the scene of the "Holy Wars" of the Crusades.

Jerusalem, the Mecca of Christian pilgrims, was generally described in unflattering terms. Sarah Searight described how English travellers saw the Holy City as a "disappointing mixture of squalor, poverty and decay." In 1858, Edward Lear, the English artist, most famous for his humorous verse, after a visit to the city commented, "O my nose! O my eyes! O my feet! How you suffered in that vile place! For let me tell you, physically Jerusalem is the foulest and odiousest place on earth. A bitter doleful soul—ague comes over you in its streets, and your memories of its interior are nothing but horrid dreams of squalor and filth, clamour and uneasiness, hatred and malice and all uncharitableness."

Despite these unflattering impressions, the country attracted archaeologists to excavate many a site in order to prove the authenticity of the Bible. The Palestine Exploration Society was founded in 1865 to guard against "the onslaught which contemporary scientists were making upon the foundations of orthodox religion". In 1870 topographical surveys of Palestine had begun. The War Office, "which had its own reasons for wanting precise details of the area", despatched a survey expedition, one of its members being Herbert Kitchener, "who was handier with the camera than the pen," mused Searight.

Syria had also been the centre for Biblical excavations in the nineteenth century. However, the country had earlier acquired a reputation as an important centre of trade, partly because of its position on the main overland trade routes with India. Aleppo, for example, was an important post for the Levant Company's factories. Damascus was generally thought of as a dangerous place for non-Muslims, especially since it was the gathering place for Muslim pilgrims on their way to the *Hadj*. Kinglake described the general European view of the city of Damascus in mid-nineteenth century as being a dangerous place. In his *Eothen*, he wrote, "Until a year or two years before the time of my going there, Damascus had kept up so much of the old bigot zeal against Christians, or rather against Europeans, that no one dressed as a Frank could have dared to show himself in the streets."

Iraq, on the other hand, was known for its celebrated city of Baghdad, the city of the *Arabian Nights*. However, Baghdad and the city of Basra were also known to the English merchants as places where the trade caravans began their overland hauls to Aleppo. But the two cities were generally unpopular with foreigners, especially after the devastating plague of 1831, in which thousands of people died daily. Despite this, English archaeologists undertook excavations in the country in an attempt to understand the past civilizations of Mesopotamia.

Arabia retained its mysterious reputation as being dangerous and inhospitable to non-Muslims. North Africa, with its Barbary Coast, although still seen as a pirates' haven, was conquered and subdued by the French in the nineteenth century.

Chapter Five

Image in Flux

The Twentieth Century

When the twentieth century opened, the British had developed both emotional and political involvements with the Arabs. On the one hand, both the desert and the Bedouin seemed to have captured the imagination of the British: the desert was clean and exciting, a place where "the senses are sharpened" and where "the Samun caresses you like a lion with flaming breath". The Bedouin, although believed to be simple and easily placated, were true aristocrats with a nobility of tradition. There was, however, another side to the image of the Arabs, in Britain: a hostile attitude which had developed towards the urban dwellers, who were represented as debased, corrupt and dangerous. The slums and bazaars of the cities were described as places where various types of animals mingled with multitudes of people: beggars, dishonest turbaned merchants, subservient veiled harems and filthy children.

On the other hand, Britain had become deeply involved both

commercially and politically with the Arab World. "Her commerce, her position as a Mediterranean power, and her Indian Empire were alike threatened by Napoleon's invasion of Egypt, which showed her the danger of allowing any strong power to secure control of the Middle East," wrote Albert Hourani.[1]

It was against this background that the British image of the Arabs continued to develop in the twentieth century. Nonetheless, this century witnessed momentous occurrences which proved to have a significant and lasting effect on the image. Perhaps the most outstanding single event was the appearance of the Zionist movement in Europe during the latter part of the nineteenth century, which began to cultivate British public opinion in order to sway it in favour of the creation of a Jewish state in Palestine.

Ideas about the Arabs in the first quarter of the twentieth century continued to accumulate, emanating from English scholars, from travellers, and also from the growing influence of the mass media of communication such as the motion pictures and the press. The long tradition of Arabic learning in Britain continued to develop. Among the many who contributed to knowledge about the Arabs were men such as Sir Thomas Arnold, whose best known works include *Preaching of Islam* and *The Caliphate*. The former work discusses the propagation of the religion of Islam and the latter traces the origins and development of the Caliphate from the legal and philosophical viewpoints. Arnold also published studies of Islamic art and painting. Guy Le Strange, another Arabist, once remarked: "If Muslim history is ever to be made interesting and indeed to be rightly understood, the historical geography of the Middle Ages must be thoroughly worked out."[2] Le Strange's publications included three well known books, *Baghdad during the 'Abbasid Caliphate*, *Palestine under Moslems* and *The Lands of the Eastern Caliphate*. A student of William Wright, A. A. Bevan, produced a study of early Arabic poetry, and he was also responsible for the standard editions of the *Naqa'id* of Farazdaq and Jarir. Other Arabists who contributed to the study of the Arabs and their culture were men such as D. S. Margoliouth, Nicholson Gibb, Storey and Arnold Toynbee.

Meanwhile, individuals who travelled to the Arab world in the twentieth century motivated by love of adventure, such as Gertrude Bell and Freya Stark, gave way to an ever increasing number of military and political personnel such as G. E. Leachman and T. E. Lawrence, who were sent by the British Government into the area for intelligence work and military operations.

Gertrude Lowthian Bell was among the English travellers in the first decade of the twentieth century. A travel enthusiast, she began her journey into the Arab World in 1899 when she visited Jerusalem and travelled widely in Palestine and Syria. Her love for travel and adventure drove her to write, "To those bred under an elaborate social order few such moments of exhilaration can come as that which stands at the threshold of wild travel. The gates of the enclosed garden are thrown open, the chain at the entrance of the sanctuary is lowered, with a wary glance to right and left you step forth, and behold! the immeasurable world."[3]

In 1913 she undertook a journey into the Arabian Peninsula with the aim of exploring the lesser-known regions of the desert. Gertrude Bell described her life among the Arabs in several publications, the best-known of these being *The Desert and the Sown* and *Amurath to Amurath*.

"I desired to write not so much a book of travel as an account of the people whom I met or who accompanied me on my way, and to show what the world is like in which they live and how it appears to them,"[4] she declared. Gertrude Bell, apparently unable to pass as an Arab, "a woman can never disguise herself effectually", approached the Arabs as an Englishwoman in order to hear them "tell their own tale". She listened to "the talk that passed from lip to lip round the camp-fire, in the black tent of the Arab." She saw the Arabs as "orientals" who according to her, although somewhat shrewd, were in the main as backward, simple and impractical as an "old child". In this somewhat condescending vein she wrote, "The oriental is like a very old child, he is unacquainted with many branches of knowledge which we have come to regard as of elementary necessity; frequently, but not always, his mind is little preoccupied with the need of acquiring them, and he concerns himself scarcely at all with what we call practical utility. He is not practical in our acceptation of the word, any more than a child is practical, and his utility is not ours. Being English," she continued, "I am persuaded that we are the people who could best have taken Syria in hand with a prospect of a success greater than that which might be attained by a moderately reasonable Sultan." But the Arabs, the children of simplicity and over whom Gertrude Bell sternly waved her superiority, could teach the Englishwoman a few lessons in both wisdom and humanity, as she also shows. On one occasion her Christian Arab guide, named Mikhail, addressed her thus:

"'Listen, oh lady,' said Mikhail, 'and I will make it clear to you. Men are short of vision, and they see but that for which they look.

Some look for evil and they find evil; some look for good and it is good that they find, and moreover some are fortunate and these find always what they want. Praise be to God! to that number you belong. And, please God! you shall journey in peace and return in safety to your own land, and there you shall meet his Excellency your father, and your mother and all your brothers and sisters in health and in happiness, and all your relations and friends,' added Mikhail comprehensively, 'and again many times shall you travel in Syria with peace and safety and prosperity, please God.' 'Please God,' said I."[5]

Gertrude Bell spent the rest of her life with the Arabs and died in Baghdad in Iraq, a country she loved and which she had made her own.

G. E. Leachman of the Royal Sussex Regiment also travelled among the Arabs during the same period; not however as a traveller as such but on an intelligence mission for the British Government, collecting information about the various Arab tribes. He spent most of his time in Iraq but made several journeys into the Arabian desert attired in native dress. "Lijman", as the Arabs called him, was described by Major N. N. E. Bray in his book entitled *A Paladin of Arabia*, as a "sportsman, explorer, leader of men, demi-god amongst the great Bedouin tribes". Gertrude Bell portrayed him as, "Lean and active, dressed in ancient riding kit, his face full of weather, so that it looked as if sun and wind and rain had had more to do with the making of it than any human progenitor. The somewhat rugged landscape of his countenance was lit by his eyes, by the acute, observant glance of one whose business it is to make a rapid appreciation of men and things and take instant action."[6]

Bray claims that the success of Leachman's activities among the Arabs was largely due to his ability to impersonate them. "Leachman was an excellent actor," writes Bray; he "could pass as an Arab amongst Arabs. He could and did so when he desired." Leachman's alleged ability to impersonate Arabs was also expounded by C. F. McPherson (as quoted by Bray):

"When I was stationed in Bahrein, a group of islands off the Arabian coast in the Persian Gulf, my Persian servant informed me that an Arab wished to see me. Entered a long, cadaverous and altogether filthy Bedu, who greeted me with 'Hullo! got anything to eat?' This was Leachman, just arrived from a six months trek across Arabia, from Damascus, by a hitherto untravelled route. He had intended to continue his overland trek to Musqat, but owing to inter-tribal trouble had been forced to make for Oqair, on the mainland opposite Bahrein, from whence he had come by native *buggalow*. They had encountered a bad storm and he had consequently spent three days on board this craft practically without food and herded up with a crowd of dirty Arab divers. I gave him what lunch there was left, but discovered him later down in the kitchen with an Arab companion of his, who had made the whole journey with him, sitting over a large dish of rice, wolfing into this ravenously and using his fingers in the true Arab fashion. I was just off to Basra by a steamer then in port and sailing almost at once and as Leachman wanted to get to Bushire he came off with me still in his Arab clothes.

"The excellence of his disguise can be gauged from the fact that, on his attempting to board the steamer by the first class companion ladder, he was roundly abused by the ship's chief officer and told that Arab deck passengers should use the other ladder."[7]

Leachman's activities in the Arab World seem to have greatly added to the already exisiting notion in England that it was comparatively easy for the *ipso facto* superior Englishman to disguise himself as an Arab and slip unnoticed into the wide expanse of the desert, withstanding the glare of the burning sun, starvation, the parched throat, mirages and the lurking danger of the fierce Arab tribesmen swooping out of nowhere.

Contrary to the claims and boastings of the various English writers concerning the ingenuity of their hero in successfully disguising himself, both Leachman's identity and his mission seem to have been well known to the Arabs. In a testimony of one Fashed Bey, a sheikh of the Amarat Anize tribe, who knew Colonel Leachman well, there is clear indication that the Arab sheikh and his men knew exactly who the Englishman was, but nevertheless tolerated and pampered him. "He (Leachman) was tolerant, and not haughty," declared Sheikh Fashed, as quoted by Bray. "During his raids he used to ride a camel leading his horse after him, just as the Arabs do, and he looked after himself, refusing to have any servant. If our men wished to minister to him, he declined, saying that he was just a man like them, and he would share their fate, eat, drink and ride, and even draw water from the wells as they did. He baked his bread on the fire and ate it, rode a camel without anyone's assistance and galloped on its back like any Bedu, whose fathers and forefathers had been used to such feats. He slept folded in his *farwa* (fur) and *aba* on the bare ground and in the scrub without any cover or tent, and endured the hardships of rain and storm and sun. His energy and indefatigable endurance of the conditions of desert life surpassed those of any of its habitués. His sojourn in the desert endeared him to all and they regarded him as one of their sheikhs, for he spoke gently with them and never vexed or enraged any of them; and if they needed anything he was ready to help them. He would not tolerate that they should be treated wrongly. He knew every hole in the desert, every wadi and hill, and all the watering places, and he knew their names correctly and could travel to them unguided. This is our knowledge of Colonel Leachman during his stay with our tribes."[8]

Leachman was also described in the diary of one Corporal Frank Wing, who served him, as believing that "Arabs are big talkers". Wing also recorded that "Colonel Leachman could talk an Arab's head off . . . There were some big Arabs, but Colonel Leachman topped them all."[9] Ironically, on 12 August 1920 Leachman went to talk to Sheikh Dhari, an Arab chief, but alas Sheikh Dhari shot Leachman dead. On 28 February 1921, Leachman's remains were taken from his grave in Felluja and reburied in Baghdad, the city he loved.

Captain W. H. I. Shakespear was another military officer whose travels among the Arabs became known in England. Prior to his appointment in 1909 as a political agent of the British Government, he had served at Bundar Abbas and Muscat.

Shakespear, like Leachman, made several journeys into the Arabian desert with the aim of making contact with the Bedouin sheikhs, discovering new routes in the desert and "filling in blanks on the map". Shakespear described the "treachery" of one Howeitat tribe, because after agreeing to conduct him to Aqaba for a fee of ten pounds, they only took him to the next section of the tribe. Shakespear also related that Sheikh Auda, Lawrence's ally, was "the worst blackmailer", for he had embezzled all his money. The account of Shakespear's journey was edited in 1922 by Douglas Carruthers, who himself made a journey to the Hijaz.[10]

Carruthers' account of his journey was recorded in his book, *Arabian Adventure to the Great Nafud*. He set out looking for the oryx, believed to be the fabled Unicorn. After a sojourn in the desert he returned, having seen his oryx, an animal of extreme shyness.

Carruthers was impressed with the colour of the Nafud desert, describing its sands as "of every shade of yellow and red, blending softly into an amazing mixture for which one can find no name."[11]

Another pre-war traveller was A. J. Wavell, who journeyed into Arabia in 1908–9, visiting the holy cities of Islam.

T. E. Lawrence

But by far the most important English personality, who was greatly instrumental in influencing the contemporary image of the Arabs in both England and the West, was T. E. Lawrence, better known as Lawrence of Arabia. Lawrence's adventures with the Arabs became so widely publicised that fact and fiction became closely interwoven and the man became a legend in his own time. Harry Broughton, in his publication *Lawrence of Arabia: The Facts Without the Fiction*, wrote, "On the 16th August 1888 Thomas Edward Lawrence was born. This is one of the facts we can be sure of among the legion of legends that have been written and told about him."[12]

Lawrence's birthplace was Tremadoc in North Wales. His childhood was spent in Jersey, Scotland and France, before his family moved to Oxford, where he attended Oxford High School and later Jesus College.

From an early age Lawrence was interested in history. He read Layard's books on the excavations of Nineveh and "knew them almost by heart."

When only eighteen he decided to go to Syria in order to visit the Crusader's castles to ascertain whether the architecture was influenced by models of Western Europe or by those of Byzantium.

As preparation, Lawrence took a number of lessons in Arabic and made contact with Charles Doughty and Lord Curzon, both of whom were familiar with the Middle East.

In June 1909 Lawrence made his first trip to Syria and visited most of the castles of the Crusading period. It is claimed that he journeyed on foot and on one occasion was attacked by Kurds who robbed and beat him. In 1910 he decided to return to Oxford to take his degree in history. The effect of his trip to Syria was described by his friend, Leonard Green, who wrote, "He returned to Oxford full of a love of the silence of the desert places. Noise—the noise of Oxford traffic—was insupportable, and, in the garden of his parents' house in Polstead Road was built a room, the walls of which were draped to keep out the noise."[13]

In 1910, after only a brief absence, Lawrence returned to Syria, studied Arabic and joined D. G. Hogarth in a tour of Palestine and Syria. Lawrence took part in the excavations started by Hogarth at Carchemish on the banks of the Euphrates, and stayed on with Hogarth's successors, Campbell Thompson and Leonard Woolley.

David Garnett, in his book *The Essential T. E. Lawrence*, stated that Lawrence had "quickly made great friends with the Arabs employed on the dig."[14] Hogarth, who headed the excavations for a time, remarked once that "Lawrence was an Arab: a street Arab."[15]

In 1911, after completing the dig, Lawrence travelled in the area and claimed to have made friends with one Sheikh Hamoudi, who on one occasion cared for him when he became seriously ill. Later Lawrence, together with Woolley, engaged in smuggling rifles ashore from a British gunboat, to protect the British Consulate in Syria.

When the First World War broke out Lawrence tried to join the British Army. His efforts, however, were frustrated by his short stature. Nevertheless, he was ordered to Egypt, where he engaged in intelligence work. This signalled the beginning of the events about which he wrote and as a result of which he became widely popular.

T. E. Lawrence was viewed in England as the British-Arab desert warrior who, according to many, became the "uncrowned King of Arabia". He was credited with uniting the Arabs and leading them into successful battles against the Ottoman Turks. In fact Lawrence was principally a liaison officer between the Arabs and the British Government. The Arabs who yearned for their independence from Ottoman rule had long before the advent of Lawrence agitated against the Turks. During the war the Arab force, which was composed of Bedouin warriors, was led into battle by Faisal, Sherif Hussein's son. Lawrence himself admitted this when he described the revolt: "It was an Arab war waged and led by Arabs for an Arab aim in Arabia."[16]

The fact that Lawrence's exploits became a legend in England was partly due to a publicity campaign conducted after the war by the American journalist, Lowell Thomas, and by the coincidental appearance of Rudolph Valentino's film, *The Sheik*,[17] in which the Arab was romantically portrayed as a desert sheikh with flowing robes and characterised by nobility, dignity, manliness, gracefulness and virility.

Lowell Thomas toured the world for four years presenting his travelogue, "With Allenby in Palestine and Lawrence in Arabia".[18] He delivered lectures and showed films depicting Lawrence as if he alone was almost personally responsible for the defeat of the Ottoman Turks. Lowell Thomas, who had been at Aqaba at the time when the Arabs overran the Turkish garrison there, related that "we never had the slightest difficulty persuading T. E. to pose for Harry Chase's camera." It seems that Lawrence wanted the world to know of his daring feats; he paraded himself in his Arab dress in front of the cameras. "Lawrence loved the sensation of wearing his sherifian regalia. He enjoyed posing for his photographs . . . While I was delivering my illustrated account of his campaign at Covent Garden, Queen's Hall and the Albert Hall," added Thomas, "Lawrence came at least five times . . . Whenever he was spotted he would crimson, laugh in confusion, and hurry away with a stammered word of apology . . . I felt that many would have found it difficult to reconcile his modesty with the fact that he frequently came to hear me tell about his Campaigns in Asia . . . He had a genius for backing into the limelight."[19]

Lawrence captured the British imagination by his reputation for daring exploits in uniting and leading the Arabs into a desert war. He presented himself in his writings as both a friend and a saviour of the oppressed Arabs. In his own words, "I meant to make a new nation, to restore a lost influence, to give twenty millions of Semites the foundation on which to build an inspired dream-palace of their national thoughts. So high an aim called out the inherent nobility of their minds, and made them play a generous part in events."[20]

However, Lawrence knew that he was acting the role of a confidence man, written for him by his government, who apparently pictured the Arabs as children of simplicity who could easily be fooled and led by promises.

"For my work on the Arab front I had determined to accept nothing," wrote Lawrence. "The Cabinet raised the Arabs to fight for us by definite promises of self-government afterwards. Arabs believe in persons, not in institutions. They saw in me a free agent of the British Government, and demanded from me an endorsement of its written promises. So I had to join the conspiracy, and, for what my word was worth, assured the men of their reward. In our year's partnership under fire they grew accustomed to believing me and to think my Government, like myself, sincere. In this hope they performed some fine things, but, of course, instead of being proud of what we did together, I was continually and bitterly ashamed."[21]

Lawrence claimed to be in sympathy with the Arab cause and expressed his indignation at the "fraudulence" of his government. Nonetheless he knew well what his mission entailed and continued his mendacity. "I risked the fraud, on my conviction that Arab help was necessary to our cheap and speedy victory in the East, and that better we win and break our word than lose," he stated.[22]

After the War Lawrence wrote his book *The Seven Pillars of Wisdom*. Winston Churchill praised the book and declared, "It ranks with the greatest books ever written in the English language."[23] The work was widely read in Britain and the West and served as a source from which pictures of Arabs were drawn. Churchill, who was one of the most influential policy makers in Britain, underlined the importance of Lawrence's book as a reliable document about the Arabs when he said that "as a narrative of war and adventure, as a portrayal of all that the Arabs mean to the world, it is unsurpassed."[24]

In his book Lawrence recorded his experiences and recounted his exploits with the Arabs. In addition, he provided a portrayal of the Arabs which generally fitted within the framework of their image in Britain. The Bedouin fascinated Lawrence and he preferred them to both peasants and townspeople. Lawrence spoke of the desert as the "naked desert under the indifferent heaven" with "the effortless, empty, eddyless wind . . . throbbing past . . . born somewhere and had dragged its way across many days and nights of dead grass, to its first obstacle, the man-made walls . . ."[25] The Bedouin represented to Lawrence the desert dweller who was "born and grown up in it, had embraced with all his soul this nakedness . . . He lost material ties, comforts, all superfluities and other complications to achieve a personal liberty which haunted starvation and death."[26] In his book he describes the Arabs as dogmatic, simple, superficial and unstable. Furthermore he saw them as narrow-minded, individualist and submissive. "Arabs could be swung on an idea as on a cord," he declared. From a position of apparent Western superiority Lawrence alluded to them as incurably depraved children: "they were incorrigibly children of the idea, feckless and colour blind, to whom body and spirit were forever and inevitably opposed. Their minds were strange and dark, full of depressions and exaltations, lacking in rule, but with more ardour and more fertile in belief than any other in the world. They were a people of starts, for whom the abstract was the strongest motive, the process of infinite courage and variety, and the end nothing. They were as unstable as water, and like water would perhaps finally prevail. Since the dawn of life, in successive waves they had been dashing themselves against the coasts of flesh. Each was broken, but, like the sea, wore away ever so little of the granite on which it failed."

However, Lawrence proceeded to assert that the Arabs at that time were incapable of maintaining the momentum of their national movements, but a day might come, he warned, although distant, when their "wave . . . might roll unchecked over the place where the material world had been, and God would move upon the face of those waters."[27] Apart from the political connotations of his work, Lawrence conveyed the image of the Arabs in their tradition-al romantic colourful role, with himself as their leader. Churchill provides us with an example of how an English reader might have been impressed upon reading Lawrence's book. "Grim camel-rides through the sun-scorched, blasted lands, where the extreme desola-tion of nature appeals to the traveller. With a motor-car or aero-plane we may now inspect these forbidding solitudes, their endless sands, the hot savage wind-whipped rocks, the mountain gorges of a red-hot noon. Through these with infinite privation men on camels with shattering toil carried dynamite to destroy railway bridges and win the war and, as we hoped, free the world." Churchill saw Lawrence not only as a soldier but a statesman as well, "rousing the fierce peoples of the desert, penetrating the mysteries of their thought, leading them to the selected points of action and as often as not firing the mine himself."[28]

Lawrence was viewed by his own nation as an Englishman who knew how the Arab mind functioned and could correctly interpret both the history and the national movements of the Arabs. More-over he was seen as possessing the ability to disguise himself as an Arab without detection. Needless to say, the Arabs did not share the view of Lawrence held in the West. Many Arab historians and writers, while giving Lawrence some credit for his military services, deny the fact that his disguise was successful and doubt whether his understanding of their national movement was correct. George Antonius, the Arab author of the book, *The Arab Awaken-ing*, points to the fact that Lawrence's image of himself as set in his book *The Seven Pillars of Wisdom* contradicts Arab evidence of the campaign, and of Lawrence. "It is doubtful," writes Antonius, "whether Lawrence was fully conscious of the extent of his limita-tions, though he frequently alluded to them in speech or in his writing. He was aware, for instance, that his knowledge of Arabic was far from perfect, yet he believed that he was sufficiently fluent in it to pass for an Arab in conversation with Arabs. In that, he showed more self confidence than powers of observation, as anyone could tell who had heard his pronunciation." Antonius stresses that "it is conceivable that now and again, in casual encounters, he may have escaped detection. But neither his accent nor his use of words, to say nothing of his appearance, could have deceived anyone in Arabia for long: and an episode in *The Seven Pillars of Wisdom* in which he tried to pass for an Arab under the scrutiny and cross examination of a suspicious stranger, shows the lengths to which he could go in deluding himself."

Antonius, who had personally met and conversed with Lawrence on one occasion for three hours, commented, "I was struck with the self assurance with which he passed judgment on certain issues, and by the startling inconsistency between the professed weakness of his Arabic and the uses to which he kept putting it."[29]

It is unlikely that a man can conform identically to such a legend as that of Lawrence, yet in the eyes of his countrymen, who were disposed to believe in their superiority, Lawrence apparently was allowed to cast a giant shadow.

H. St J. Philby and J. B. Glubb

At the time when Lawrence in 1917 was working with the Arabs in Syria, H. St. J. Philby was dispatched to Arabia by Sir Percy Cox, the British political officer in charge of the territory already occupied from the Turks in Iraq, to "watch over" Ibn Saud.

Philby began his Government career in 1908 as a civil servant in India. He first came into contact with the Arabs when he was sent as a military political officer to Iraq in 1915. It seems that the only reason for Philby to be sent to the Arab World was his knowledge of the Arabic language. In Iraq he assisted in organising the administration of districts won from the Turks and was also in charge of collecting taxes from Arab merchants. He became friends with Gertrude Bell, especially because of their mutual interest in tribal lore and genealogies, and also because they both agreed that "good manners, not the brusque methods practised by Leachman, were the best way of getting what one wanted out of the desert Arabs."[30]

While in Iraq he toured the country and travelled up the Euphrates, where the "marsh Arabs . . . with skirts lifted above their waists splashed through the shallows alongside to sell eggs and chickens."[31]

In 1917 Philby was dispatched to Arabia as the political representative of his Government. His mission was to "smooth over the difficulties" between Sherif Hussein and Ibn Saud and to "secure a working arrangement between them in the interests of Arab

unity".[32] Arabia was to become Philby's home for many decades
and the country played a significant role in shaping his future life.
Philby travelled widely in the Arab World. He described Cairo as
the "most beautiful city I have ever seen" and observed that the
old city of Jerusalem looked beautiful despite its "filth" and the
poverty of its inhabitants. Philby became a close friend of Ibn
Saud, the King of Saudi Arabia, and as a result of this he became a
convert to the religion of Islam and became known as Abdullah.
"He needed Islam not as a faith, but as a convenience," remarked
Elizabeth Monroe who wrote his biography.[33]

Philby became known and admired in England mainly for his
feat of South Arabian exploration. The story of his journeys into
the desert were narrated in several books, the most widely-known
being *The Heart of Arabia*, *Arabia of the Wahabis* and *The Empty
Quarter*.

Although he was ostensibly a sympathiser with Arab aspirations
for unity and independence, some of his views exhibited glaring
inconsistencies, especially when it came to the Palestine question.
On the one hand Philby branded the Balfour Declaration as "an
act of betrayal for whose parallel, the shekels and the kiss and all
the rest of it, we have to go back to the garden of Gethsemane," and
on the other he proclaimed his support for the Declaration on the
grounds that the Jews had the right to settle in Palestine. Nonetheless Philby described the Arabs as a "noble race". Like many of his
countrymen, he preferred the desert and its dwellers to the cities
and their inhabitants, of whom he wrote: "Life in towns is
wretched, and all day long they do nothing but pray, eat, drink
coffee and lie with their wives."[34] His admiration of the Bedouin
sense of humanity and warmth is best depicted in a scene when on
a desert journey he had to bid farewell to some of his tribesmen
guides who were leaving his party by a different route. He writes:
". . . each of them saluted me with a kiss on the forehead. Forgive-
ness for our failing!! said Ali. There is nothing to forgive, I
replied, but I thank you for your services. In the keeping of God!
And so I parted from eight of the companions of two months
wandering in the wilderness. The farewell of the Arab is manly
indeed. With fair words on his lips he strides off into the desert
and is gone. He never looks back."[35]

In his narratives, the Arabs are seen through the eyes of the
Englishman, but occasionally we have the opportunity to see the
foreign traveller as perceived by the Arabs. On one occasion Philby
was thus addressed by his Arab guide:

"Firstly, you are hot-tempered and easily get angry if we do not do as you please. And, secondly, you are ever ready to disbelieve what the guides say." Then he continued candidly, "Tell me, were you like that from the day God created you? Or what is the reason for it? Surely you know that the guides do not lie deliberately, and this is their own country, where they should know every bush and every hummock. Why then should you suspect them of lying?"

"As for the guides," Philby replied, "I know that they should know this country, and you say they do not lie deliberately. Do you remember that day marching down to Ain Sala when I wanted to go aside to visit Adraj on the way and Ali told us it was distant a day's journey? Afterwards we went to Adraj, as you know, and when I drew it on my map I found it was but an hour's ride from our route. Tell me, did Ali really not know or was it otherwise?" "You speak sooth," the Arab guide replied. "Ali lied, but he was thinking of our need of water."[36] A far cry between the English outbursts of righteousness and the Arab silent sobriety.

Philby spent most of the rest of his life in Saudi Arabia both as a businessman, helping American oil companies to acquire oil prospecting rights in the country, and as a friend and adviser to Ibn Saud the Saudi Arabian monarch. In 1960 Philby died in Lebanon and was buried in the city of Beirut.

Another Englishman whose work with the Arabs became somewhat popular in Britain was John Bagot Glubb. Glubb served in the British Army in Iraq immediately after the First World War and was commissioned by his government in 1930 to command the Arab Legion in Trans-Jordan. According to Glubb the Arab Legion was the "heir" of the Arab army originally formed by Amir Faisal and T. E. Lawrence. John Glubb served as the head of the Arab Legion from 1930 until 1956, when he was dismissed by King Hussein of Jordan. While serving in Jordan, Glubb earned the title of "Pasha" and became known in the Jordan military forces as "Glubb Pasha". In one of his books, *The Story of the Arab Legion* published in 1948, Glubb describes the image of the Arabs as held by some of his countrymen as follows. "The majority of Englishmen who land in the Middle East," he wrote, "believe the Arabs to be a backward race not yet civilized." Glubb then sets out the manner in which Arabs are stereotyped in Britain. "The English cartoonist has accustomed us to visualize the Arab as a rather lanky individual with a long black beard, riding a camel over an endless flat plain with a single palm-tree in the middle of it!" He adds, "Even the more initiated are still inclined to believe that a great proportion of the Arab race consists of wild nomads living in tents. Such a picture is greatly distorted."[37]

Although Glubb glorified the nomadic Arab, he stated that the Bedouin were passing away in the Arab World and were ceasing to exist as a concrete political force.

The Arab World according to Glubb consists mostly of peasants: ". . . one tenth of the Arabs belong to nomadic tribes." He wrote, "The majority of the Arab race, today, are villagers engaged in agriculture. Even the city dwellers are probably more numerous than the bedouins."[38]

Glubb's work and his fame proved a main factor in popularising the Arab Legion in Britain. He portrayed them as Arab tribesmen who are to be "first-class military material . . . I am convinced that they are the same men who conquered half the world 1,300 years ago."[39] In Britain the Arab Legion were favourably viewed and nicknamed "Glubb's Girls"; they were seen as brave and colourful Bedouin, trained by British officers and ready to fight on the side of Britain.

The British in Egypt

It is important at this juncture to give a brief survey of both the political and the military situation in the Middle East in the first quarter of the twentieth century. As will be recalled, the first Arab country to fall under European domination was Algeria, occupied by France in 1830. Tunis next fell to France in 1881. Britain invaded and occupied Egypt in 1882, primarily to safeguard the Suez Canal, which was important for her trade route to the East, especially to India. The presence of the British rule, primarily in the urban areas of the Arab countries, began to adversely affect the nineteenth-century romantic image of the Arabs in Britain.

In Egypt, the British developed a contemptuous attitude towards the Egyptians. They despised and snubbed them, referring to them as "Wogs" (a term of disparagement and contempt connoting "germs" and "parasites"). Moreover the British soldiers, who mostly interacted with the depraved and degenerate segment of the Egyptian population such as pimps and prostitutes, believed that their presence in Egypt was to defend the Egyptians and thus, "to keep the skins on the backs of the Wogs". This attitude of contempt towards the Egyptians was not limited to the British troops alone but seemed to include the whole British community in Egypt. Dr A. Cecil Alport, an English physician, who taught medicine in Egypt in the thirties, described the snobbish attitude towards the Egyptians in his book *One Hour of Justice*. "English officials of the Egyptian government, and members of the British community generally, live as insular a life at Gezira (a club) as they do in England. They spend all their time between their homes and places of business on the one hand and the club on the other. They know little or nothing of Egypt and the Egyptians, and care less . . . I cannot understand the attitude of Englishmen who take everything from a country and give nothing in return," he declared. Dr Alport then related how he was unable to acquire a club membership for an Egyptian friend and colleague due to the lofty attitude of the British Club members. "About a year ago," he wrote, "I proposed one of the ablest physicians of Fouad I Hospital for membership of Gezira. He had been my assistant for five years, and was a man of the highest character and culture, yet two English professors of the Faculty refused to second him. Both of them said, 'We cannot have these people in the Club.' In every respect this Egyptian is a gentleman. Both he and his wife are charming, and they would be an acquisition to Gezira. He is an M.R.C.P. of London, and one of the cleverest men in Egypt. Moreover, having lived for some time in England he is fully conversant with English ways."[40]

The sense of superiority with which the English sternly regarded the Egyptians is best illustrated in a parable used by an English writer Douglas Sladen, in the first quarter of the twentieth century. "The value of the English to Egypt is of a different kind," he wrote. "It is the custom in noble English families, where the heir is of weak character, to engage a tutor, who is not only good at education of the ordinary kind, but is looked up to by all his fellows for the strength of his character and his excellence in manly sports. He is given complete authority over the boy in the hope that his influence will make a man of him.

"Egypt has the same results to expect from the tutelage of England," he concluded.[41] Contempt, disregard and disgust seemed to characterise the British attitudes towards the Egyptians throughout their occupation of Egypt.

Zionism in Palestine and in Britain

It is to Zionism that we must now turn in order to briefly examine the manner in which it has influenced the image of the Arabs.

In the first quarter of the twentieth century Britain made two promises: one to the Arabs and the other to the Jews. The Arabs were explicitly promised their freedom and independence in return for their support in the First World War. This pledge was made in a number of letters between Sherif Hussein, the then leader of the Arab national movement, and Sir Henry McMahon, the British High Commissioner in Egypt.[42] On the other hand, the British Government, two years later, made a commitment to the Zionists in 1917 in the Balfour Declaration,[43] which promised to assist the establishment of a national home for the Jews in Palestine. Moreover these two promises were compounded by a third promise made to the French in the Sykes-Picot Agreement: to dissect and divide the Arab nation between Britain and France. The promise to the Arabs was broken, whereas the promises to both the Jews and the French were honoured. This indicates the disregard the British seemed to have for the Arabs, believing that "the incorrigible children" could easily be lied to and could be put off by a few apt political promises.

After the victory of the allies in the First World War, a British Mandate was established over Palestine, Trans-Jordan, and Iraq. France held mandate over Syria and the Lebanon.

The British Mandatory Government in Palestine proceeded to encourage and aid Jewish immigration and facilitate their colonization of the country in the face of intense Arab opposition. Thus the British were determined to uphold their promise to the Jews and Zionism.

Zionism found its way into British Society at the beginning of the twentieth century through two main channels: the Poale Zion (Workers of Zion), who first infiltrated the British Labour movements and eventually established itself as an element in the newly formed Labour Party; and Chaim Weizmann, a Jewish chemist from Russia who emigrated to England in 1904. He became a personal friend of many of the aristocratic and influential members of the ruling class in Britain.

Although these two Zionist influences seemed to stand at opposite sides of the scale, yet they both aimed at the same goal: to steer both the Government and public opinion in Britain to support a Jewish State in Palestine, and to this end, to provide an unfavourable portrayal of the Arabs. At the time when Poale Zion was making inroads in the British Labour movement and later in the Labour Party, Chaim Weizmann and his group of Zionists and converts to Zionism were working to gain influence with the British Conservative Party, then in power.

Weizmann converted many important English leaders to the

cause of Zionism, men such as Lloyd George, James Balfour, Herbert Samuel (himself Jewish), Winston Churchill, and C. P. Scott, then the editor of the *Manchester Guardian*. Weizmann became their personal friend. He conversed and corresponded with them. Through these contacts he was able to encourage support for Zionism and to portray the Arabs in an unfavourable light. His tactics were to seize upon and emphasize those unfavourable and disapproved traits attached to the Arabs' image in Britain. In a telling letter which he wrote to Balfour in 1918, Weizmann depicted the Arab as tricky, a nuisance and untrustworthy. He wrote: "It is with a great sense of responsibility that I am attempting to write to you about the situation here and about the problems which confront the Zionist Commission . . . The Arabs, who are superficially clever and quick-witted, worship one thing and one thing only—power and success. Hence, while it would be wrong to say that British prestige has suffered through the military stalemate it certainly has not increased . . . The British Authorities . . . knowing as they do the treacherous nature of the Arab, . . . have to watch carefully and constantly that nothing should happen which might give the Arabs the slightest grievance or ground for complaint. In other words, the Arabs have to be 'nursed' lest they should stab the Army in the back. The Arab, quick as he is to gauge such a situation, tries to make the most of it. He screams as often as he can and blackmails as much as he can.

"The first scream was heard when your Declaration was announced. All sorts of misinterpretations and misconceptions were put on the Declaration. The English, they said, are going to hand over the poor Arabs to the wealthy Jews, who are all waiting in the wake of General Allenby's army, ready to swoop down like vultures on an easy prey and to oust everybody from the land . . .

"At the head of the Administration we see enlightened and honest English officials, but the rest of the administrative machinery is left intact, and all the offices are filled with Arab and Syrian employees . . . We see these officials, corrupt, inefficient, regretting the good old times when backsheesh was the only means by which matters administrative could be settled . . . The fairer the English regime tries to be, the more arrogant the Arab becomes. It must also be taken into consideration that the Arab official knows the language, habits and ways of the country, is a 'roué' and therefore has a great advantage over the fair and clean-minded English official, who is not conversant with the subtleties and subterfuges of the oriental mind. So the English are 'run' by the Arabs."

Weizmann, in the same letter, attacks the Arabs of Palestine for being so numerous, "for there are five Arabs to one Jew," he writes. However, in the same breath Weizmann minimises the superiority of the number of Arabs by dismissing them as backward peasants and corrupt effendis. He even attempts to deny the existence of Arabs in Palestine: "The present state of affairs would necessarily tend toward the creation of an Arab Palestine, if there were an Arab people in Palestine. It will not in fact produce that result because the fellah is at least four centuries behind the times, and the effendi (who, by the way, is the real gainer from the present system) is dishonest, uneducated, greedy and as unpatriotic as he is inefficient . . ."[44]

The theme that Palestine Arabs did not exist has present echoes in the words of Golda Meir, the former Prime Minister of Israel, who said in an interview with the *Sunday Times* in 1961 that there had never been such a thing as Palestinians.

Ormsby-Gore, who was a British member of Parliament and held several Government posts, including Assistant Secretary in the War Cabinet from 1917 to 1918, also used this theme in a speech he gave on 16 August 1918 at a meeting in London of the Zionist Political Committee. Ormsby-Gore spoke about the Arab National Movement, asserting that "the true Arab movement really existed outside Palestine. The movement led by Prince Faisal (son of Sherif Hussein) was not unlike the Zionists' movement. It contained real Arabs who were real men. The Arabs in trans-Jordan were fine people," he proclaimed, but he continued "*The west of the Jordan people were not Arabs but only Arabic speaking*"[45] (italics added by the author).

Nevertheless, there were those in the British Government who challenged the Zionist claims that the Arabs did not exist in Palestine; among them was Lord Curzon, who had served as Foreign Secretary. Curzon was of the opinion that the Zionist presentation of facts about the Arabs and the situation in Palestine was a distortion of reality. He further believed that Zionist designs in Palestine could prove harmful to the national interest of the British Empire. Curzon saw the need for his Government to take account of the Arab majority in Palestine and to respect their wishes. Curzon's warning fell on stony ground, for Balfour seems to have been far gone in his involvement with Zionism; and in a memorandum to Curzon on 11 August 1919, he fired the following barrage: ". . . For in Palestine we do not propose even to go through the form of consulting the wishes of the present inhabitants of the country. The four Great Powers are committed to Zionism, and Zionism, be it right or wrong, good or bad, is rooted in age-long traditions, in present needs, in future hopes, of far profounder import than the desires and prejudices of the 700,000 Arabs who now inhabit that ancient land."[46]

The Zionists and their allies in the British Government were quick to react to anyone who deviated from the picture they portrayed of the Arabs and of the situation in Palestine. A good case in point is that of Major Hubert Young, who served in the Foreign Office from 1919 to 1921. Young, while in England, had held favourable views about Zionism and believed that the situation in Palestine was as the Zionists presented it; namely, that the Arabs in Palestine were not to be taken seriously because they were both backward and insignificant. In October 1921 Young paid a visit to Palestine. What he found and saw did not seem to tally with what he had been led to believe. In a letter to John Shuckburgh, who worked in the political department, Young noted that Arab opposition to Zionism was serious and that the Arabs "have lost confidence in our straightforwardness." Young suggested that "what is required is some public action which will show the people of Palestine that the H.M.G. is determined its policy shall follow the lines which they themselves approve, but that the Zionists have been told so, and warned that unless they conform both in appearance and reality they cannot expect the continued support of H.M.G...."[47]

Richard Meinertzhagen, at that time Military Adviser in the Middle East Department of the Colonial Office, reacted to Young's letter in the following manner: "I am distressed to see that Major Young has seceded from the views held on Zionism before he left England. He has obviously been influenced by the local atmosphere and the Arab bogey."[48] Upon learning that there were disturbances in Palestine against the Balfour Declaration on 2 November 1921, in which four Jews and an Arab were killed in Jerusalem, Meinertzhagen suggested that drastic and severe action should be taken against the Arabs in Palestine: "... action on our part, if of a strong nature, will not fail to appeal to a race who are by nature cowards, and who have from time immemorial been accustomed to strength and dictation,"[49] he declared.

The Zionist organisation in London had by this time developed an efficient propaganda machine. It had established contacts with the Foreign Office and provided it with "information" about the situation in Palestine. In a letter to the Foreign Office dated 3 May

1921, the Zionist organisation presented the Arabs as terrorists and fanatical murderers, as the result of a riot that had earlier broken out between Arabs and Jews in Jaffa: "On first May a riot broke out in Jaffa (old city) resulting in serious casualties. The Jewish labour procession sanctioned by the authorities was absolutely peaceful notwithstanding the attempt of a handful of communists to cause disturbances; advantage was taken of the occasion for attacks on the Jews in the streets and shops were pillaged. The most terrible attack was the storming of the immigrants' houses by a gang of rioters who attacked men, women and children. There is general testimony to the participation of the Arab Police in the riots and of the fanaticism of murderers. The Arab crowd was stirred up by parties opposing the British Mandate and the Jewish National Home. These rioters used knives, pistols and rifles,"[50] the letter asserted.

In the meanwhile the Poale Zion that had started early in the century continued its work. Prior to its affiliation to the Labour Party, Poale Zion was active in waging large-scale campaigns in order to "enlighten" the public about the Zionist Socialist Aspirations in Palestine. These campaigns were apparently effective, especially when the special Labour Party conference held in 1917 recommended that Palestine should be internationally guaranteed to become a Free State, to which, "Such of the Jewish people as desire to do so may return, and may work out their salvation free from interference by those of alien race or religion."[51]

Members of the Labour Party who "have been brought up in the belief that Zionism equals socialism"[52] believed the Zionist allegations that the majority of the Arabs in Palestine welcomed the Zionists in their midst and that it was only the few Arab aristocrats who opposed the idea. Josiah Wedgwood, Labour's spokesman, portrayed the following image in a speech in the House of Commons in 1922, according to David Watkins: "He expounded the view that Zionism was bringing democracy and progress to Palestine, that it was welcomed by the Arab common people and opposed only by feudal landlords."[53]

This same theme has been used recently by the Zionists, who presented the Palestine resistance movement as a small group of "terrorists" unsupported by the majority of the Palestinian people.

The Labour Party was concerned in general with alleviating the miseries of the working classes in the world. Poale Zion presented the case of Palestine in such a way as to appeal to the principles and ideals of the Party. The main issue was depicted as being a conflict between both Arab and Jewish workers on one hand and the Arab feudal landlords on the other. Furthermore the feudal Arabs were identified with both imperialism and capitalism, the two arch-enemies of socialism. Therefore to many unsophisticated and unsuspecting minds of the Labour Party the picture seemed clear: both Jewish and Arab workers had a common enemy: the "exploiters". In October 1936 at the Labour Party Conference held in Edinburgh, Alex Gossip moved: "Believing that the interests of the Jewish and Arab workers in Palestine are identical, and that the Jewish Arab capitalists and landlord exploiters are the enemies of both, this annual conference of the Labour Party . . . urges them to unite together against the exploiters of both races."

However, when the motion was seconded by H. Lester Hutchinson, who classified Zionism with both Arab landlords and British imperialists, the motion was lost, and instead "a Zionist motion moved on behalf of the National Executive Committee and seconded on behalf of Poale Zion was carried overwhelmingly."[54]

Poale Zion succeeded in encouraging an unfavourable attitude towards the Arabs among the members of the Labour Party. David Watkins states that "Labour Party members have been brought up in the belief that Zionism equals socialism and that Arabs are aggressors and intruders."[55] Furthermore, the Zionists constantly bombarded Labour Party members with slogans such as "To make Palestine as Jewish as England is English", and that "Trans-Jordan must be open for the displacement of landless Arabs and for the settlement of Jews."[56]

In 1944 the official policy of the Labour Party regarding Palestine was stated as follows: "Here we have halted half way, irresolute between conflicting policies. But there is surely neither hope nor meaning in a Jewish National Home unless we are prepared to let Jews, if they wish, enter this tiny land in such numbers as to become a majority. There was a strong case for this before the War. There is an irresistible case now, after the unspeakable atrocities of the cold and calculated German Nazi plan to kill all Jews in Europe. Here, too, in Palestine surely is a case, on human grounds and to promote a stable settlement, for a transfer of population. Let the Arabs be encouraged to move out, as the Jews move in. Let them be compensated handsomely for their land and let their settlement elsewhere be carefully organized and generously financed. The Arabs have very wide territories of their own; they must not claim to exclude the Jews from this small part of Palestine, less than the size of Wales. Indeed, we should examine also the possibility of extending the present Palestinian boundaries by agreement with Egypt, Syria, or Trans-Jordan. Moreover, we should seek to win the full sympathy and support of American and Russian Governments for the execution of this Palestine policy."[57]

In the late forties, Ernest Bevin, the Labour Foreign Minister, challenged the unfavourable Arab image that was continually promoted by the Zionists. He made several remarks such as: "We must also remember the Arab side of the case—there are, after all, no Arabs in the House," and that the Zionists "demanded far more from the Arabs than they could or should be expected to accept peacefully,"[58]—for which he was labelled an anti-Semite and suffered bitter recriminations.

In 1970 a celebration of the fiftieth anniversary of the affiliation of the Zionist organization Poale Zion to the British Labour Party was held in London. On this occasion, Ian Mikardo, in a speech in the presence of Labour Prime Minister Harold Wilson, attacked Bevin and called him "not only an anti-Zionist . . . (but) an anti-Semite". Mikardo in his speech also attacked Foreign Office officials, whom he described as "public school boys who share with the Arabs a common tendency towards homosexuality, romanticism and enthusiasm for horses."[59]

Newspapers and Radio

The mass media of communication played an important role in informing and educating members of British society about the Arabs. The images of Arabs that are produced through the media are created by an army of "specialists" to become part of reality to their beholders. Generally speaking, the materials used in portraying various races and nationalities in modern societies are primarily drawn from three sources: information and stereotypes that already exist in society; new information collected by various individuals and groups such as reporters, writers and "fact-finders"; and propaganda establishments and interest groups motivated by specific intentions and aims.

Nevertheless, the existing stereotypes influence both the reporters and the propagandists. Reporters as a rule are unconsciously conditioned to perceive and interpret what they see or hear in terms of their past experiences and the predispositions acquired from their own cultures. Propagandists must also take into consideration the existing image in order to be able to create and project specific impressions, notions and ideas.

Finally it must be remembered that any new information contrary to prevailing beliefs and stereotypes is hard to accept and therefore initially seems to be either rejected or resented.

In the twentieth century, the mass media in Britain contributed to the formation of the Arab image: the press, radio, television and motion pictures provided both a political and social portrayal of the Arabs. Ideas, notions and impressions about the Arabs from various sources were used with little discrimination, particularly those taken from historical fiction and non-fiction such as the *Arabian Nights* and the tales of the Crusaders, from travel books, the writings of diplomats, soldiers and reporters, and from interests and pressure groups such as the Zionists, and also from various public-relations organisations.

In general the portrayal of the Arabs in the twentieth century in the press and broadcasting in Britain has been for the most part unfavourable. This is primarily due to a bias both cultural and political. The Arabs are perceived as an "outgroup", whose religion and values are seen as alien to those of the West. Furthermore the Arabs are seen fighting the State of Israel, which is an important part of Christian millenarianism. Christopher Mayhew, former British Labour Member of Parliament and an Arab sympathiser, writing on the bias against the Arabs in British radio and television stated that "bias in British broadcasting has been for the most part inbuilt and unconscious, a true reflection of our cultural prejudices, which are founded on half-remembered and inaccurate impressions of the Old Testament, the Crusades, the era of British colonialism, and most of all by our sense of guilt over the way we Europeans have behaved in the past towards the Jews in our midst." Mayhew also observes that the direct and indirect Zionist pressures on the media of communications render the portrayal of Arabs unfavourable. "The bias also came—often without deliberate intent—from the influence of sympathisers with Israel inside and outside the broadcasting organizations," he wrote.[60] Mayhew in his book *Publish it Not* . . . relates a conversation he had with an important British television producer about a projected television epic on the life of Moses. He relates: "'How will the Egyptians come out of it?' I asked. He had not given the question much thought. 'How do you mean?' 'Well, will you show them as goodies or baddies?' I asked. He saw the danger ahead and pondered. But then the safe sensible answer came to him. 'As it is in the Bible,' he said. 'That's fair, isn't it? Just as it is in the Bible.'" Mayhew continues, "Sadly I calculated that what seemed fair to him would also seem fair to the viewers and to the Independent Broadcasting Authority. Scene after scene of the proposed television epic filled my mind's eye. I heard the cries of the helpless Jewish baby in the bulrushes. I saw a handsome young Moses confronting an ugly old Pharaoh. I watched as the waters of the Red Sea parted, and the heroic children of Israel escaped from their well-armed, anti-Semitic pursuers. Above all, I saw the trailer to the series, repeated over and over again at peak hours, with Palestine being promised by God to Abraham, and Abraham being portrayed not, as the Old Testament in fact presents him, as the ancestor of both the Jews and the Arabs of Palestine, but exclusively—and inaccurately—as the forerunner of the Children of Israel."[61]

The Cinema: Early Days

Another important medium of communication which has significantly influenced the Arabs' image in Britain in the twentieth century is the film. To realise the importance attached to the feature film in particular, as both an image maker and image reflector in society, a detailed study of the film portraying Arabs is necessary. The film has long been recognised as a principal and effective means of disseminating information to large masses of people and as an instrument to be used in modifying and changing attitudes. For example, in 1937 an English film maker, Alexander Korda, was planning a movie on Lawrence of Arabia. However, the British Government, aware of the potential influence of the film and foreseeing a European war, did not want to offend the Turks and asked Korda to drop the project, which he did.[62]

In the middle twenties some people in England considered the American film a great threat to the British Empire. The *London Chronicle* asked apprehensively whether the British Empire could be conceived of as holding together indefinitely with American movies appealing directly to the natives of Asia.[63]

Ever since its inception the motion picture industry both in England and in the United States has shown interest in Arabs and Arab countries. Some of the earlier films depicted the Arabs as entertainers and associated them with both guns and magic.

A picture issued as early as 1898 by Thomas A. Edison was entitled *A Street Arab*. The content of the film, as described by Kemp R. Niver in his book *Motion Pictures from the Library of Congress Paper Print Collection 1894–1912*[64] states, "A boy is seen doing back bends, hand stands, head spins and back handsprings.

He is dressed in the conventional attire of a pre-adolescent boy of the era." Though the child portrayed was probably American, we see here an interesting and offensive use of the word "Arab" to mean an impoverished child of any nationality.

This film was followed in 1899 by another, called *Arabian Gun Twirler*, which was released by the American Mutoscope and Biograph Company, and showed the Arab as a bearded man "dressed in the costume of an Arab infantryman". He was associated with guns and demonstrated "his skill at twirling a standard army rifle."

In 1902 the Arab was portrayed as a clever magician in a picture entitled *Allabad: The Arab Wizard*, produced by A.M. and B. This film showed an Arab wizard "as he conjures out of space eggs, chickens, trees and animals, etc., and then makes them disappear". In 1903 the Arabs were again shown as performers and entertainers in the film *Arab Act, Luna Park*, in which "four tumblers performed for a crowd of customers in the mid way of an entertainment area."

In the same year at least eighteen pictures, newsreels or documentaries, concerned with Arabs and their countries were produced. This came on the heels of a trip around the world arranged by Thomas A. Edison in order to procure footage for the company's productions. The subjects in these pictures, described as being of "human interest" were taken from Egypt, Palestine, Syria and Jordan.

More than half of the documentary films showed Egyptian markets, historical monuments, native people and different types of animal. Four films referred to markets in their titles: *Egyptian Market Scene, Market Scene in Old Cairo; Going to Market; Luxor, Egypt, Panoramic View of an Egyptian Cattle Market*. These depicted Egyptians wearing "burnooses, turbans and fezzes", many carrying objects on their heads, "milling about" with donkeys, camels and cattle in market places, where "merchandise is spread out on mats". The Pyramids and the River Nile were also shown as tourist attractions in pictures such as *Tourists Starting on Donkeys for the Pyramids of Sakkarah, Excavating Scene at the Pyramids of Sakkarah* and *Fording the River Nile on Donkeys*, in which "approximately a dozen little donkeys are being pulled, pushed, ridden and driven across the ford toward the camera by drivers who wear turbans and burnooses, or by naked little boys riding them across." Other subjects of interest dealt with *Egyptian Faker with Dancing Monkey, Egyptian Boys in Swimming Race* and *Primitive Irrigation in Egypt.* The last showed "a counterbalanced pole with a rope and a bucket attached. An operator wearing a turban and a burnoose dips the bucket into a well. A tethered donkey can also be seen." The film also presented a scene of "an irrigation project where an ox-powered water-wheel is in operation."

The Holy City of Jerusalem and Jaffa, a coastal town in Palestine, were shown in three films: *Jerusalem's Busiest Street, Showing Mount Zion, Herd of Sheep on the Road to Jerusalem*, in which "four men dressed in the costume of desert shepherds of Jerusalem" were shown escorting a herd of sheep. *Tourists Embarking at Jaffa* and *Street Scene at Jaffa* presented the Arab natives dressed in "burnooses, turbans, fezzes . . . wrap-around pants . . . some leading camels or donkeys and others in rowboats."

Two pictures were filmed in Syria and the city of Beirut. In the first, entitled *Tourists Returning on Donkeys from Mizpah*, "The camera was positioned among rocks and brush of desolate countryside in order to show some tourists passing. All are mounted on donkeys, each led by a man who appears from his attire to be a native." The other film, *Panoramic View of Beirut, Syria, Showing Holiday Festivities*, showed a large group of people milling about "in an area that resembles a fairground or amusement area. In the foreground are men wearing fezzes, and women with their faces covered with veils."

Filmed in Jordan, a picture entitled *Tourists Taking Water from The River Jordan* showed scenes of a group of tourists on the banks of the River Jordan.

All these were, of course, made and presented in the very early days of the cinema, with the simple aim of showing the potentialities of the new medium. Their attraction lay in the depiction of the exotic, of scenes which the ordinary American could never hope to see in actuality. The Middle East offered great scope: here were people and places as remote as could be from the culture of the West, and interesting for this reason alone. The effect of such films would be not to bring the Arabs nearer but to make them appear all the more alien and strange.

Although fictional entertainment did not become the primary product of motion pictures until 1910, as early as 1905 feature films had given highly fictionalised portrayals of Arabs and Arab countries. In 1905 the French director, George Melies, issued a serial which was shown in England and the United States entitled *The Palace of the Arabian Nights.* This marked the beginning of a torrent of fantasy pictures based on tales from the *Arabian Nights.*

Two of them were seen in 1909: *A Tale of the Harem* (1908) and *The Cobbler and the Caliph* (1909), both released by the Vitagraph Company of America.

Further utilising the Arab countries as a background for action, in 1912 Crown Feature Film Company issued *The Battle of Two Palms*, based on the battle of 12 March 1912 at Benghazi and Tripoli between the Italian and the Turkish armies. In 1913 Western heroes and Arab villains were shown in a picture entitled *Fire and the Sword* (Kismet Feature Film Company). This film dealt with an American girl abducted by the Grand Vizier of a mythical Arab country. In the midst of a revolution involving spectacular hand-to-hand fighting, she is finally rescued from the Sultan by an American reporter. It is worth noting that elements such as the fantasy of the *Arabian Nights* and a background of action associated with the Arab countries began to be woven together in a single plot.

Almost from the beginning the theme of mystery was associated with Arabs and their lands, especially Egypt, in such films as *The Egyptian Mystery* (Edison Mfg. Co., 1909) and *Vengeance of Egypt* (Gaumont Company, 1912).

This element of mystery which became associated with Arabs was furthermore used successfully in the early 1900s in a campaign which made an actress named Theda Bara a star. Derivatives of the word "vampire"—"vamp" and "baby vamp"—were introduced into the English language as a result of the movie career of this actress. Frank J. Powell, a film producer, was looking for an unknown actress to play the aggressive *femme fatale*. He found her in a girl from Ohio. Richard Griffith and Arthur Mayer in their book entitled *The Movies* describe her as "dark-haired, big-eyed", and comment: "This circumspect and demure girl was at once whisked out of sight and an entirely new personality was manufactured for her. She was renamed Theda Bara, which the publicity office insisted was an anagram for 'Arab death'. She was alleged to be the daughter of a French father and an Egyptian mother and to be inscrutably but frightfully evil. A dead white limousine attended by 'Nubian' footmen drove her to the Chicago Hotel where she gave an unforgettable interview in a dim room hung in black velvet and filled with incense fires . . . The campaign, apparently the first designed specifically to create an artificial movie star, was successful. *A Fool There Was* made Miss Bara famous overnight . . . and offered the sublime 'Kiss me, my fool,' which was quoted for a generation.

"Thereafter, Miss Bara was wicked through forty subsequent films in four years. Constantly photographed with skulls and snakes, she became the public's permanent symbol of evil . . ."[65]

The Last Egyptian (1914) showed the Egyptian in the role of a villain and ascribed to him a desire for vengeance. The plot dealt with a descendant of the Pharoahs pledged by his dying grandmother to avenge her wrongs at the hands of an English Earl. The attempt to fufil this oath led to the downfall of the Egyptian.

In 1915 an important picture, *The Arab*, was issued by Jesse L. Lasky Feature Play Company. The film, originally a play by Edgar Selwyn, had been successful on Broadway. *The Arab* was advertised as "the most spectacular production ever made by the Lasky Company";[66] furthermore it was remade and released in 1924. The importance of this picture lies in the fact that firstly, the Arab was portrayed as a central character in a saga of sand and heroism, draped in princely costumes and shown as an unexcelled horseman; secondly, the main theme in the story was concerned with both Christianity and Islam; thirdly, an Arab Muslim male falls in love with a Western Christian female (however, this relationship was not allowed to develop beyond certain limits). The story depicted an Arab, named Jamil, a son of a Bedouin tribal leader, who is disowned by his father for a desert raid at the time of the Muslim Feast of Ramadan. Eventually he becomes a tourist guide in a Turkish city, where he falls in love with Mary, the daughter of a Christian missionary. Jamil, with the aid of the Bedouin, foils the Turkish Governor's attempt to massacre the Christians. Later Jamil is made a leader of his tribe and accepts the girl's promise to return to him as she departs for America.

In the twenties the Arabs were mostly presented as belly dancers, lovers, bandits, robbers, pirates, and as villains against French and British heroism in North Africa and Sudan.

In 1920 John Franklin Meyer released a picture entitled *Little Egypt*, based on the story of the Egyptian girl who introduced belly-dancing to America. Belly-dancing was inseparably associated with Egypt and the Egyptians. Many pictures were produced later linking Egypt with dancing; for example, *The Egyptian Dancer* (John Franklin Meyer, 1920) and *The Dancer of the Nile* (William P. S. Earle Pictures, Inc., 1923).

The Cinema: *The Sheik* and Others

But by far the most important film of this early period was *The Sheik* (Famous Players Lasky Corporation, 1921), an adaptation from a best-selling novel by Edith M. Hull, first published in London in 1919.

As a motion picture about Arabs, *The Sheik* was important for several reasons. First, the film became a great popular success. Second, the lead was played by one of the most "perfect lovers the screen has ever known".[67] Third, it started a cycle of dramas of the "great throbbing desert".[68]

There are many views on the success of *The Sheik* at the box office. Lewis Jacobs stated that: "In the prevalent post-war disillusionment most people sought 'escape'. The movies obligingly offered substitutes for life in the form of exotic and erotic costume dramas, all affording vicarious satisfaction, extravagant visual magnificence. The phenomenal success of *The Sheik* (1921) climaxed the series of exotic 'red hot romances'."[69]

Park Taylor commented on the popularity of *The Sheik*: "The great popularity of Valentino's best-known film *The Sheik* was owing to the anachronistic glamour of the sheik's erotic technique: he kidnaps a beautiful woman and compels her to fall in love with him. The essential primitiveness of this technique recalls those elements of ancient ritual in which a bride was won by feats of physical daring or lost by failing in such feats. It is also illustrated by a popular version of the legend of 'caveman love', the figure of Tarzan."[70]

Others dismissed the story of *The Sheik* as "cheap fiction" and gave all credit to Valentino personally for making it into a genuine love legend.

Some of the traits ascribed to Valentino in the role of *The Sheik* include manliness, sex appeal, gracefulness and virility.

The film may have been greatly instrumental in introducing a new trait to the image of the Arab in both Britain and the United States: that of the perfect lover surrounded by terror, mystery, the spell of the east and the lure of the desert.

The Sheik,[71] which is listed among the one hundred great movies of all times, started a cycle of dramas of the desert: *Arabian Love* (William Fox, 1922), *Burning Sands* (Famous Players Lasky Corporation, 1922), *When the Desert Calls* (Pyramid Pictures, Inc., 1922), *The Tents of Allah, Sons of the Desert* (Metro Goldwyn Mayer Corporation, 1933). In all these films the leading men were "passionate and aggressive lovers who casting aside all prudence swept the women off their feet."[72] Also as the result of the tremendous success of *The Sheik* many pictures released in 1922 featured "sheik" in their titles: *The Sheik of Araby* (R.C. Pictures Corporation, 1922), *The Sheik's Wife* (Harilal C. Twiwedi, 1922), *Soak the Sheik* (Pathe Exchange, Inc., 1922), *The Village Sheik* (William Fox, 1922), and others. Although none of these pictures acquired the popularity of *The Sheik*, they helped introduce the word "sheik" into popular usage.

Another picture, made in the same year as *The Sheik* and directed by Ernest Lubitsch, a German director, *One Arabian Night* (Associated National Pictures, 1921), is worth mentioning. This picture set a new standard in movie history for its innovations in photography and scenery. For the first time in movies an Arabesque was shown on the screen. *One Arabian Night* introduced a new "light and sexy" theme which was to have a lasting influence on film productions about the Arabs.

In 1926 Valentino played the role of an Arab in a new picture entitled *Son of the Sheik* (Feature Productions, Inc.) and once more the film became a "smash hit". Again Valentino portrayed the Arab in his colourful and now famous role. *Son of the Sheik*, tells an exotic, romantic story. The Arab here in this picture, as in *The Sheik*, was characterised as a gentleman with dishonourable although unrealised intentions. *Son of the Sheik* has been revived on television and in the theatres. In addition to the fact that the picture had Valentino in it, "[It] packs in all the essential ingredients of mass culture entertainment . . . fates worse than death, desert chases, dagger stabbing and furious fighting . . . apart from being a grand entertainment, *Son of the Sheik* did come closest to being a masterpiece, in its own particular way."[73]

The photography in the film was "superb", "rich and luxurious", utilising Yuma, Arizona, which was a popular double for Arabia in the mid-twenties. Valentino died before *Son of the Sheik* was released. His death, it seems, brought to an end a highly romanticised era of the portrayal of the Arab on the screen.

Son of the Sheik was followed by *Beau Geste* (Paramount Famous Lasky Players, 1927), the most popular of the Foreign Legion films. This film has been described as ". . . the best silent picture ever made."[74] Based on P. C. Wren's best selling novel about the French Foreign Legion, it portrayed the Arabs as menacing marauders. The film was remade twice, the first time in 1939 with Gary Cooper in the role originally played by Ronald Coleman, and secondly in 1966.

Wren's story was a mixture of intrigue, romance and adventure: three brothers, determined to protect their mother and retrieve a fabulous jewel which had disappeared mysteriously, found them-

Charlie Chan in Egypt

Son of the Sheik

Beau Geste

Beau Sabreur

Thief of Bagdad

Ben Hur

Lawrence of Arabia

Lawrence of Arabia

selves together in the Legion fighting not only Arabs, but also the treachery of their commanding officer.

The Arabs were shown in *Beau Geste* as villainous. The climatic scene showed a French outpost in Morocco, Fort Zindernerf, stormed by a horde of Arab tribesmen, who came riding furiously over the sand dunes from all directions. Lasky describes the story behind the scene as follows: "The scene was so important that a dozen extra cameramen had been brought from Hollywood to photograph it, and Brenon was anxious for them to pick up plenty of action when the besieging Arabs were fired on from the fort. 'A ten dollar bonus to every man who takes a fall!' At the first burst of fire from the piddling Legion guard all the riders, two thousand strong, 'dropped dead' in their tracks!"[75]

Beau Geste intensified the theme of adventure, involving the French Legionnaires as heroes with on the opposing side the Arabs as villains. The stories usually took place in North Africa; Algeria, Morocco, the Sahara, and Tunisia. The Arab was portrayed as bad, dangerous, and as treacherous as the desert, the heat and the harshness of life in North Africa. Some of the Legion pictures that followed *Beau Geste* are *Beau Sabreur* (Paramount Lasky Players, 1928), *The Foreign Legion* (Universal Pictures Corporation, 1928), and *Outpost of the Foreign Legion* (Brown-Nagel Productions, 1931).

In 1928 a comedy was released, *Two Arabian Knights* (The Caddo Company, Inc.). This picture was directed by Lewis Milestone and proved to be one of the most outstanding[76] in cinematography in the years 1927–28. William Boyd starred in the leading role and portrayed a colourful and "self-assured" Arab.[77]

The Cinema: The Thirties

In the twenties, then, a highly romanticised portrayal of the Arab was seen on American and British screens in *The Sheik* and *Son of the Sheik*, and the same period also witnessed the beginning of a new theme depicting the Arabs as villains against French heroism in Legion stories.

The thirties brought a recurrence of most themes treated during the twenties: mystery, adventure and romance. One notes, however the intensification of political and religio-political themes. The Arabs were portrayed in films of this decade mostly as mysterious villains, but at times as colourful and noble.

Islam against Christianity became the central theme of several pictures in the thirties. Religious war and adventure involving

Arabs and the Crusaders were shown on the screen, beginning with the release of *A Tale of the Crusades* (The Vitagraph Company of America, 1908), and later *The Crusaders, or Jerusalem Delivered* (World's Best Film Company, 1911).

In the thirties an important film, *The Crusaders* (Paramount Productions, Inc., 1935), based on the book of the same title by Harold Lamb, presented Arab Moslems fighting Christians against the background of the Holy City of Jerusalem. The third crusader, Richard the Lion-Heart, King of England, was fighting Saladin in the period when "All Christendom made war against all Islam."[78] The Arabs (called Saracens) were portrayed as "dark, fierce . . . with their razor-like scimitars and indomitable courage."[79] Saladin was favourably portrayed as the great and noble Sultan of Islam. *The Christian Science Monitor* went so far as to comment: "Why it was necessary to drag Christianity into the picture is not clear from anything on the screen. The one character with clarity and greatness of spirit is the Sultan of Islam, Saladin."[80]

Christianity and Islam were brought together again in 1936 in a romantic theme set against the background of Old Algiers. *The Garden of Allah* (Selznick International Pictures, Inc.) showed how the personal conflicts of Christians were resolved in a romantic setting belonging to Islam. Filmed in technicolor and based on the novel and play of the same title by Robert Hichens, the picture featured Charles Boyer and Marlene Dietrich. It was described as "unquestionably the finest thing yet done in technicolored films and one of the most impressive offerings, all round, of a prodigal season."[81] It is the story of a "self-tortured trappist monk" who breaks his final vows and escapes to the desert (the Sahara) where he falls desperately in love with a woman who has also gone to the desert to find peace. "Torn by love and his awakened sense of religion he leaves the woman to return once again to his celibate's cell."[82]

Although the Arabs were not involved directly in the plot, they and their country were an important part of the love story. The story in itself was a secondary issue to the "exotic . . . settings." Colourful scenes of the hubbub of life in Arab bazaars, the "lovelorn caravan" pushing along the Sahara horizon and the seductive movements of an Arab dancing girl were as significant as the story, if not more so. *The Garden of Allah* seems to have unveiled the scenic potentials of the Arab World, especially that of North Africa. Other pictures in the same period showing scenes of the desert and "life of the native" Arabs were *Morocco* (The Van Beuren Corporation, 1936), *Trouble in Morocco* (Columbia Pictures Corporation, 1937), *Adventures in the Sahara* (Columbia Pictures, 1938), and *In Morocco* (Columbia Pictures, 1939).

The film *Algiers* (Wagner-United Artists, 1937), which introduced the popular line "Come with me to the Casbah," was another picture made in North Africa. Charles Boyer portrayed a Parisian jewel thief who hid away in the Casbah, the native quarter of Algiers. While he lived among the native Arabs he could not be molested by the police, who lay in wait for him to set foot outside. The heroine (Hedy Lamarr) was a beautiful Parisian girl who came to the section as a tourist. They fell in love and through a ruse arranged by the police he followed her, only to be arrested while she sailed away, unaware of his fate.

The Casbah began to be portrayed in films as a romantic retreat, but one with sinister, lurid and gaudy connotations.

Egypt retained its mysterious reputation in the 1930s when Charlie Chan, the famed Chinese detective, was featured in a picture entitled *Charlie Chan in Egypt* (Fox Film Corporation, 1935). The plot involved the misappropriation of treasures found by archaeologists in the employ of the French Government. The Arabs (Egyptians) were not directly involved in the plot, but the "shadowy tombs at Luxor" apparently served as a fine background in a tale of mystery and intrigue for the inscrutable "Chinese of the mystery films".[83] Egypt was also used in the thirties as background for films dealing with the Suez Canal. The film *Disraeli* (Warner Brothers, 1930) portrayed Egypt at the time of the Khedive Ismail Pasha as a bankrupt country. Disraeli, the then British Prime Minister, was shown borrowing funds from an international Jewish banker, Hugh Meyers, in order to "buy the Suez Canal from Egypt and ensure England's India Empire".[84] In another picture, entitled *Suez* (Twentieth Century Fox, 1938), Ferdinand de Lesseps was depicted as the hero, who was working in order to construct the Suez Canal in the face of political intrigue and attacks by the Arabs.[85]

The Arabs were again shown in the thirties as the villains against British heroism in *The Four Feathers* (United Artists, 1939). This film, based on Kitchener's Egyptian-Sudan campaign, was first made in the twenties. The hero, an Englishman, "his engagement broken, and branded as a coward . . . sets off for Egypt determined to prove himself . . . He disguises himself as a native and joins the Khalif's army as a spy."[86] The Arabs were shown as slave traders and treacherous bloodthirsty fanatics.

The Cinema: The Forties

In the forties, British and American films portraying Arabs were for the most part comedies, fantasies, tales of war and espionage, mysteries and love stories.

In 1942 a comedy, *Road to Morocco* (Paramount), featuring Bob Hope and Bing Crosby, was released. It was described by one reviewer as the "biggest smash Paramount has had in years."[87] Crosby was shown selling Hope to an Arab slave dealer. Later Hope appeared reclining luxuriously in the palace of an Arabian princess. A camel was also shown talking, admitting "this is the craziest picture I have been in."[88] The Arabs were shown in an Arabian Nights setting where Caliphs lived in palaces while slaves were bought and sold in the market place. A sheik of the desert, Anthony Quinn, wearing flowing white robes and caressing a girl, was shown in an advertisement for the film with the caption: "Quin-Tessence of Wolfery". The advertisement continued: "Anthony Quinn, who loves his art, is here shown enthusiastically expressing his regard for delectable Donna Drake . . . Quinn, who bears some resemblance to the late Valentino is termed Milly Kasum in the picture. Donna? Just call her Mihrama."[89]

A sheik was also shown in *Lost in the Harem*, as the ruler of a "mystical eastern land and who has defrauded his nephew of the throne. The nephew (John Conte) knowing his uncle's weakness for blondes, hires Marilyn Maxwell, the troupe's prima donna, and Abbott and Costello, the troupe's magic act, to regain his kingdom by stealing some magic rings his uncle wears . . . The quartet's efforts involve them in varied escapades, mostly centred about the sheik's extensive harem, until the youthful prince regains his throne."[90]

Arabs were not involved directly in the plot of *A Night in Casablanca*, but one of the Marx brothers ran a "camel company".[91]

The fantasy image of the Arab seems to have begun to take shape on the screen in the forties; not only did the fantasy features based on the *Arabian Nights* increase in number in this decade, but also the films were successes. At present many of these pictures are being revived on television. *The Thief of Baghdad* (Alexander Korda, 1941), which was first made in the 1920s, *Arabian Nights* (Universal, 1942), *Ali Baba and the Forty Thieves* (Universal, 1944), *Kismet* (Loew's Inc., 1944), *A Thousand and One Nights* (Columbia, 1945), and *Sinbad the Sailor* (RKO, 1947) were among the many fantasy pictures which portrayed the Arabs during the forties.

All these pictures showed the Arabs in a highly romanticised manner. Most showed the Arabs in colourful settings, with intrigue, desert chases, battles, flying carpets, genii and flying horses. *The Thief of Baghdad* tells a typical Arabian fantasy story: "Through the wickedness of Jaffar, his Grand Vizier, Ahmed, the rightful king of Bagdad, is thrown into prison. There he meets Abu, the little street thief. They manage to escape and get to Basra, where Ahmed sees the Sultan's lovely daughter and immediately falls in love with her. The Sultan, however, promises her hand to Jaffar. She escapes, while Ahmed and Abu are captured. By Jaffar's magic, Ahmed is blinded and Abu turned into his dog. The ship on which the princess has escaped is attacked by slavers and she is brought back to Basra and sold to Jaffar, in whose house she must lie in a magic trance until Ahmed comes to awaken her. She is taken off to sea by Jaffar, but as he embraces her so the spell on Ahmed and Abu is broken. The rest of the film tells how by the help of a Djinni in a bottle Abu steals the All-seeing Eye and finally on the magic carpet arrives in the nick of time to slay the Grand Vizier and reunite the lovers."[92]

The Arabian Nights utilised fictional and historical characters side by side in the plot. Harun El Rashid, an historical Arab Caliph, was juxtaposed with such fictional characters as Shahrazad, Aladdin and Sinbad.[93] The picture was advertised on two full pages with a caption that read, "Just glimpse into Arabian nights—no magic carpets . . . just blood, sand and romance in technicolor."[94]

While in the twenties and thirties the Arabs had been pictured as villains against both British and French heroism, implicitly accepting and condoning French and British imperialism and colonialism in Arab countries, during the forties, in such espionage and war melodramas as *A Yank in Libya* (Producers Releasing Company, 1942), *Passport to Suez* (Columbia, 1943), *Adventures in Iraq* (Warner, 1943), *Sultan's Daughter* (Monogram Pictures, 1944), and *Action in Arabia* (R.K.O., 1944), Arabs were depicted as Nazi spies and shown as blackmailers and kidnappers.

At this time there was another development: more westerners were shown as able to disguise themselves as Arabs and assume a position of leadership among them. This reminds us of the early western adventurers such as Ludovico Varthema, some of the explorers such as Burckhardt and Burton, and British officers such as Lawrence of Arabia, who were said to have lived successfully among the Arabs in disguise. In *Desert Song* (Warner Brothers, 1943) an American (Dennis Morgan), formerly a soldier of fortune "who's been fighting Franco in Spain", and who turns "piano player in a Morocco night spot," assumes the identity of an Arab leader, Al-Khabor. He leads an Arab tribe, the "Riff" in an uprising against Nazi agents constructing a new railroad, and circumvents Nazi plans "by periodic appearances in the desert." He persuades the French Colonel (Bruce Cabot) to obtain eventual freedom and rights for the Riffs through an edict of France. This was one of the few films to hint that Arabs under French colonialism in North Africa did not have complete freedom and rights.

With North Africa much in the news in the early forties, feature films utilised the cities of North Africa as a background for action, espionage and romance. *Casablanca* (Warner, 1942) was the first of such pictures, followed by *Five Graves to Cairo* (Columbia, 1943) and *Sahara* (Columbia, 1943). *Casablanca* told the story of an American night club owner in Casablanca (Humphrey Bogart) who helps the husband of the woman he loves (Ingrid Bergman) to escape to America because he "can do so much for the United Nations." *Casablanca*, having to do with espionage and intrigue, emphasised the love theme, for which the North African cities by now were famous. *Five Graves to Cairo* and *Sahara* were war pictures, utilising the desert for the action against the Germans. *Five Graves to Cairo*, however, portrayed an Arab innkeeper who was described as a "terrified host to three armies".

The theme of miscegenation, love between Arabs and non-Arabs, appeared as early as the twenties, particularly in *The Sheik* pictures. The relationship between the Sheik (Valentino) and the foreigner, an Englishwoman, was forced love: the Sheik kidnapped an English woman and "compelled" her to fall in love with him. However, in the late forties a theme of mutual love between foreigners and Arabs appeared in *Outposts in Morocco* (United Artists, 1949) and in *Casbah* (Universal, 1948). *Outposts in Morocco* reworked the French Foreign Legion theme, setting Arab villainy against French heroism. However, the Legionnaire officer (George Raft), who was commissioned to break up a rebellious conspiracy among the Arab tribes, fell in love with the daughter of the rebel chief. In *Casbah*, an Arab girl fell in love with a Parisian thief. The solution offered in both cases was tragic: the death of one of the lovers. In *Outpost in Morocco*, the Arab girl was killed when she tried to stop her father from fighting the Legion, which, by the way, did "wipe out the insurgents". In *Casbah* the thief was lured to his death by the police.

Egypt was still featured as a background for mystery in the

forties. Some of the pictures released include *Dark Streets of Cairo* (Universal Pictures, 1940) and *To the End of Earth* (Columbia, 1948). The latter picture told a story of the United States Bureau of Narcotics, whose pursuit of smugglers took them from San Francisco to China and Cairo. The Arabs were shown as planters and smugglers of dope.

Towards the end of the forties and the beginning of the fifties, a new political theme appeared on the screen, involving Arabs and Jews. *Sword in the Desert* (Universal, 1949) was one of the first films to treat the subject of the Palestine problem. The film was shown in London for only three days, and then withdrawn by order of the Home Office because of "violent disturbances organised by a fascist minority."[95] The film was prejudiced in favour of the Jews. It explicitly accepted the premise that the Jews were right in fighting for Palestine. The British on the one hand were made to appear as "stupid and not very effective villains"; and yet the film allowed "the British officers to point out that they were merely carrying out an unpleasant duty". On the other hand the Arabs were shown as the real danger to the creation of a Jewish State in Palestine. Placing the struggle on the shoulders of all humanity, an Israeli commanding general ponders: "This isn't a Jewish, Arab or British problem, it's a problem of all mankind."[96] The picture, furthermore, gave some indication of the broad international base of those who fought for Israel. The same political theme was to appear again in the sixties and later in pictures such as *Exodus* (1960) and *Rosebud* (1975).

The Cinema: The Fifties and After

In the fifties, feature films brought Arabs and Jews together several times. In *Ben Hur* (M.G.M., 1959), set in Palestine at the time of Christ, an Arab sheik living in luxurious tents in the desert was the host of a Jewish aristocrat seeking vengeance on a Roman officer who had banished him and his family. The Arab sheik owned three white stallions which he called "my darlings". Fond of horses, races, and betting, the Arab sheik allowed the Jewish aristocrat to drive his horses in the chariot races, which the Jew won, avenging himself by killing his adversary. The Arab appeared to be highly pleased with the outcome.

Enmity between Arabia and Judea was depicted in a religious film entitled *The Big Fisherman* (Buena Vispana Vision, 1959). Arabs were shown as vengeful, but in sympathy with the cause of Christianity, in a story set in the beginning of the Christian era.

The plot revolved around Fara, the daughter of a political marriage
between the Judean king, Herod Antipas, and an Arab princess,
who came in disguise to Galilee to kill her father for deserting her
mother, an act that heightened the hatred between the two countries. The princess became a friend of a fisherman called Simon,
who became a Christian and aided the Arab to return to her country and marry an Arab prince who was in love with her.

In the fifties, fantasy characterised a large number of feature
films portraying Arabs. The early fantasy theme of the *Arabian
Nights* seemed to have returned to the screen.

Of 53 major feature films portraying Arabs or set in the Arab
World in the fifties, 23 (44 per cent) had *Arabian Nights* settings
with colour and costumes, 20 (38 per cent) were mysteries, adventure, comedies and musicals, six (12 per cent) were war pictures
and four (6 per cent) were Foreign Legion films.

Most of the fantasy films were adventurous tales in the *Arabian
Nights* tradition: scheming grand viziers, scantily clad dancing
girls, wild riding, breathtaking rescues. Zinsser comments on the
general state of the films portraying Arabs in the fifties as follows:
"To . . . many . . . producers, the Middle East is one vast harem,
where the Arabian Nights never end. It is a place where lovely
young slave girls lie about on soft couches, stretching their slender
legs, ready to do a good turn for any handsome stranger who
stumbles into the room. Amid all this decolletage sits the jolly old
Caliph, miraculously cool to the wondrous sights around him,
puffing on his water pipe while his vizier announces that Tamerlane is riding towards the city at that very moment with his fero-
cious legions. This is history at its best."[97]

Arab history, as reflected in these fantasy films, seemed to be re-
written and tailored by film producers and writers to fit situations
out of the *Arabian Nights*. Fiction and fact were crowded together;
historical personalities interacted with imaginary characters.

A typical fantasy picture of the fifties, *Son of Sinbad* (RKO,
1955) is a good example. The picture was made in Superscope and
Technicolor with Dale Robertson and Sally Forest in the leading
roles. The plot had the Son of Sinbad, together with Omar, poet
and tentmaker, and the daughters of the Forty Thieves, save Baghdad from Tamerlane. One reviewer had the following to say:
"Straight from the realm of old-time burlesque comes this garish
and giant-screen opus in technicolor, based ever-so-loosely on the
Arabian Nights. Here are 'Girls, Girls, Girls,' swivel-hipped and
revealingly costumed, in harems and out, suggestively dancing

with near-Arabian bumps and grinds. There is obviously ample opportunity for young Sinbad, the son of Sinbad, to have acquired his reputation as the great lover. Even the second generation descendants of his father's Forty Thieves turn out to be an all-girl troupe. A mad mix-up of spies, intrigues and chases, plus a touch of hypnosis and a burst of 'Greek Fire' keep the action humping along. The humor is low and broad; dialogue is full of double meaning."[98]

William Zinsser in a lengthy parody of the film states: "I don't think many people know how Bagdad was saved from Tamerlane. The scholars have never written the story down. Luckily, Hughes (the producer) reconstructed the event in *Son of Sinbad* . . . He assembled so many leggy maidens in the harem that I didn't pay any attention to the plot. This is called leading from strength, or so the captions might say. To us history fans, authentic costumes mean a great deal. The girls were draped in garments of finest gossamer that fluttered apart with every zephyr. (Many are the uses of the wind-machine in Hollywood.) Hughes was not stuck with any excess fabric—in fact, there was not quite enough to go around once. Occasionally one of the girls found the energy to get up and do an oriental dance—that is, a dance devised in East Hollywood—and then such a flourishing of hips, such a rotating of navels you never saw. Be it ever so humble, there's no place like the Caliph's palace. With the setting thus established—a process which, as I recall, didn't take more than forty-five minutes—Hughes felt that he could safely begin telling the story. Its hero, the son of Sinbad, was very fond of girls, and he was forever scaling the palace wall to visit the Caliph's favorite wife in her bath. She enjoyed this kind of devotion, but one night the Caliph caught Sinbad. The intruder could hardly pretend that he came up there just to take a bath, and the Caliph threw him in a dungeon. There he was comforted by various semi-nude beauties and by a poet named Omar Khayyam, who also dabbled in tent making. Omar kept improvising lines like 'A jug of wine, a loaf of bread and thou' and they had many a good laugh over what a lousy poet he was.

"Well, then a terrible thing happened. Tamerlane and his men (Abbasides? Mamelukes?) swooped down and kidnapped a slave girl who knew Bagdad's precious military secret—something to do with magic fire in a cave outside the city. She was a cute dish, and Sinbad was eager to rescue her. Another cute dish sprung him from jail and he went out to fight Tamerlane. Suddenly a band of warriors appeared out of the desert to help him. They said they were descended from Ali Baba's forty thieves, and would you believe it, all forty of them were girls. It seems that their daddies were killed in a vile plot, and the girls formed this darling little platoon to carry on the old tradition . . . These lady fighters were all real lookers, needless to say, but when they took up their bows and arrows and magic fire, Tamerlane's boys didn't know what hit 'em. They retreated across the painted sands, past the cardboard palm trees, and left the girls to fight and love another day. And that's how Bagdad was saved."[99]

Son of Sinbad was condemned by the American National Legion of Decency on the grounds that: "This film, in its character and treatment, is a serious affront to Christian and traditional standards of morality and decency because of its blatant and continuing violation of the virtue of piety. Throughout, it contains grossly salacious dances and indecent costuming. This picture is a challenge to decent standards of theatrical entertainment and as an incitement to juvenile delinquency, it is especially dangerous to the moral welfare of youth."[100]

Many other fantasy pictures that were released before and after *Son of Sinbad* were objected to (mainly for their suggestive costuming and dancing) by the American National Legion of Decency. Such pictures include *Aladdin and His Lamp* (Monogram, 1952), *Thief of Damascus* (Columbia, 1952), *The Veils of Bagdad* (Universal, 1953), *Adventures of Hajji Baba* (20th Century Fox, 1954).

Although the Arab was portrayed in improbable situations, the heroes were well known actors who lent popularity and prestige to the characters and nationals they portrayed. For example, in a movie entitled *The Prince Who Was a Thief* (Universal, 1951) Tony Curtis played a kidnapped prince who became a thief before he was returned to his throne. In spite of the fact that the Arab was shown to practise a criminal occupation, he tended to gain the sympathy and admiration of Tony Curtis' followers. Other popular American actors who played the roles of Arabs in fantasy pictures included Jeff Chandler in *Flame of Araby* (Universal, 1952), Tony Curtis in *Son of Ali Baba* (Universal, 1952), Victor Mature in *The Veils of Bagdad* (Universal, 1953) and Rock Hudson in *The Golden Blade* (Universal, 1953).

However, other films released in the same decade dealt unfavourably with the contemporary Arab. *Saadia* (M.G.M., 1954) depicted the Arab of the time as backward, superstitious and dangerous. Set in Morocco, the plot dealt with an Arab girl who undertook hazardous tasks to help the French doctor who cured her of the plague and rescued her from a tribal sorceress. The theme of *Saadia* seems to be in keeping with the tradition of Legion films in general. Witchcraft, black magic and primitive rituals of the Arabs are contrasted with modern French medicine, scientific outlook and humanity.

The theme of love between a Westerner and an Arab reappeared in this picture. The French doctor fell in love with Saadia, but when he found that she was in love with a "good caid" (nobleman) he attended "a colorful . . . native ceremony and the doctor gives them his blessing."

In another film, in a western set in Death Valley in the United States, the Arab was presented as villainous in contrast with American Indian heroism. *Desert Pursuit* (Monogram, 1952) depicted three Arabs mounted on camels chasing an American miner (loaded with gold) and a girl, across Death Valley. "The camels and Arabs were leftovers from those imported by the American government at the time it was figured the hump-backed mounts would be the solution to domestic desert travel."[101] The Arabs were mistaken by "Mission Indians" for the Three Wise Men during a Christmas Eve ceremony. However, in the end the Arabs were wiped out when the "same redskins aid the couple the next day."

War pictures released in the fifties, utilising Arab countries as background, did not deal directly with the portrayal of Arabs but emphasised the conflict between the Allies and the Axis in such pictures as *The Desert Fox* (Twentieth Century Fox, 1951), *Hotel Sahara* (Universal, 1941), *El Alamein* (Columbia, 1954), etc.

Although films portraying Arabs in the sixties were fewer in number than in previous decades, three important pictures appeared which became significantly popular in Britain. These films were *Exodus* (United Artists, 1960), *Lawrence of Arabia* (Columbia, 1962), and *Khartoum* (United Artists, 1966). In all these pictures the Arabs were portrayed dressed in flowing robes; they were fierce looking and possessing alien values contrary to western beliefs.

Exodus is a three and a half hour dramatisation of the Jewish struggle for Palestine. The real enemy of the Jews, in the film, were the Arabs. Young Jewish and gentile fighters were shown fighting for the Jewish cause and against both the Arab "terrorists" and to a lesser degree the British army stationed in Palestine. The Arabs were generally tolerated but pictured in the background in their traditional robes and depicted as backward. Nonetheless the

Arab "terrorists" were the menace to the Jews; these were shown to be organised and led by an "Arab Nazi".

Lawrence of Arabia placed the Arabs in an historically remote situation. Although the Arabs were colourfully portrayed they were depicted as fierce-looking desert warriors led by the Englishman T. E. Lawrence. Lawrence was glorified in the film and shown as the man without whom the Arabs could not have united nor won the battle.

The alien and bizarre value system of the Arabs was best exemplified in a scene where Lawrence's thirsty guide is shot down by Sherif Ali for drinking water from the Sherif's well. (Incidentally, such conduct is unheard of in the tradition of the desert Arabs.)

In the motion picture entitled *Khartoum*, Arabs were shown in 1883 as fighting General Gordon, the British officer in Sudan. The Arabs in this film were mainly depicted as "fanatics" led by a "fanatical religious leader known as the Mahdi." The humanity of the English was contrasted with the inhumanity of the Arabs, who were shown as slave traders and savage spear-fighters.

In another film in the sixties called *Two Women*, the Arabs were shown in only one scene, raping the mother and her daughter in the church.

In short, the favourable and unfavourable portrayals of the Arabs in British and American feature films appear to be equally unrealistic. On the one hand the Arab is over-romanticised, on the other he is presented as completely villainous.

The present trend on the screen seems to be to present the Arab more or less favourably in historically remote situations, but in an unfavourable and unsympathetic light in contemporary situations.

The End of the Romantic Image

The favourable side of the nineteenth century image of the Arabs underwent basic transformation in Britain in the twentieth century. Although in the first quarter of this century the Bedouin was still admired and colourfully portrayed, the "despised" urban Arabs began to push their way into the important events of the day. As a result, the picture of the "contemptible" Egyptian city dweller became emphasised in the popular literature in Britain. Thousands of British troops and officials who served in Egypt and returned home disseminated an ugly image of the Egyptian.

Zionists, who represented a pressure group in Britain, depicted the Arabs as a corrupt, untrustworthy and backward people, who had "absorbed all the vices of the Levant."[102]

There can be little doubt that the mass media also, especially the press and broadcasting, portrayed the Arabs unfavourably. This is primarily due to their "built-in" prejudices against the social and political conditions of the Arabs. The feature films, which at one point early in the century depicted the Arabs colourfully and favourably, eventually reverted to presenting them as villains and portraying them unrealistically.

It seems that with the gradual disappearance of the Bedouin and their way of life from the Arab World, the image of the Arabs in Britain began to be adversely affected. Needless to say, most of the favourable attitudes the British had towards the Arabs were directly related to their love of the desert and their admiration of the Bedouin. They considered the desert to be "clean" and saw the Bedouin as a free aristocrat who in the face of adversity bravely held on to his values and way of life.

When W. Thesiger, an Englishman who travelled into Arabia during the first half of the twentieth century observed the passing away of the Bedouin, he lamented: "Here in the desert I had found all that I asked; I knew that I should never find it again. But it was not this personal sorrow that distressed me. I realised that the Bedu with whom I had lived and travelled and in whose company I had found contentment, were doomed . . . I shall always remember how often I was humbled by those illiterate herdsmen who possessed, in so much greater measure than I, generosity and courage, endurance, patience, and light-hearted gallantry. Among no other people have I ever felt the same sense of personal inferiority."[103]

It seems that with the "doomed" Bedouin the highly romanticised portrayal of the Arabs in Britain had come to an end, or at least to a standstill.

At present the image of the Arabs is in flux in Britain. This is due to many new factors and developments both in and outside the Arab World. For example, the vast oil resources are endowing the Arabs with significant economic power. The Arab-Israeli war of 1973 showed clearly that the Arabs could also become an effective military force. In addition, the increasing numbers of Arab tourists and travellers abroad, especially to Britain and to Europe, and the initiation of cultural exchanges are facilitating personal contacts between the Arabs and the outside world.

It is hoped that other scholars in the future will interest themselves in the study of the development of the image of the Arabs in
both Britain and the West. For it is through such studies that we
shall be better able to understand the ways in which peoples perceive one another.

Notes

A Bird's-eye View

1. Herodotus *The History of Herodotus*, trans. George Rawlinson (Tudor Publishing Company, New York 1943) pp. 185–187.
2. Strabo *The Geography of Strabo*, trans. H. L. Jones (William Heinemann, Cambridge, Mass. and London 1930, reprinted 1954, 1961) Book I, p. 373.
3. Paterculus, Velleius *Res Gestae Divi Augusti* (*Compendium of Roman History*), trans. Frederick W. Shipley (William Heinemann, London 1924, reprinted 1955, 1961) p. 389.
4. Strabo, op. cit., Book 7, p. 301.
5. Ibid. p. 303.
6. Ibid. p. 347.
7. Ibid. p. 349.
8. Montgomery, James A. *Arabia and the Bible* (University of Pennsylvania Press, Philadelphia 1934). See Chapter 2, pp. 27–36.
9. Fisher, H. A. L. *A History of Europe* (Edward Arnold & Co., London 1940) p. 137.
10. Daniel, Norman *Islam and the West* (University Press, Edinburgh 1966) p. 4.
11. Hitti, Philip *The Arabs* (University Press, Princetown 1943) p. 1.
12. Ibid. p. 2.
13. Ibid. p. 185.
14. Daniel, Norman, op. cit., p. 200.
15. Hitti, op. cit., p. 188.
16. Polo, Marco *The Travels of Marco Polo* (Everyman's Library No. 306, London 1946) pp. 73–76.
17. See Hakluyt, Richard *The Principall Navigations Voyages Traffiques and Discoveries of the English Nation* 12 vols. (James McLehose and Sons, Glasgow 1904) Vol. V, pp. 367–368.
18. Varthema, Ludovico Di *The Travels of Ludovico Di Varthema*, trans. from the Italian by John Winter Jones (Hakluyt Society, London 1858) pp. 17–18. See also Bayard Taylor (editor) *Library of Travel: Arabia* (Scribner's Sons, New York 1892) p. 9.
19. Neibuhr, Carsten *Travels Through Arabia* (Edinburgh 1792) 2 vols., passim. For more details on Neibuhr's life and journey, see D. G. Hogarth *The Penetration of Arabia* (Lawrence and Buller, Inc., London 1904) pp. 39–62.

20. *World Encyclopedia* (The Quarrie Corporation, Chicago 1947) Vol. I.
21. Flaubert, Gustave *Flaubert in Egypt* (The Bodley Head, London 1972) p. 95.
22. Daniel, Norman *Islam, Europe and Empire* (University Press, Edinburgh 1966).
23. Ibid. p. 72.
24. Ibid. p. 73.
25. Ibid. p. 74.
26. Ibid. p. 74.
27. Ibid. pp. 98–100.
28. Ibid. p. 104.

The Beginnings

1. Villehardouin and De Joinville *Memoirs of the Crusades*, trans. Sir Frank Marzials (Everyman's Library No. 333, London 1908, reprinted 1965) p. 276.
2. As quoted by Lewis, Bernard *British Contributions to Arabic Studies* (published for the British Council by Longmans, Green & Co, London 1941) p. 11.
3. Mandeville, John *Travels* (London 1900) passim.
4. Hakluyt, Richard *The Principall Navigations Voyages Traffiques and Discoveries of the English Nation* 12 vols. (James McLehose & Sons, Glasgow 1904) Vol. V, pp. 62–63.
5. See Wood, Alfred C. *History of the Levant Company* (Cass, London 1964).
6. The Hakluyt Society *The Original Writings and Correspondence of the Two Richard Hakluyts* (Hakluyt Society, London 1935) Second series Vol. XXVI, p. 72.
7. Shakespeare, William *Macbeth*, Act I, Scene iii, lines 7–10.
8. Hakluyt, Richard *The Principal Navigations Voyages and Discoveries of the English Nation* 2 vols. (Imprinted in London 1958, published for the Hakluyt Society by the University Press, Cambridge 1965) Vol. I, p. 208.
9. See also Searight, Sarah *The British in the Middle East* (Weidenfeld and Nicolson, London 1969) p. 51.
10. Purchas, Samuel *Hakluytus Posthumus or Purchas His Pilgrims* (James McLehose & Sons, Glasgow 1905) Vol. I, p. xliv.
11. Montagu, Mary Wortley *The Complete Letters of Lady Mary Wortley Montagu* (Oxford 1763).
12. Daniel, Norman *Islam, Europe and Empire* (University Press, Edinburgh 1966) p. 14.
13. Hakluyt, Richard *The Principall Navigations* op. cit., Vol. I, p. 231.
14. Hakluyt, Richard *The Principall Navigations* op. cit., Vol. V, pp. 465–466.
15. See Lewis, Bernard, op. cit., p. 12.
16. Ibid. p. 13.
17. Daniel, Norman, op. cit., p. 17.
18. Lithgow, William *A Most Delectable and True Discourse of a Painful Peregrination*, 1614, passim.

19. Sandy, George *Relation of a Journey*, 1652, passim.
20. Blount, Henry *Voyage into the Levant*, 1637, passim.
21. Moryson, Fynes *Itinerary*, 1617.
22. Mundrell, Henry *A Pilgrimage from Aleppo to Jerusalem*, 1697, p. 80.
23. Hakluyt Society *The Red Sea and Adjacent Countries at the Close of the Seventeenth Century* (Hakluyt Society, London 1935) p. x.
24. Pitts, Joseph *A Faithful Account of the Religion and Manners of the Mohametans* (London 1738, republished Gregg, 1971) passim.
25. Hall, Joseph *Satires* VI, i.
26. Chew, Samuel *The Crescent and the Rose* (Oxford University Press, New York 1937) p. 521.
27. Spenser, Edmund *The Faerie Queene*, I, vi.
28. Marlowe, Christopher *The Jew of Malta*, I, i.
29. Fletcher, John *The Bloody Brother*, V, ii.
30. Milton, John *Paradise Lost*, iv.
31. See Chew, Samuel, op. cit., pp. 536–538.
32. Shakespeare, William *Henry VI, Part I*, I, iii.
33. Knight, Francis *Relations of Seaven Yeares Slaverie*, 1640, p. 32.

The Arabian Nights

1. Ockley, Simon *History of the Saracens* (London 1874) p. xi.
2. Conant, M. P. *The Oriental Tale in England in the Eighteenth Century* (New York, Columbia University Press 1908) p. xv.
3. Pope, Alexander *The Correspondence of Alexander Pope* edited by George Sherburn (Clarendon Press, Oxford 1956) Vol. 1, p. 369.
4. Montagu, Mary Wortley *The Complete Letters of Lady Mary Wortley Montagu* (Oxford 1763) Vol. 1, p. 385.
5. Ockley, Simon *History of the Saracens* (London 1874) passim.
6. Sale, George *Preliminary Discourse to the Koran* (Warne, London 1900) passim.
7. Pococke, Richard *Description of the East* (London 1743) passim.
8. Perry, Charles *View of the Levant* (London 1743) passim.
9. Russell, Alexander *Natural History of Aleppo* (London 1757) passim.
10. Bruce, James *Travels to Discover the Source of the Nile* (London 1790).
11. Searight, Sarah *The British in the Middle East* (Weidenfeld and Nicolson, London 1969) pp. 58–59.
12. As quoted by Searight, ibid. p. 86.
13. Eton, William *A Survey of the Turkish Empire* (London 1799) passim.
14. Ibid. Also see Daniel, Norman *Islam, Europe and Empire* op. cit., pp. 103–104.

The Romantic Image

1. Meester, Marie de *Oriental Influences in the English Literature of the Nineteenth Century* (Carl Winters Universitats-buchhanburg, Heidelberg 1915) p. 13.

2. *Edinburgh Review* Vol. 164, July 1886. See also Brodie, Fawn M. *The Devil Drives* (Eyre & Spottiswoode, London 1967) p. 309.
3. Thackeray, W. M. *Journey from Cornhill to Grand Cairo* (London 1846).
4. Disraeli, Benjamin *Home Letters Written in the East in 1830 and 1835* (London 1885) XII, XIV, pp. 107 and 126.
5. Russell, W. H. *British Expedition to the Crimea* (London 1858) p. 38.
6. Twain, Mark *The Innocents Abroad or The New Pilgrims Progress* (Bantam Books, New York 1964 edition) pp. 235 and 241.
7. Payne, John *The Book of the Thousand Nights and One Night: Its History and Character* (London).
8. Longfellow, Henry Wadsworth *The Poetical Works of* (Oxford University Press, London 1910) p. 340.
9. See W. F. Kirby in his bibliographical notes in Benton's *Nights* Vol. X, pp. 512 ff. and supplemental *Nights* Vol. VI, pp. 370 ff.
10. Dickens, Charles *Christmas Books* (*A Christmas Carol*) (Oxford University Press, London 1966) p. 28 and also Dickens *The Old Curiosity Shop* (Oxford University Press, London 1967) pp. 475–476.
11. Carlyle, Thomas *Sartor Resartus* and *On Heroes and Hero Worship* (London 1940) p. 192.
12. Hogarth, D. G. *The Penetration of Arabia* (Lawrence and Buller, Inc., London 1904) p. 88.
13. Burckhardt, John Lewis *Travels in Nubia* (John Murray, London 1822) p. 45.
14. Burckhardt, J. L. *Bedouins and Wahabys* (Henry Colburn and Richard Bentley, London 1930) passim.
15. Lewis, Bernard *British Contributions to Arabic Studies* (published for the British Council by Longmans, Green & Co., London 1941) p. 20.
16. Lewis, Bernard, op. cit., p. 21.
17. Lane, Edward William *An Account of the Manners and Customs of the Modern Egyptians* (Everyman's Library No. 315, 1908, reprinted 1966) passim.
18. Lane, E. W. *Arabian Society in the Middle Ages* (London 1883).
19. Palmer, Edward Henry *The Desert of the Exodus* 2 vols. (Deighton, Bell & Co., Cambridge 1871) passim.
20. Lewis, Bernard, op. cit.
21. Burton, Richard *Pilgrimage to Al-Madinah and Meccah.*
22. Burton, Richard *The Gold-Mines at Midian* (C. Kegan Paul and Co., London 1878) p. 1.
23. Burton, Richard *Zanzibar, City, Island and Coast* 2 vols. (London 1872) see Vol. II, p. 377. Also see Brodie, Fawn *The Devil Drives* (Eyre and Spottiswoode, London 1967) p. 91.
24. Brodie, Fawn M., ibid. p. 91.
25. Blunt, Wilfred Scawen *My Diaries 1888–1914* 2 parts (Martin Secker, London 1919) Part One, pp. 134–135.
26. Ibid. p. 136.
27. Ibid. p. 133.

28. Blunt, Wilfred Scawen *Secret History of the English Occupation of Egypt* (T. Fisher Unwin, London 1907) see Chapter 1.
29. Blunt, Wilfred Scawen, ibid.
30. Ibid.
31. As quoted by Searight, Sarah *The British in the Middle East* (Weidenfeld and Nicolson, London 1969) p. 102.
32. Blunt, Wilfred S. *Diaries*, op. cit., p. 153.
33. Blunt, Wilfred S. *The Future of Islam* (Kegan Paul, London 1882) p. 172.
34. Assad, Thomas J. *Three Victorian Travellers* (Routledge and Kegan Paul, London 1964) p. 93.
35. Doughty, Charles M. *Travels in Arabia Deserta* (Jonathan Cape, London 1926) passim.
36. See T. E. Lawrence: introduction to Doughty's *Travels in Arabia Deserta*, op. cit.
37. Fairley, Barker *Charles M. Doughty; A Critical Study*.
38. As quoted by Assad, Thomas J., op. cit., p. 96.
39. Assad, Thomas, op. cit., p. x.
40. Ibid.
41. Curzon, Robert *Visits to Monasteries of the Levant* (John Murray, London 1849) passim.
42. Palgrave, William Gifford *Narrative of a Year's Journey Through Central and Eastern Arabia* (Macmillan and Co., London 1908).
43. Layard, Henry Austen *Discoveries in the Ruins of Nineveh and Babylon* (London 1851) passim.
44. Kinglake, A. W. *Eothen* (Harrison, London 1864) passim.
45. Warburton, Eliot *The Crescent and Cross* (London 1844) passim.
46. Hogarth, David *The Wandering Scholar* (Humphrey Milford, Oxford University Press, London 1925) pp. 46 and 262.
47. Fisher, H. A. L. *History of Europe* (Edward Arnold and Co., London 1940) p. 1033.
48. Assad, Thomas, op. cit., p. 7.
49. Disraeli, Benjamin *Tancred*.
50. Scott, Walter *The Talisman*.
51. Lord Byron, *The Poetical Works of* (Oxford University Press, London 1960) p. 683.
52. Longfellow, Henry *The Poetical Works of*, p. 131.
53. Shelley, Percy Bysshe *The Complete Poetical Works of* (Oxford University Press, London 1961) p. 552.
54. Moore, Thomas *Lalla Rookh* (London 1861).
55. Montgomery, James *Poems*.
56. Moore, Thomas, op. cit.
57. Spaeth, Sigmund *Read 'Em and Weep* (Doubleday, New York 1927).
58. Blanch, Lesley *The Wilder Shores of Love* (John Murray, London, 1965, reprinted by Panther Books 1966) p. 14.
59. As quoted by Sarah Searight, *The British the Middle East*, pp. 157–158.
60. Kinglake, op. cit., p. 92.
61. Searight, Sarah, op. cit., p. 157.
62. Blanch, Lesley, op. cit., p. 24.

63. Ibid. p. 76.
64. Burton, Isabel *The Inner Life of Syria, Palestine and the Holy Land* 2 vols. (Henry S. King and Co., London 1875).
65. Blanch, Lesley, op. cit., p. 97.
66. Blunt, Lady Anne Noel *A Pilgrimage to Nejd* 2 vols. (John Murray, London 1881) see Vol. I, p. 68 and Vol. II, pp. 16–17.

Image in Flux

1. Hourani, Albert H. *Great Britain and the Arab World* (John Murray, London 1945) p. 15.
2. As quoted by Lewis, Bernard *British Contributions to Arabic Studies* (published for the British Council by Longmans, Green & Co., London 1941) p. 28.
3. Bell, Gertrude Lowthian *The Desert and the Sown* (William Heinemann, London 1970) p. 1.
4. Ibid. p. ix.
5. Ibid. p. 340.
6. Bray, N. N. E. *A Paladin of Arabia* (John Heritage, The Unicorn Press Ltd., London 1936) pp. vi–vii.
7. Ibid. p. vi.
8. Ibid. pp. 254–255.
9. Ibid. p. 400.
10. See Carruthers, Douglas *Arabian Adventure: To The Great Nafud in Quest of the Oryx* (Witherby, London 1935).
11. Ibid. p. 123.
12. Broughton, Harry *Lawrence of Arabia: The Fact Without the Fiction* (Pictorial Museum, Wareham, Dorset 1969) p. 1.
13. As quoted by David Garnett in *The Essential T. E. Lawrence* (Jonathan Cape, London 1951) p. 16.
14. Ibid. p. 16.
15. Ibid. p. 17.
16. Lawrence, T. E. *The Seven Pillars of Wisdom* (Jonathan Cape, London 1973) p. 21.
17. For details on the film *The Sheik* see pp. 146 ff.
18. As quoted by Garnett, David, op. cit., p. 20.
19. Ibid.
20. Lawrence, T. E., op. cit., p. 23.
21. Ibid. pp. 23–24.
22. Ibid. p. 24.
23. Churchill, Winston S. *Great Contemporaries* (Thornton Butterworth, London 1937) p. 161.
24. Ibid.
25. Lawrence T. E., op. cit., p. 38.
26. Ibid.
27. Ibid. p. 41.
28. Churchill, Winston S., op. cit., p. 164.
29. Antonius, George *The Arab Awakening* (Hamish Hamilton, London 1938) p. 321.
30. Monroe, Elizabeth *Philby of Arabia* (Faber and Faber, London 1973) p. 54.

31. Ibid. p. 52.
32. *Arab Bulletin* No. 77, Cairo, 27 January 1918, p. 21.
33. Monroe, Elizabeth, op. cit., p. 164.
34. As quoted by Elizabeth Monroe, op. cit., p. 92.
35. Philby, H. St J. *The Empty Quarter* (Constable and Co. Ltd., London 1933) p. 299.
36. Ibid. p. 211.
37. Glubb, John Bagot *The Story of the Arab Legion* (Hodder and Stoughton, London 1948) pp. 7–8.
38. Ibid. p. 8.
39. Ibid. p. 355.
40. Alport, Cecil *One Hour of Justice* (Dorothy Crisp and Co., London 1946) pp. 52–53.
41. Sladen, Douglas *Egypt and the English* (Hurst and Blackett, London 1908) p. 6.
42. See Ingrams, Doreen *The Palestine Papers 1917–1922* (John Murray, London 1972) p. 2.
43. Ibid. p. 7.
44. Ibid. p. 31.
45. Ibid. p. 33.
46. Ibid. p. 73.
47. Ibid. pp. 151–152.
48. Ibid. p. 152.
49. Ibid. p. 153.
50. Ibid. p. 121.
51. As quoted by Watkins, David *Labour and Palestine* (published by Labour Middle East Council, 1975) p. 8.
52. Ibid. p. 3.
53. Ibid. p. 8.
54. Ibid. p. 15.
55. Ibid. p. 3.
56. Ibid. p. 13.
57. Ibid. p. 16.
58. Michael Adams and Christopher Mayhew *Publish It Not . . .* (Longman Group Ltd., London 1975) p. 17.
59. Ibid. p. 26.
60. Ibid. p. 93.
61. Ibid. p. 96.
62. Zinsser, William "In Search of Lawrence of Arabia" (*Esquire* June 1961) p. 10.
63. Merz, Charles "When the Movies Go Abroad" (*Harpers Monthly Magazine*, 1926).
64. Niver, Kemp R. *Motion Pictures From The Library of Congress Paper Print Collection 1894–1922*, (University of California Press, 1967).
65. Griffith R. and Mayer A. *The Movies* (Simon and Schuster, New York 1957) p. 66.
66. Lasky, Jesse L. *I Blow My Own Horn* (Doubleday, New York 1957) pp. 114–115.
67. Ibid. p. 148.

68. Jacobs, Lewis *The Rise of the American Film: A Critical History* (Harcourt, Brace and Company, New York 1939) p. 402.
69. Ibid. p. 402.
70. Tyler, Park *The Three Faces of the Film* (Thomas Yoseloff, New York 1960) pp. 84–85.
71. *The Film Daily Yearbook of the Motion Picture*, Forty-second edition (New York 1960) p. 63.
72. Jacobs, Lewis, op. cit., p. 402–403.
73. Franklin, Joe *Classics of the Silent Screen* (The Citadel Press, New York 1960) p. 74.
74. Taylor, Dennis *A Pictorial History of the Movies* (Simon and Schuster, New York 1950) p. 173.
75. Lasky, Jesse L., op. cit., p. 116.
76. Jacobs, Lewis, op. cit., p. 332.
77. Ibid. p. 411.
78. *Motion Picture Review Digest* Vol. I, 30 March 1936, p. 35.
79. Ibid. p. 35.
80. Ibid. p. 35.
81. Ibid. 28 December 1936, p. 48.
82. Ibid. p. 48.
83. Jones, Dorothy B. *The Portrayal of China and India on the American Screen* (Center for International Studies M.I.T., Cambridge 1955) p. 16.
84. *Variety.*
85. *Monthly Film Bulletin of the British Film Institute*, Vol. 5, no. 59, November 1938, p. 264.
86. *Monthly Film Bulletin of the British Film Institute*, Vol. 6, no. 65, May 1939, p. 91.
87. *Variety*, 2 December 1942, p. 8.
88. Ibid. 7 October 1942, p. 8.
89. Ibid. 4 November 1942, p. 8.
90. Ibid. 23 August 1944, p. 8.
91. Ibid.
92. *Monthly Film Bulletin of the British Film Institute*, Vol. 8, no. 85, January 1941, p. 2.
93. *Variety* 23 December 1942, p. 8.
94. Ibid. 9 December 1942, p. 8.
95. *Monthly Film Bulletin* published by the British Film Institute, Vol. 17, no. 196, April/May 1950, p. 62.
96. Ibid.
97. Zinsser, William, op. cit., p. 72.
98. *Variety* December 1955, p. 8.
99. Zinsser, William, op. cit., pp. 72–73.
100. *Motion Pictures Classified by National Legion of Decency* February 1936–1955, p. 186.
101. *Variety* 10 July 1953, p. 8.
102. Ingrams, Doreen, op. cit., p. 33.
103. Thesiger, W. *Arabian Sands* (Longmans, Green & Co. Ltd., London 1959) p. 310.

Index

Abulfida Ismail, 23
Adelard of Bath, 19–20
African Association, 58
Alexander, Michael, 105
Alexander the Great, 2
Algeria, 22, 37, 132, 151
Alport, A. Cecil, 132–3
American National Legion of
   Decency, 158
antiquarianism, 49–50
Antonius, George, 128–9
Arab Empire, 5–6
Arab horse, 78, 82, 96, 103, 114–
   115
Arabi Pasha, 67, 76, 80
Arabia, 35, 117, 129–31
Arabian Nights, 8, 13–14, 16, 39–
   41, 42, 48, 52, 53–7, 141
  films based on, 144–5, 152–3, 156
  influence of, 55–7, 66, 75, 90,
    104, 107
Arabic language, 41, 43
Arabic studies, 26–7, 39, 41, 119;
   see also scholars
Arab–Israeli war 1973, 161
Arab Legion, 131–2
Arabs, 34
  and *Arabian Nights*, 39–41, 42,
    53
  and explorers, *see* Blunt; Burton;
    Curzon; Doughty; King-
    lake; Layard; Palgrave
  in films, *see* cinema
  in literature, 56–7, 106–10
  and scholars, 41–2, 43, 46–7
  and Turks, 21–2, 30–1, 43, 51–
    52, 53, 63, 104
  and Zionism, 135

  see also Bedouin; city Arabs
archaeology, 116–17
Arnold, Sir Thomas, 119
Assad, Thomas, 82, 89, 105
assassins, 9, 18

Bahira, 5
Balfour, James, 135, 136
Balfour Declaration, 130, 134, 137
ballads, 109–10
Bara, Theda, 145–6
Barbary pirates, 22, 37
Baring, Sir Evelyn, 80
Bedwell, William, 26
Bedouin, 3, 4, 11, 12–13, 15–16, 20,
   118, 160–1
  in travellers' tales, 28, 29–30, 34,
    45, 47–8, 59–60, 67–8, 71–
    75, 78, 82, 83–9, 91–3, 94,
    96–8, 102, 127, 130
Bell, Gertrude, 119–21, 129
Bevan, A. A., 119
Bevin, Ernest, 140
Bible, the, 4, 18, 36, 83, 85, 89, 104,
   141
Blanch, Lesley, 110–11, 112–14
Blessington, Lady, 106
Blount, Henry, 29–31
Blunt, Lady Anne, 76–8, 110, 112,
   114–15
Blunt, Wilfred Scawen, 69, 76–83,
   84, 89
Boccaccio, Giovanni, 8
Bodenham, 22
Boyd, William, 149
Boyer, Charles, 150, 151
Bray, N. N. E., 121–2

171